Social Planning

ASPECTS OF SOCIAL POLICY

GENERAL EDITOR: J.P. Martin
Professor of Sociology and Social Administration, University of Southampton.

Planning for Welfare
edited by TIMOTHY A. BOOTH

The Social Context of
Health Care
PAUL BREARLEY, JANE GIBBONS,
AGNES MILES, EDA TOPLISS AND
GRAHAM WOODS

Social Policy
edited by MICHAEL H. COOPER

Images of Welfare
PETER GOLDING AND
SUE MIDDLETON

The Poverty Business
JOAN HIGGINS

State of Welfare
JOAN HIGGINS

Understanding Social Policy
Second edition
MICHAEL HILL

Voluntary Social Services
NORMAN JOHNSON

The Family, the State and the
Labour Market
HILARY LAND

Health, Wealth and Housing
edited by R.A.B. LEAPER

The Child's Generation
Second edition
JEAN PACKMAN

The Sociology of Welfare
GRAHAM ROOM

The Organization of Soviet
Medical Care
MICHAEL RYAN

A Charter for the Disabled
EDA TOPLISS AND
BRYAN GOULD

Provision for the Disabled
Second edition
EDA TOPLISS

Alternative Strategies for
Coping with Crime
edited by NORMAN TUTT

Community Care
ALAN WALKER

Efficiency in the
Social Services
ALAN WILLIAMS AND
ROBERT ANDERSON

Reserved for the Poor
*The Means Test in British
Social Policy*
ALAN DEACON AND
JONATHAN BRADSHAW

SOCIAL PLANNING

A Strategy for Socialist Welfare

ALAN WALKER

Basil Blackwell

For B and R, in gratitude

© Alan Walker, 1984

First published in 1984 by
Basil Blackwell Publisher Ltd.
108 Cowley Road, Oxford OX4 1JF.

British Library Cataloguing in Publication Data

Walker, Alan
    Social planning. — (Aspect of social policy series)
    1. Social policy
    I. Title   II. Series
    361.6'1   HN18

    ISBN 0-85520-453-2
    ISBN 0-85520-454-0 Pbk

Typeset by Cambrian Typesetters,
Aldershot, Hants.
Printed and bound in Great Britain by
Billing and Sons Ltd., Worcester

Contents

Preface

Planning is widely discredited. The market ideology that currently dominates government in Britain views it as a threat to individual liberty, especially to the freedom of capitalist enterprise to make its own investment, employment and other decisions. In the realm of the welfare state, planning is associated with bureaucracy and waste. At the same time, many people on the Left reject planning as being inherently undemocratic. Popularly, the memory of planning in wartime, the numerous planning disasters, the experience of nationalized industries and the image of Soviet-style centralism all combine to give planning a justifiably bad name.

So why write a book about planning when the mere mention of the word is likely to invoke, at the very least, a hostile reaction across a broad front? The straightforward answer is that, dare I say it, there is no alternative. If it is recognized that capitalism is unable, on its own, to provide any consistently effective social authority over the distribution of resources and the essentially private decisions that determine the living standards of individuals and families, for example whether or not they will be employed; if, in short, it is recognized that capitalism is unable to employ national resources efficiently and effectively in the interests of all citizens, then the alternative is likely to involve some form of planning. If, however, it is also accepted that the dangers of centralized, bureaucratic planning outweigh most of the advantages, then the proponents of planning find themselves in an apparently difficult position. The conviction that planning is essential in order to distribute resources efficiently and effectively in meeting need is countered by the belief in democratic freedom.

The cause of the impasse is that the main models of planning that we have to go by are restricted, undemocratic, or both: namely, the planned economies in Eastern Europe and, in the West, central government intervention to promote economic growth or welfare. In view of this, it is not surprising that planning is so discredited, and that ordinary people would take a great deal of convincing that they could actually take part in the planning process. Our experience of public sector planning has provided a very limited model of planning – bureaucratic, unresponsive, undemocratic, not geared to meeting need – very similar, in fact, to what happens in the private sector: decisions are made by unaccountable small groups of people in private. A new model of planning is required, one that is open and democratic, the antithesis of all that is commonly associated with the practice of planning. Indeed, the term is so strongly tainted that, if it would not be so confusing, an alternative one might be proposed.

One of the main aims of this book is to outline, and so begin a discussion about, an alternative form of planning – alternative in both scope and methods. Discussion of planning, particularly on the Left, has tended to concentrate on economic planning, while popularly it is associated more often with environmental and land use planning, and so with planning blight and 'great planning disasters' (Hall, 1981). The 'planning system', however, is usually the province of professional environmental and town planners (Amos et al., 1982). This book, however, is about *social* planning. In essence, this is planning that is directed at the distribution of resources, status and power; in other words, it is social policy planning. Along with other forms of planning, social planning has been discredited to some extent among policy-makers and policy analysts. In the first place, experience has been with a very narrow form of priority planning; once set, priorities have been quickly overridden by economic contingencies, and this has not inspired confidence in further rounds of planning. Second, the idea of planning to meet need through the welfare state conflicts with an influential body of opinion in modern social policy that supports some forms of privatization and, more generally, the promotion of a mixed economy of welfare. These developments would frustrate, to some considerable extent, the aims of planning for need and democratic involvement. Third, an as yet less influential strand of thinking in the field of social policy holds that the clients and claimants of the welfare state must be involved to a large degree in managing and running their own services. Although, as I argue in chapter 9, this position can be reconciled with the notion of planning – and indeed it is my own starting point in thinking about an alternative social planning process – the experience of Fabian-style centralist, or blueprint, planning tends to suggest a conflict between planning and democracy in the welfare state. Social planning, therefore, must be transformed if it is to provide a basis for the planned distribution of resources according to need and at the same time allow for the democratic involvement in service provision of those served by the welfare state — that is, if it is to provide a basis for socialist welfare.

As a starting point, this book provides a critique of the dominant conceptions of social policy and social planning. It is argued that they are narrowly constructed, and that this is due particularly to the influence of orthodox economics in the political system. As a result, explicit goals of social policy to meet need and promote social welfare are always mitigated by narrow economic assumptions. If social objectives, such as meeting need, are to be established as the purpose of both social and economic development, then alternative approaches to social policy and social planning (and economic policy and planning) are called for.

To this end much of the book is directed towards constructing alternative forms of socialist social policy and planning, which are aimed at distributing resources according to need. The book is intended to encourage, and also to contribute to, a discussion about the possibility of achieving distribution according to need, or socialist welfare, within a democratic society; about how we identify and meet social needs most efficiently and effectively, and how we build socialist social services on top of the existing welfare state apparatus.

The approach adopted is 'critical' in that it questions both the theory and the practice of social policy and planning. It contrasts, therefore, with the current vogue for 'rational' policy analysis. Indeed, issue is taken with the myth of value neutrality in which the application of microeconomic techniques to social policy masquerades. The rationale for this approach is a growing personal dissatisfaction with the dominant thinking in the field of social policy about the relationship between economic and social policy. This is derived, in turn, from an increasing awareness over the last 15 years of the inadequacy of, at best, ameliorative welfare state benefits and services in the face of structural inequality and dependency. Of particular importance was my participation in the national survey of household resources and standards of living (Townsend, 1979). This confirmed the structural nature of poverty, the limitations of institutionalized social policies and the need for distributional justice.

The analysis adopted here is also 'radical', or what Rein (1983, p. x) calls 'value-committed'. I argue explicitly for distribution based on need, or socialist welfare, as the only means of tackling the unequal structure of resources, status and power and of realizing the goal of social welfare. This reflects a commitment not only to understand and illuminate the social structure, but also to change it.

My approach to social policy derives principally from the work of R.H. Tawney, Barbara Wootton, Richard Titmuss and Peter Townsend. I gratefully acknowledge my debt to them and accept full responsibility for the use to which their work has been put. I am grateful to Sue Corbett, Adrian Sinfield and Peter Townsend for their comments on individual chapters and for their encouragement throughout this project. I would also like to express thanks to Vic George, Nigel Parton, Eric Sainsbury and John Westergaard for their helpful comments on the paper that first set out in detail my approach to social policy (A. Walker, 1981) and from which chapter 2 is derived, and to Huw Edwards for his helpful comments in chapter 1.

Christine Bell, Sheila Fuller and Jeanette Leaman typed the manuscript with their usual patience, accuracy and good humour. The copy editor, Susan Hughes, brought order to an untidy manuscript with great skill. Special thanks are due, finally, to Carol and Alison for sustaining me and enabling this book to be completed. None of those named is responsible for any views expressed or any remaining deficiencies in the book.

Alan Walker
September 1983

List of Abbreviations

ADSS	Association of Directors of Social Services
AES	Alternative Economic Strategy
AHA	Area Health Authority
AMA	Association of Metropolitan Authorities
CDP	Community Development Project
CIPFA	Chartered Institute of Public Finance and Accountancy
Comecon	Council for Mutual Economic Assistance (CMEA)
CPRS	Central Policy Review Staff
CSE	Conference of Socialist Economists
CSD	Civil Service Department
DEA	Department of Economic Affairs
DHA	District Health Authority
DHSS	Department of Health and Social Security
DoE	Department of the Environment
EDC	Economic Development Committee
EEC	European Economic Community
FIS	Financial Information System
GNP	Gross National Product
GRE	Grant-related Expenditure
HMSO	Her Majesty's Stationery Office
IMF	International Monetary Fund
JCC	Joint Consultative Committee
JCPT	Joint Care Planning Team
LAPS	Local Authority Planning Statements
NEDC	National Economic Development Council
NIAC	National Insurance Advisory Committee
NHS	National Health Service
PAR	Policy Analysis and Review
PESC	Public Expenditure Survey Committee

PPBS	Planning—Programming—Budgeting System
PSBR	Public Sector Borrowing Requirement
PSU	Policy Strategy Unit
QUANGO	Quasi-autonomous Non-governmental organization
RAWP	Resource Allocation Working Party
RHA	Regional Health Authority
RSG	Rate Support Grant
SBC	Supplementary Benefits Commission
SMR	Standardized Mortality Ratio
SSAC	Social Security Advisory Committee
UDC	Urban Development Corporation

We all have our values and our prejudices . . . . At the very least, we have a responsibility for making our values clear; and we have a special duty to do so when we are discussing such a subject as social policy which, quite clearly, has no meaning at all if it is considered to be neutral in terms of values.

R.M. Titmuss, *Social Policy: An Introduction.*

1
Introduction

Social planning in Britain and most other capitalist societies is under-developed. In particular, it is narrowly bureaucratic, centralized, un-responsive to need and subordinate to economic policy and planning. Its application is no less restricted in state socialist societies. One of the three prime and interrelated aims of this book is to put the case for an alternative form of concerted social planning. This would ensure the efficient and effective use of resources, and would further the achievement of social development based on need and on the promise of social policy which has yet to be realized: social welfare. At the same time, the concept of social planning may be re-established alongside social policy in academic inquiry. Since the advent of the new classical macro-economics or 'monetarism', which favours private motivation and is ideologically opposed to explicit social planning (Hayek, 1967, pp. 96–105), social planning has been relegated to an even more minor role than previously. The abolition of the Central Policy Review Staff, or government 'think tank', in June 1983 is but one manifestation of this antipathy.

A major factor in the underdevelopment of social planning is a restricted construction of the role and function of social policy as dependent on the economy. This has resulted in the adoption of minimal definitions of need as a means of rationing resources (see Foster, 1983, pp. 18–38). Also, it has led traditional social administration into an impasse. Social administration describes social deprivation based on structural differences in resources, status and power between different groups, yet has to devise policies that operate within the very structure that creates the deprivation it is concerned to overcome. There is a conflict, in other words, between the ethic and structure of capitalism (and the authoritarianism of state socialism) and some of the welfare goals of social policy. The second aim of this book, therefore, is to propose the reconstitution of key aspects of social policy into a new structural form. This *structural social policy* would be not ameliorative, but transformative: the major vehicle of social development. In capitalist societies structural social policy would be usually, though not necessarily, socialist in character (see chapter 4). The counterpart to structural social policy would be structural social planning.

As its third aim the book is intended to counter the automatic subordination of social policy to narrow economic assumptions and, as a result, of social priorities to economic priorities. It is argued, in fact, that the crude separation between economic and social policy is misleading and obstructive. Structural social policy and planning for need require the reintegration of social and economic policy and the reordering of priorities between them. Thus, social objectives would be openly stated and economic policies recognized as simply one of the means by which they may be achieved. This would pave the way for the transformation of social planning from a mechanism of control into one of development, from a cost- to a needs-orientation and from a bureaucratic to a democratic form.

In a sentence, then, this book is about the process of planning social policies: why it is so narrowly constructed in theory and practice, and what shape an alternative form of planning, aimed at promoting socialist welfare, might begin to take.

SOCIAL PLANNING

As with social policy (see chapter 2), social planning has been defined and practised in many different ways. These range from the societal level development planning, aimed at bringing about social change and achieving social objectives, which is found in some Third World countries (Gans, 1972; Midgley, 1978; Conyers, 1982; see also chapter 8 below), to the concentration on the planning of public social services, characteristic of advanced capitalist societies (Falk and Lee, 1978; Booth, 1979; Glennerster et al., 1983). In recent years the tendency in some Third World and state socialist societies has been for social planning to be concerned increasingly with development planning (Conyers, 1982, pp. 8–11; Ferge, 1979, p. 68). In contrast, in Britain and other capitalist societies social planning has been directed more and more towards the social services. This has included the co-ordination between public social services (Abel-Smith, 1967) or local voluntary welfare activities (Mayer, 1972), the rationing of public expenditure (Glennerster, 1975; Booth, 1979; Glennerster et al., 1983) and the social work role (the Barclay Committee, 1982, coined the term 'social care planning'). In practice, then, social planning has usually been equated with social services planning or personal social services planning.

The definition adopted in this book encompasses all of these approaches, for similar reasons to those advanced in chapter 2 in respect of social policy. Most importantly: unless the scope of social planning is cast sufficiently widely to include all social institutions, and not just those of the state, significant sources of social deprivation and social welfare will fall outside the competence of social planners. As with traditional social administration, social planning has been associated chiefly with the activities of the state and particularly the public social services (see chapter 2). As a result, social policies and social plans are always responding to, ameliorating, or being circumvented by, developments in the private sector. The scope of social planning, therefore, has been unnecessarily narrowly constructed. A broader conception of social planning is required to encompass relations in both public and private sectors and to reflect the scope of the approach to social policy taken here.

The definition of social planning derives from that of social policy: it is the process of developing, implementing and evaluating social policies. Social policies are those that determine the distribution of resources, status and power between different groups (see |p. 39). Social planning, like social policy, is concerned with the distribution of welfare.

The essence of social planning, therefore, is the determination of social priorities (A. Walker, 1982a, pp. 20–2; Glennerster et al., 1983, p. 2). Unless social priorities are established, social welfare is not likely to be created by the unplanned operation of social institutions, including the social services. In the words of the House of Commons Social Services Committee (1982, p. xxi), which was encouraging the DHSS to publish strategic priorities for the health and personal social services, 'In the absence of declared priorities, we fear that the most vulnerable groups may lose out.'

This definition is broader than that adopted in much of the literature on planning in advanced industrial societies. It has three connected stages (Rein, 1968, p. 144):

(1)   policy development;
(2)   policy implementation;
(3)   policy evaluation.

Policy development involves the construction and modification of social policies and the determination of strategic priorities. This includes the search for alternative policies and plans. Some definitions of social planning concentrate on this first stage. For example, Kahn (1969, p. 15) says it is 'a process of policy determination for orderly development to achieve given objectives'. Thus, according to this approach, 'policies are standing plans.'

Policy implementation covers the distribution of resources between different policy objectives — this may be at the level of national goals, between different programmes, departments or agencies or within programmes. In addition, it includes the determination of (primarily operational) priorities and the design of delivery and administrative mechanisms. It is on this second stage that most conventional definitions of social services planning are centred. Sometimes the planning process is equated with budgeting or rationing procedures, but this is only one part of the process. In practice, explicit social planning is often reduced to rationing or budgeting (see chapter 7), and this signals the fact that its application is often extremely restricted.

Policy evaluation concerns the assessment of the effectiveness of policies in practice. Monitoring is frequently mistaken for evaluation and sometimes also assumed to be planning. This is particularly true in the DHSS (see p. 181). But monitoring is backward-looking (Hambleton, 1982, p. 424), and the planning process as a whole should be forward-orientated. Equally, programming — the forward projection of increments to existing services — or forward accounting are not fully developed forms of planning, without, that is, policy evaluation and reconstruction. (Since the abolition of Programme Analysis and Review (PAR) in 1979 — one of the few mechanisms for evaluating policies — social planning in central government has become even less fully developed.) The results|of policy evaluation are fed back into the planning process to inform further policy developments. Thus, 'planning is a continuous and circular process, rather than an occasional event initiated to solve a specific problem' (Rein, 1968, p. 144). Research is crucial to each stage of this process and might be seen as one of the key dynamic elements in planning.

IDEOLOGY AND SOCIAL PLANNING

Planning is usually associated with an explicit, written blueprint (Kahn, 1969, p. 12) and the above outline of the three key stages of the social planning process tends to emphasize this characterization. This is misleading because, again like social policy, approaches to social planning are based on ideology and values.

So, for example, if it is believed that the market is the most important means of distributing resources and that public welfare is a burden on it, then explicit social planning will be confined to a narrow role, primarily in the control of welfare expenditure. If, on the other hand, the intention were to restructure the distribution of resources throughout society in order to create social welfare and to make the market subordinate to that goal, then social planning would be explicit, comprehensive and transformative. Thus, governments of all political persuasions conduct social planning in one form or another. The difference between them is in the *objectives* of planning and the *methods* of planning (see p. 91).|Social plans, therefore, are not necessarily 'good' or beneficial, and certainly are not necessarily socialist. As a broad rule of thumb we might say that, the more formal and explicit the social planning machinery, the more transformative the social goals of that planning are likely to be (but see chapter 8). Thus, as Mitchell (1966, p. 28) points out with regard to economic planning, 'Economic planning was originally, and still is largely, a policy advocated by socialists.'

Governments tending towards *laissez-faire* policies in economic and social life, such as the Conservative administrations elected in Britain in 1979 and 1983, have plans for the sort of social relations they want to create or re-create and the distribution of resources they favour, but these are rarely made explicit (see for example Brittan, 1982, p. 14). Equally, evaluation of policy effectiveness is often informal — perhaps as informal as whether it confirms one prejudice or another (social security policy-making is an obvious case; see for example, Golding and Middleton, 1982; C. Walker, 1983). The point is that the planning process does not have to be open, institutionalized and rational for planning to take place. Moreover, it does not have to be complete for planning to proceed. For example, opposition political parties plan social policies and may evaluate them by use of research or devices such as the Treasury's model of the economy, but they cannot implement them without being elected to government.

In chapter 4 different models of planned change are contrasted. The two extremes of my social planning continuum are 'bureau-incrementalism' and 'structural planning' or 'structural incrementalism'. The major difference between them is in their objectives. The first is concerned with small adjustments to existing institutions and services, and therefore never questions the present institutional framework. It is a form of planning found predominantly in large bureaucratic organizations, and favours the continuance of the existing structure (Castles et al., 1978, p. 64). The search for alternatives is very limited or non-existent (Perrow, 1973, p. 286), and change is often conducted only by means of tackling anomalies. This form is the one that is characteristic of planning in most advanced industrial societies, including state socialist societies.

The second model is a normative concept in those societies. It is concerned with planning the transformation of existing institutions and with radical change in the distribution of resources, status and power between different groups. It sets out to question existing policies and services, not as an end in itself, but in terms of their adequacy as means of distributing resources. One of the main functions of this book is to develop the concept of structural incrementalism as the basis of planning for need.

There is a danger, as Marris (1982) has pointed out, that the use of a structural metaphor will create the daunting image of a system that is immutable to change. On the other hand, it does emphasize the connection between deprivation and the structure of values, resources and social relations. The resolution of this dilemma, discussed in chapter 9, is a recognition of the dynamic nature of the social structure, which is constantly changing and being *reproduced*. This opens the door for intervention and change in the process of reproduction – that is, for structural policy and planning.

A concrete example may help to illustrate the essential differences between the two approaches to planning. Official concern is frequently expressed about the projected growth in the numbers of elderly, and especially very elderly, people up to the end of the century. Planning is rightly considered essential to cope with the impact of this major and wholly unprecedented population change. But the starting point for planning is the existing institutional framework, rather than the needs of elderly people. Thus, in the first Green Paper on the elderly, the DHSS (1978b, p. 33) argued, with regard to domicilary services, that

Overall the scope of these services seems to be right and no completely new professional skills need to be developed. However, it is vital to make the best use of all available resources . . . . This means improving co-ordination between the statutory services.

It was assumed that relatively minor adjustments to the existing framework were all that was needed to create 'a happier old age'. Moreover, the only innovations considered were, apparently, among social service professionals. There is no account, in either this document or the subsequent White Paper (DHSS, 1981a), of the needs of the elderly, or of the role of social services in creating or reinforcing dependency among the elderly (A. Walker, 1982a).

An alternative analysis that took account of these would suggest that major structural changes in policy and institutions, rather than minor modifications, are necessary in order to minimize dependency on the state, and to ensure that elderly people are able to exercise a dignified freedom of choice over how they lead their lives.

This shows that underlying the two approaches to social planning there is a fundamental conflict. Bureau-incrementalism supports the status quo in capitalist societies, and structural social planning would attempt to transform it. The form of social planning that any society or social institution adopts is a reflection of a political conflict over the distribution of resources, status and power. It is a conflict 'between the beneficiaries of the status quo and those who wish to change the status quo' (Sweezy, 1977, p. 68).

Although planning objectives may be established within the framework of bureau-incrementalism, as for example in the case of the DHSS guidelines for the growth of day care and domiciliary services (DHSS, 1976a, 1977a), these are more properly regarded as incremental or programming *targets*. The distinction is important, because these planning targets are modifications to the existing pattern of services, and do not rest necessarily on an assessment of needs and objectives. In this framework, the fundamental reappraisal of the welfare services necessary to overcome the problems of widespread poverty, deprivation and deep-seated inequalities is never considered as a realistic option. Policy analysts and social planners have tended, too readily, to support this bureau-incrementalism, either tacitly or more actively by attempting to sharpen the tools of budgeting and rationing. Because of their preoccupation with the institutionalized public services, many policy analysts and planners have overlooked the *goals* of policy (Miller, 1975). Embroiled in incremental planning, they have ignored the political components of that method of planning.

SOCIAL DEVELOPMENT AND THE FRAGMENTATION OF PLANNING

Our wide definition of social planning as the explicit or implicit planning of the distribution of welfare extends far beyond the realm of public social services. This reflects the fact that, to paraphrase Townsend (1975, p. 3), social policy and planning are no more synonymous with the activities of government than social behaviour is with government behaviour. It includes, therefore, much of what has been traditionally regarded as economic planning or physical, land use or town planning. The crude fragmentation or 'social division of planning' (A. Walker, 1981, p. 242; Booth, 1982, p. 205) has prevented a unified assessment of and response to social need and has sustained the false notion of competition between the objectives of different forms of planning. The planning of public expenditure, for example, is divorced from any consideration of private consumption (Townsend, 1972). The 'planning system' is usually the province of professional town planners, in either the public or private sector, and only rarely of the subjects or 'victims' of planning.

When we consider social development as a whole, an approach that tends to occur more often in underdeveloped than in so-called 'developed' societies (see p. 218), the separation between social, economic and physical planning 'soon ceases to have validity' (Kahn, 1969, p. 5). The most important and deeply entrenched division is between economic and social policy and planning (chapter 3). Yet this division in objectives is false and misleading. As Abel-Smith (1967, p. 16) has pointed out, all ends are social, and economic growth and development is only one of the means of achieving them: 'Why do we want economic growth if it is not to promote social and not economic ends – higher levels of living whether they are gained through collective provision or private provision?' This much has been recognized in several Third World countries (see chapter 8). But in advanced nations social and economic planning remain administratively and intellectually divided. Like the social division of welfare (Titmuss, 1968), the social division of planning reflects the distribution of power and the division of labour (A. Walker, 1981, p. 237). The division between social and economic planning and physical planning is based on similar processes of social differentiation in which classes and occupational groups, including professional planners, have attempted to promote their own interests.

In contrast to economic policy and planning, physical planners have been recognizing more and more the social components and assumptions of their work (see for example, Simmie, 1974; Pahl, 1975; Harvey, 1976; Paris, 1982). The dominant practice, however, in both economic and physical planning is to exclude critical questions about the distribution of resources, often through the development of supposedly value-neutral microeconomic techniques (Simmie, 1974, pp. 220–4; chapter 7 below); and it is a major task of social planning to impose them on the other sectors of planning. This retreat into techniques has occurred within social services planning too and may be seen as an attempt to depoliticize planning. This reflects an 'end-of-ideology' or 'convergence' belief in the superiority of existing institutions, a belief that is held particularly strongly by civil servants, and which helps to sustain the firm hold that bureau-incrementalism has over the machinery of government in all industrial societies (see p. 26).

There is not only a division between planning in the public and private sectors but also a division *within* the realm of the state. Social planning is administratively separated between central and local government, between different departments, and even within the same department (see chapter 7). This helps to explain why the goal of co-ordination has become so important in the pursuit of social planning. However, this usually means co-ordinated bureau-incrementalism (see p. 92), which attempts to align the operation of different services or different levels of the same services. The need for co-ordination is more acute the more developed is the fragmentation of planning machinery and division of labour in planning. Thus, in advanced industrial societies, in which it is believed that the structure of services is correct and all that is required is the 'fine-tuning of heaven', the main motivation for planning is the need for co-ordination (Myrdal, 1960, p. 63; Kahn, 1969, p. 14). Of particular importance in social services planning is co-ordination between the planning of strategic and operational priorities.

Strategic and operational priorities

What is meant by these two different levels of planning?

Strategic priorities are concerned with the overall allocation of resources between different services and different client groups (Algie, 1979, p. 179). They are usually expressed in terms of general objectives — for example, to increase community care — and are contained in policy statements or forward plans. Thus the document *The Way Forward*, published by the DHSS in 1977, which set out the government's national strategy on priorities for health and personal social services in England, had three broad aims (1977a, p. 6):

— to emphasise prevention;
— to remedy past neglect of services, particularly those for the mentally ill and the mentally handicapped;
— to make provision for the continuing increase in the elderly population and for the increasing number of children in local authority care.

Four years later, in a 'handbook' of policies and priorities for the health and personal social services, it was stated that the 'Secretary of State expects authorities to give priority to the further development of services, both statutory and voluntary, for . . . the following priority groups' (DHSS, 1981b, p. 20). The groups were elderly people, especially the most vulnerable and frail; mentally ill people; mentally handicapped people; and physically and sensorily handicapped people. Strategic plans were also established locally, within the framework of the national guidelines.

Having established strategic priorities, the major problem is how to put them into practice. The observation that, predictably, there is not always a simple connection between national indicative, or paper planning, and local service operation and practice has resulted in increasing attention being paid to *operational priorities* (see for example Hall, 1975; Algie, 1979; Hill, 1979). This level of planning is concerned with the distribution of resources by individual practitioners or teams within the framework of strategic priorities (Algie, 1979, pp. 179–80):

They articulate 'professional policy and practice'; are usually implied in the way work is actually carried out, though they may be more explicit in guidelines related to workloads, case-loads, case reviews, bed allocations, places in day centres, and so on; they are often justified by specific arguments in favour of one client receiving a service in preference to another.

Individual authorities, departments, teams or workers effectively make policies in the precise way that they deliver services and ration resources. They may, therefore, frustrate or further the aims of strategic planning. Two separate issues must be distinguished here.

There is the autonomy of social service professionals, which encompasses the power to allocate resources. The medical profession, for example, can authorize the expenditure of considerable sums of money in medical care on particular groups, while the social work profession can determine the allocation of substantial sums in different forms of care.

Second, there is the constitutional relationship between central and local government. Conflict may arise between the aims of central government's strategic planning and strategic or operational planning by local authorities. This relationship is further complicated by the fact that the bulk of funds for services over which the local authorities have some responsibility are provided centrally from general taxation. There is, therefore, bound to be tension between central government attempting to restrict public expenditure and taxation and local authorities seeking to respond to local need (see chapters 6 and 7).

In practice, these two conflicts of interest often coincide in the planning process. The personal social services are a good example. Statutory responsibility for the personal social services rests with elected local government. As a result, there is greater flexibility for local strategic planning in the personal social services than, for example, in the more centralized, hierarchical and managerial NHS structure. The formal position is that central government sets out broad priorities, within which local authorities determine the distribution of resources between different groups. In practice, however, local strategic plans are constructed within the context of central resource provision and (more especially) constraint, and also within the social, economic and political climate created by forces over which they may not have much influence.

A sharp distinction between strategic and operational priorities is impossible to sustain because operational priorities are also established within the context of national policies and to a significant extent are determined by them. For example, the statutory duties placed on social services departments with regard to the care of children, have resulted in a greater proportion of expenditure per head of population being devoted to child care than to other groups such as the elderly. In periods of resource constraint the dependence of operational on strategic priorities is even more pronounced, because the activities of social service workers are often restricted primarily to statutory requirements. However, since operational planning rests on individual action, there is greater potential for flexibility than in strategic planning.

The incongruence between strategic priorities determined by central government and local authorities, and operational priorities determined by social service workers, has resulted in the construction of various models aimed at matching the two more closely in a 'rational' order.

The Operational Priority System (Hall, 1975; Whitmore and Fuller, 1980) is one such method for making decisions about priorities in social work. It aims to equate the two levels of planning by recognizing that fieldworkers make operational decisions, defining these decisions and then attempting to feed them into the debate about long-term strategic planning at divisional or departmental level.

The main problem with these operational priority-scaling systems is that, in seeking to align two levels of planning more effectively, they put the fieldworker at the centre of the planning process. This places a greater reliance on the ability of professionals to represent the needs and aspirations of the consumers of these services than is justified by existing evidence about their priorities (see for example, Wilding, 1982; Goldberg and Connelly, 1982). It also puts undue weight on the role of social workers above those of other social service workers such as home helps, health visitors and care assistants.

Despite such innovations as priority-scaling and the Barclay Committee's (1982) proposal to turn social workers into 'social care planners', the problem of a lack of co-ordination between strategic plans made predominantly at the central level and the practice of social services workers is likely to remain until those responsible for carrying out the plans and those being served by them have some role in their construction. The proposals in chapter 9 are intended to secure both of these goals and thereby to achieve a closer match between strategic and operational priorities.

PLAN OF THE BOOK

The three aims of this book were outlined above. They represent the three themes that run throughout it: the narrow construction of social policy and the need for a broad, structural or socialist social policy in order to realize social welfare; the stultifying separation between economic and social policy and the need for their reintegration; and the narrow conception and underdevelopment of social planning and the need for an alternative structural form, which would be the mechanism through which social welfare is achieved.

In Part I each of these themes is taken up and expanded. Together they provide the basic arguments on which the book is based and the rationale for the proposals in chapter 9. At the heart of this section on social policy, economics and social planning is the conflict between economic efficiency and what might be termed 'social efficiency'. Economic efficiency entails a judgement about the production of a good or service at the lowest possible cost (see p. 57). In contrast, social efficiency is concerned with the impact of policy changes on the distribution of resources, status and power between different groups in society. A socially efficient policy is one that maximizes equality in the distribution of these three. The free market is not socially efficient because it does not base decisions about production and distribution on social priorities, such as need. (If the distinction between social and economic efficiency is too confusing for readers trained in economics, it might be made less so by substituting 'social equity' for social efficiency.)

An example might make this clearer. People with disabilities are a severely disadvantaged group in the labour market (see Townsend, 1981a). The orthodox economist concerned with efficiency approaches this 'problem' from the perspective of the return on the outlay of wages, or productivity. For the planner concerned with social efficiency, the key issue should be the need to secure a more equal distribution of resources, status and power between unemployed people with disabilities and others. This may require access to employment in order to ensure that this group is able to participate in social roles, relationships and consumption. Social priorities are normally subordinate to economic efficiency, and chapters 2–4 take issue with this 'natural order'.

Part II concentrates on a description of the actual practice of social and economic planning. Inevitably, the focus of attention is on the state, because of its overarching role in the economy. This Part critically appraises the subordination of social and economic planning to the financial orthodoxy of the Treasury. It traces the transition of central social planning from an already minimal system of programming and evaluation to one of control. It illustrates the underdevelopment of both official social and economic planning, and the restricted definitions of need underlying this planning.

In Part III the main alternatives to bureau-incrementalist planning are examined, including the planning in opposition of the Labour Party and the Alternative Economic Strategy. The assumption that the alternative to bureau-incrementalism is centralized, authoritarian state socialism is dismissed in favour of a more diffuse and democratic model based, in part, on aspects of development planning in Third World countries.

In the final chapter some proposals are made for a framework within which structural social planning, or planning for need, might begin to take place within a capitalist society. These suggestions reflect my conviction that social planning is the only mechanism through which the democratic transition from capitalist to socialist welfare is likely to be achieved. The reader is invited to refine and extend these, or to make alternative proposals. The book will have served its purpose if it encourages a debate about social planning and the potential for socialist welfare.

2

The Social Construction of Social Policy

INTRODUCTION

Social policy is commonly defined, studied and discussed as if it were identical to the activities of the welfare state, or to publicly provided social services. This is the prevailing tendency in Britain and other western industrial societies, and therefore in the comparative study of these societies (see for example, Rodgers, Doron and Jones, 1979). Thus, social policy is usually taken to mean state provision of social security, housing, health, personal social services and education, with the relatively recent addition of employment services. 'Social expenditure' is then defined as state expenditure on these services (Gould and Roweth, 1980; A. Walker, 1982b).

One of the main themes of this book is that this is a narrow conception, concealing as many activities that should come within the compass of social policy analysis as it reveals, and therefore stultifying the prospects for social inquiry, social planning and social development. At best, social policy is regarded as a largely passive response to the problems or 'dis-welfares' created by industrialization or economic development, rather than occupying a more positive role in producing social and economic change. *It is reactive rather than creative.*

The purpose of this chapter is to show that this concept of social policy is not a natural law, which must be accepted by successive generations of students, but is only one particular construction — albeit one that has severely restricted the scope of social policy and, at the same time, the potential for social planning. The elements of this social construction are discussed, together with some of the factors that explain the persistent hold it retains. To date, the main limitations of this approach have been exposed most clearly by recent Marxist critiques of the welfare state, and by the realization that it has failed in important respects to realize the need-orientated aspirations of much postwar social policy. Some aspects of this failure are considered as the basis for a more detailed examination in subsequent chapters. Finally, an alternative conception of social policy is outlined which provides a more comprehensive framework within which to analyse the distribution of welfare, both within and between societies, and lays the foundation for the discussion of the need for an explicitly unified social and economic policy in the next chapter.

THE SOCIAL ADMINISTRATION TRADITION

The literature on social policy and social administration encompasses a large number of definitions of social policies. There are, in fact, almost as many definitions as authors on the subject (see Baker, 1979; A. Walker, 1981). The dominant theme they share is the idea of collective, or state, intervention in the private market to promote individual welfare. According to one of the leading figures of postwar social policy analysis in Britain, T.H. Marshall (quoted in Townsend, 1975, p. 2), social policy is:

> 'the policy of governments with regard to action having a direct impact on the welfare of citizens, by providing them with services or income' − the central core of which includes 'social insurance, public (or national) assistance, housing policy', education and 'the treatment of crime'.

Although this definition does not appear in precisely the same form in subsequent editions of *Social Policy* (Marshall, 1975), it remains typical of this dominant tradition in social administration (see for example Cooper, 1973; Parker, 1975; Brown, 1976; Marsh, 1979; Hill, 1980).

If students in this tradition do not share a precise definition of social policy, in practice they do have in common their almost exclusive concern with the activities of the state through the public 'social services'. These always include the provision of social security, housing, health, education and personal social services, and sometimes extend to employment services and penal policy. The activities of what I will refer to as the private sector (covering all non-public institutions) are rarely considered, except in so far as they interact with, rely on or are encouraged by public services, such as private health care and voluntary social services.

Second, they share the view that the purpose of the welfare state is the enhancement of individual welfare. Recently a few authors have overcome the 'general reluctance' noted by Pinker (1971, pp. 147–8) to move far away from a focus on individual welfare, and have stressed the importance of *social* welfare as a goal of collective action (see for example, Ferge, 1979; Mishra, 1981). Titmuss (1963) and Donnison (1962) were at the forefront of this development.

The third common feature of this tradition is the rigid distinction between economic and social policies on the basis of the wholly different values underpinning each of them. (The first two assumptions are considered in this chapter, and the third in the following chapter.)

Since the social administration tradition has a long and distinguished history, stretching back to the work of Booth and Rowntree among others, and now forms the main intellectual and ideological context within which social policy is both studied and practised, it is important to consider its strengths and weaknesses.

On the positive side, social administration offers practical answers to a range of important problems in the operation of the social services. It is an essentially pragmatic approach to social policy and social welfare, being more concerned to prevent simpleminded acceptance of anti-collectivist theories than to develop alternatives systematically. It is empirical and reformist rather than theoretical and revolutionary (Mishra, 1981, pp. 3–4). Thus there is no generalized body of normative theory and, indeed, no clearly defined discipline of social administration (Donnison, 1962, p. 21):

> The distinctive feature of our subject is neither its body of knowledge (for most of this could be incorporated into other disciplines), nor its theoretical structure (for it has very little), and we are not interested in methodology for its own sake.

Pinker (1971, p. xii) writes in a similar vein that social administration 'has developed an impressive empirical tradition while lacking any substantial body of explanatory theory'.

The absence of theory may be seen as one of the subjects' main strengths, or alternatively as a fundamental weakness. It is a fact that, while other branches of the social sciences have tended to be obsessed with the theoretical purity of their disciplines, social administration has concentrated on empirical research and the painstaking demonstration of the survival of poverty and various forms of deprivation throughout the lifetime of the welfare state. The students of sociology, economics and politics who do not share their colleagues' singleminded interest in theory as an end in itself have tended to gravitate towards the study of social policy (Townsend, 1975, p. 1).

Second, social administration has provided a framework for the expression of altruistic and humanitarian values in teaching and research, and for the development of an academic field of study committed to modest social changes. The close association between members of this profession and political organizations and pressure groups, such as the Fabian Society and Child Poverty Action Group, as well as with postwar (especially Labour) governments, is one expression of this commitment.

Third, the study of social administration has been able to draw on expertise from the whole range of social sciences and to be more sensitive than other branches of social science to the artificial rigidity of many of the boundaries between these disciplines.

Limitations of traditional social administration

Against the considerable strengths of this legacy, however, must be set its severe limitations. Their existence should not be surprising in such a relatively young field of study, and one that may be an emergent discipline (Titmuss, 1968, p. 23; Carrier and Kendall, 1977). But my concern here is less with the largely academic question concerning the development of a fully fledged social science discipline than with the more important ones associated with the severely circumscribed basis on which social policy is perceived, studied and practised. It is not entirely certain that the achievement of the goal of a 'genuine disciplinary approach to the subject' (Mishra, 1981, p. 23) will necessarily broaden the compass of analyses in social policy. There are two sets of factors to be considered, and while progress on the former has been made, if slowly and falteringly, there is little sign of similar progress on the latter.

First, there is the traditionally atheoretical, factual and empirical stance of social administration, which has been subjected to a good deal of constructive criticism in recent years (see for example Pinker, 1971, pp. 3–14; George and Wilding, 1976; Mishra, 1981, pp. 18–25). Although this empirical approach was an understandable reaction against *laissez-faire* economic theories and the conditional welfare policies they fostered (Pinker, 1971, p. 49; 1979, p. 98), it has been sustained by a 'concern with social amelioration within a framework of social and moral consensus' (Mishra, 1981, p. 18) on the part of those working within, as well as those sponsoring research in, social administration. As a result of this exclusive concern with social reform, insufficient attention has been paid to the structural causes of social problems such as poverty, and to the need for changes in the social structure if they are to be overcome.

The absence of a theoretical framework within which to study and formulate social policies and plan social change is a major limitation to social planning and social development. Without this framework social policy is likely to remain reformist and parochial and most importantly, therefore, will not provide the basis for the realization of social welfare through social planning. Significant steps have been taken recently in laying some theoretical foundations for the conceptualization of welfare and the study of social policy through the approach based on the delineation of different ideological attitudes to, or models of, welfare (Titmuss, 1974; Parker, 1975; George and Wilding, 1976; Mishra, 1981; and, for their application to the comparative study of social policy, Higgins, 1981). Despite this, new theoretical developments are either incorporated into standard practice in social administration or rejected out of hand (Taylor-Gooby and Dale, 1981, pp. 12–13).

Second, and apparently much more intractable, there is the overriding interest of the social administration tradition in Britain in state intervention through the public social services. This excessively narrow focus imposes at least five major limitations on the analysis of social policy and of the central concept in this field, social welfare (Townsend, 1975, pp. 2–3).

The social production of needs

There is the constant danger that significant sources of social inequalities and social welfare will be overlooked because attention is focused only on social reform and only on one form of government action. Thus, in exclusively 'welfare statist' approaches to social policy, the agenda of need is set by the public social services (A. Walker, 1983). But needs are produced and met by a wide range of social institutions and groups. These include, but also stretch beyond, the institutions of the state. The point may be illustrated with references to the important problem of low pay.

Measures to meet the needs of low paid workers may be based on state tax, incomes or minimum wage policies, as well as through the social security system or institutions such as wage councils. In addition, the problem may be tackled at source by employers in different industrial sectors, perhaps as a response to trade union pressure. But as well as meeting some of the needs of the low paid, state social security policies may also reinforce and perhaps encourage low pay through the creation of the 'poverty trap' and the subsidy that is effectively given to low paying employers by the provision of a means-tested benefit such as Family Income Supplement in respect of poor wages (Jordan, 1973; A. Walker, 1982). Similarly, wage councils may have depressed, rather than increased, the wages of the employees they cover (Winyard, 1976).

Some of the causes of low pay are closely related to industrial structure or to the type and scale of production, which particularly influences the cohesiveness of the workforce. Low pay is also created in declining areas as the structure of industry changes, with the break-up of the skilled workforce and the introduction of new production, often calling for part-time unskilled workers. But the industrial structure of an area does not simply change according to some law of nature; the state itself plays a major role in determining the pattern of industry, through its investment and purchasing policies and through its industrial location policies. The living standards of individuals in communities are intimately related to the complexion of local industry, which in turn rests on national and multinational organizations (CDP, 1977; Foster, 1982). Thus, over time, industrial investment and pay policies are more important than social security policies in determining living standards.

Social policy analysis that includes only the explicit intentions of state relocation or regional development policies and social security policies will ignore many factors that actually cause low pay, including the social consequences of different forms of investment and the pay policies of different firms and industries. In view of this narrow focus on the state, it is not surprising that the analysis of the social creation and distribution of needs and dependencies is so underdeveloped in social policy, in relation to the study of the social responses to those needs (A. Walker, 1980a).

The role of power

The one-dimensional approach to social policy tends to oversimplify the nature and operation of power. In particular, it overlooks the 'second face' of power, an implicit or non-decision-making face, as opposed to an explicit decision-making one (Bachrach and Baratz, 1970, pp. 3–16; Lukes, 1974). But those alternatives that are excluded from policy proposals are as important to an understanding of social policy as the officially published record.

Bachrach and Baratz (1970, p. 8) have argued convincingly against this simplistic pluralist position that identifies power with concrete decision-making: 'to the extent that a person or group — consciously or unconsciously — creates or reinforces barriers to the public airing of policy conflicts, that person or group has power.' Lukes (1974, p. 23) goes further to show that power may be exercised directly over an individual or group, but also indirectly in determining their response to that exercise of power:

A may exercise power over B by getting him to do what he does not want to do, but he also exercises power over him by inflencing, shaping or determining his very wants. Indeed, is not the supreme exercise of power to get another or others to have the desires you want them to have — that is, to secure their compliance by controlling their thoughts and desires?

Approaches that concentrate only on the outcome of deliberations, and not on those options that were never considered, are unquestioningly accepting the prevailing distribution of power as expressed in the political agenda. For example, in the study of poverty the crucial interconnection between poverty and inequality may be forgotten in the overwhelming desire to make acceptable ameliorative proposals. Thus the structure of inequality may be accepted in the false belief that, within it, the problem of poverty can be solved by reform

(Westergaard, 1972, p. 155). Social problem-solving can be carried on in isolation from a critique of the social structure only if the meaning of power and the mechanisms by which it is reproduced are distorted and the causes of poverty and deprivation are ignored. Similarly, accounts of the making of social policy that give too little attention to the multidimensional operation of power are apt to over-emphasize the influence of individuals in the policy-making process, and to under-emphasize both the structural determinants of social change and the position of individuals in the social structure (see for example Crossman, 1977; Hall, 1976; Banting, 1979; Donnison, 1982).

'Social' v. 'public'

As a result of the narrow focus of social administration, policies without explicit 'social' objectives are neglected by policy analysts. The main examples are those policies labelled as 'economic', which are discussed at length in the next chapter. Others include the transport policies of government, local authorities and private bus companies, which can have a significant impact on the well-being of citizens. Defence policy may not be explicitly social, but the level of employment in some areas of the country is closely related to it (CDP, 1977, pp. 78–9), and poverty among some soldiers' families is determined by the level of forces pay. In addition, there is the provision of housing and other social facilities for the armed forces.

Social policy extends beyond the boundaries of state provision. Social policies cover not only the welfare policies of the central and local state, but also those of industry and commerce and voluntary bodies. This tendency in traditional and some radical approaches (see for example Jones and Novak, 1980, p. 143) derives from the dominance of the empirical approach which describes and evaluates service provision and the explicit rationales of policies. It does not, moreover, include all forms of state intervention in social life, but only those defined as 'social services'.

Comparative social policy

Pinker (1971, p. 48) has pointed to the small number of comparative studies of social policy and to the continuing 'stubborn resistance' to conducting them (see also Higgins, 1981, p. 31). Comparative social policy forces us to recognize that we cannot study state activities alone to understand how societies produce and distribute welfare. In order to compare social policies in health care between Britain and the United States, it is necessary to look at both public and private sectors, including the medical policies of industry and the state, since concentration on one alone will reveal only part of the actual practice of health care. Also, a thorough analysis would include the even wider range of interests and institutions that are involved in the social *creation* of ill health and disablement (A. Walker, 1980; 1983).

Social planning

As well as restricting the scope of social policy, traditional social administration has limited severely the potential of social planning. Thus, as I argue in detail in chapter 4 below, social planning has come to be associated primarily with public administration and particularly with the administration of the social services. Social planning, again like social policy, is administratively fragmented within the realm of government, outside it and between the two. Within government, planning is regarded either as a technical adjunct to administration or as a mechanism for controlling resources − or both. It has not been comprehensively addressed to overall social development. Instead, social planning has been assigned a restricted bureaucratic role.

Paradoxically, then, the professed aim of social policy to promote welfare is seriously inhibited by the restrictions placed on its scope and competence. It may ignore sources of inequality and dis-welfares that fall outside the realm of public policies. It does not provide an adequate framework in which to analyse those 'social' institutions that do not 'foster integration and discourage alienation' or that have dual functions (Titmuss, 1968, p. 22). It tends to be parochial, paying insufficient attention to systems of distribution in other countries, and therefore it rejects solutions to similar problems in other countries (see for example the consideration given to compensation schemes in other countries by the Royal Commission on Civil Liability and Compensation for Personal Injury, 1978, pp. 51−9). It restricts the role of both social policy and planning in social development.

THE SOCIAL CONSTRUCTION OF THE WELFARE STATE

Social policy consists of institutionalized principles or intentions; while the welfare state is the social services provision by the state. Through the social administration tradition in Britain the two have become equated. Thus, according to Marshall (1975, p. 15),

> *Social policy* uses political power to supersede, supplement or modify operations of the economic system in order to achieve results which the economic system would not achieve on its own, and that in doing so it is guided by values other than those determined by open market forces.

In a similar vein Briggs (1961, p. 228) argues that:

> A *'welfare state'* is a state in which organized power is deliberately used (through politics and administration) in an effect to modify the play of market forces in at least three directions — first, by guaranteeing individuals and families a minimum income irrespective of the market value of their work or their property; second, by narrowing the extent of insecurity by enabling individuals and families to meet certain 'social contingencies' ... and third, by ensuring that all citizens without distinction of status or class are offered the best standards available in relation to a certain agreed range of social services.

The parallel growth of social administration and welfare state services and the close relationship between the two is one important factor in explaining the perpetuation of a limited conception of social policy. The growth of the social administration teaching profession has been closely associated with welfare state institutions, particularly social work. Starting out as a practical guide to the social services, 'mainly for the benefit of intending social workers', it has grown along with social work and the public social services over the postwar period (Brown, 1976, p. 18). The historical link between social administration and social work training probably helps in large measure to account for the focus of many definitions on the individual and personal welfare.

The close association between social administration and the state — in terms of research funds the latter is usually the hand that feeds — has at best fostered a relatively uncritical stance towards the state. At its worst, this association can breed the belief that the primary function of those working in the field of social policy is to produce research and ideas that will be of practical value to policy-makers in government (see for example, Rodgers et al., 1979, p. 220).

The dominance of consensus

It is not mere coincidence that the social construction of social policy as representing beneficial public services is matched by a similar social construction of the welfare state; the two views are interrelated. Both have their roots in a theory, or rather in a group of similar theories, which are broadly classified as order theories of society. In contrast to conflict theories, they stress consensus, stability and functional integration. 'Individuals in society, according to this theory, share the same basic social values and are thus agreed on the way they behave towards each other as individuals and as members of groups' (George and Wilding, 1976, p. 2). The inadequacies of these sociological theories as explanations of social order and social change have been long exposed (Lockwood, 1956; Goldthorpe, 1962). But benign functionalism maintains a firm hold on public and academic conceptions of social policy and the welfare state, partly because the dominant tradition in the postwar (Butskellite) political consensus is one of social reform.

The institutional form of the 'welfare state' was founded on the work of social reformers such as Booth, Rowntree and especially Beveridge. The liberal, or 'neo-mercantilist' (Pinker, 1979), values from which this tradition draws its inspiration are consensus-based, as are the pluralist political theories associated with it. (The classic statement of pluralism is Dahl (1961). For a recent application to social policy see Hall et al. (1975); and for a critique, see Gough (1978).) Because social administration is concerned with the reform of practical problems in the operation of the welfare state, it has attempted to foster a social and moral consensus around the aims of welfare services (Mishra, 1981, p. 18). This, coupled with the close association of many of those working in social administration with the welfare services and the policy-making process, helps to explain why it has not produced a more fundamental appraisal of the welfare state.

One important expression of this consensus approach to welfare, on which the postwar settlement was founded and on which basis support for the welfare state has been periodically reaffirmed, at least until the election of the Conservative government in May 1979, is the end-of-ideology thesis. Writing in the late 1950s and early 1960s, social scientists such as Bell (1965) were arguing that the major ideological battles were over and that the welfare provisions of all countries would converge. More recently, Wilensky (1975, p. 86), in a similar vein, attempted to argue that growth is the 'main explanation' for the development of welfare states and that, with economic growth, 'all countries develop similar social security programs'.

The pervasive impact of this thesis can be discerned through both general public and professional attitudes to welfare services. In a survey of people in EEC member countries in 1976, the UK had the lowest proportion of people attributing poverty to injustices in society (16 per cent, compared with 35 per cent in France) and the largest proportion attributing it to laziness and lack of willpower (43 per cent, compared with 16 per cent in France). Altogether, one-fifth of the UK sample felt that *too much* was being done to combat poverty (the largest proportion outside the UK was one-tenth in Luxembourg and Denmark) (Riffault and Rabier, 1977; but see also Lansley and Weir, 1983).

The end-of-ideology thesis is also pervasive among those administering the social services, as the following quotation from the first annual report of the Supplementary Benefits Commission (1976, p. 11) demonstrates:

Whatever the starting points of their social security systems, all governments endeavour gradually to correct their weaknesses, and thus to produce patterns of service which tend to converge. It is no accident that the main debates about social security in Britain have for a decade or more focused on pensions, on family support, and more recently on the needs of the severely disabled. Contentious though they originally were, these debates have at last created a large measure of consensus among the political parties . . . .

Thus services have come to be seen as ends in themselves. It may be argued that a service is inadequate in coverage, but never misguided in operation. The wider structural context is forgotten in the belief that the existing framework of service provision is the best starting point. As Galper (1978, p. 38) argues,

> Conventional service providers view services either as containing a solution to the problem, as an end in themselves, or they view them as potentially enabling clients to go forth in the world and individually battle their way to health and success.

Stemming from the influence of consensus theory are the ideas that the welfare state has been achieved and that, in an international context, the British solution is the best, the 'envy of the world'. The battle for social welfare was won during the war and in the immediate postwar period; all that is needed now, as the above quotation from the SBC illustrates, are various technical adjustments to ensure smooth running or, as Rose (1978, p. 3) puts it, the 'fine-tuning of heaven'.

In place of a dynamic concept, over which some groups' views may be at variance with others and which itself may create dis-welfares, or the instrument through which the effects of social changes are managed, the welfare state is seen as a once-and-for-all achievement, and is assumed to create welfare. Marshall (1975, p. 99) notes that 'The British Welfare State was the culmination of a long movement of social reform that began in the last quarter of the nineteenth century.' Other writers have also traced that 'evolution' of the welfare state, or have mapped out 'milestones' along the road to its achievement (Bruce, 1961).

However inadequate this social construction of the welfare state may appear, there can be no doubt about its influence on social policy and planning. It has inhibited social inquiry and social change by encouraging the attitude that the welfare state is a finite achievement and a shining example to the world, that the activities of the welfare state represent progressive increments to welfare, and therefore that major social changes are not necessary to eliminate poverty and deprivation. The inadequacies of these assumptions, and particularly the two central ones — that welfare rests on the activities of the state and that these activities are necessarily beneficial — have been exposed by the critique of the welfare state that developed from the work of Titmuss and has been enjoined, more recently, by some of the clients

of welfare services and those working with them. It is to a discussion
of these developments that I turn now.

THE SOCIAL DIVISION OF WELFARE

Criticism of two of the key components of the social administration
tradition — the equation of social with public services and the assumption
that the purpose of social policy and of the welfare state is the
enhancement of welfare — was expressed for the first time from within
its ranks by Titmuss (1963). In his seminal essay, 'The Social Division
of Welfare', Titmuss outlined the basis for a definition of social services
based on their functional similarities rather than on administrative
boundaries: 'The definition of what is a "social service" should take
its stand as aims; not on the administrative methods and institutional
devices employed to achieve them' (Titmuss, 1963, p. 42).

By distinguishing between social welfare, or more properly 'public
welfare' (the public social services), fiscal welfare (tax allowances and
reliefs) and occupational welfare (benefits and services provided by
employers), Titmuss demonstrated that social policy may be implemented through a range of institutions and not simply through
those conventionally recognized as 'social services'. By questioning the
assumptions that the performance of welfare has fulfilled the promise
of welfare, and that the welfare state has redistributed resources from
rich to poor (Titmuss, 1963, p. 38), he cast doubt on the prevailing
belief that the sole purpose of the welfare state is the enhancement
of welfare.

Welfare as a public burden

The enduring force of the social division of welfare analysis lies in its
exposure of the alternative sources of welfare that there are to public
social services. Thus, as Titmuss (1963, p. 53) noted, the welfare
state depends on a 'stereotype of social welfare which represents only
the more visible part of the real world of welfare'. This has important
implications for social policy and for the politics of welfare.

In the first place, it ensures that the public are aware of only public
expenditure on the welfare state, and not of public expenditure on tax
reliefs and on subsidizing fringe benefits, or of private expenditure on

welfare. This forms the basis for the proselytization of the 'public burden' view of welfare, which holds that public social services are a drain on the productive sector, a view that has recently been enjoying a new lease of life (Bacon and Eltis, 1976; A. Walker, 1982b, p. 11). Public expenditure on the social services is constantly under the scrutiny of politicians and the media, a close attention that is not afforded to other sectors of welfare. This bias reinforces the social construction of social welfare as a burden (Golding and Middleton, 1982, p. 167). The growth of 'private' welfare provision for professional and other non-manual groups is seldom debated, though is as surely paid for out of public contributions, through prices or subsidies, as the public sector of welfare is paid for through taxation. The public burden model of welfare, together with the increasing unfairness of the tax system (Pond, 1982), are important factors in explaining the increasing opposition to public expenditure on the social services in the 1970s and early 1980s.

The social construction of welfare as *public* welfare also creates reactions against those people, especially the 'undeserving' poor such as the unemployed, who rely solely on this source of income (Golding and Middleton, 1978; 1982). A more balanced view of welfare across the three sectors distinguished by Titmuss would, in all probability, considerably reduce the tendency to label only those clients of public welfare as 'scroungers'. This social construction of welfare also militates against the reform of public social services. By disguising transfers of public resources through the fiscal and occupational sectors, a distorted picture of the beneficiaries of the welfare state and of the extent of redistribution is created (Sinfield, 1978, p. 148). Thus it is believed that redistribution has been in one direction only — from rich to poor — and, despite the large body of evidence to the contrary, that this has gone too far.

The divisions between different institutions in the implementation of social policy remain as sharp today as when they were outlined by Titmuss. The Treasury grudgingly acknowledged that there may be less justification for its division between 'social' and 'fiscal' welfare, but this has not resulted in any fundamental change in its analysis of the relationship between the two. Since 1978 the annual White Paper on the government's public expenditure plans has contained some limited information on tax reliefs, including the tax relief and option mortgage subsidy going to owner—occupiers, as well as subsidies to public sector tenants in local authority and new town housing and support through rent rebates and allowances. According to the Treasury (1979, p. 17),

> Public expenditure ... presents only part of the picture. For an improved understanding of the role of fiscal policy it is necessary to look also at certain of the reliefs embodied in the taxation system. Such reliefs can have broadly the same effect on the Government's borrowing requirements as public expenditure ... there is a case for saying that, where a tax relief benefits a particular group of tax-payers, or a particular sector of the economy, it should be taken into account along with direct public expenditure related to those tax-payers or that part of the economy.

Although the force of the social division of welfare thesis is enduringly strong, particularly in explaining the social construction of welfare, it has several major drawbacks. Titmuss limited his analysis of social policy to those that are influenced directly or indirectly by government. When noting the great expansion in occupational welfare benefits in cash and in kind, he reasoned that 'Their ultimate cost falls in large measure on the Exchequer' (Titmuss, 1963, p. 50). While he classified occupational fringe benefits as 'social services', 'duplicating and over-lapping social and fiscal welfare benefits', this classification appears to rest on the fact that they are legitimized and subsidized by the state (Titmuss, 1963, p. 51; 1968, p. 192). Moreover, while recognizing the often self-interested exercise of professional power, he failed to sustain this analysis to include class conflict as a basis for the development of social policy (Wedderburn, 1965, p. 138).

Although there are limitations, the social-division-of-welfare thesis continues to be the source of new inspiration for students of social policy and to demonstrate a remarkable analytic capacity (Sinfield, 1978; Graycar, 1983). Unfortunately, this has only rarely been exploited, and the paradigm itself has been only partially implemented (Rose, 1981, p. 493). Titmuss provided a framework within which to relate the social policies of different institutions, but this has not been taken up subsequently in order to extend the compass of social policy analyses.

Moreover, although he recognized that policies may have unintended as well as intended consequences (Titmuss, 1968, p. 22), the former are related solely to the production of dis-welfare and the latter to the production of welfare or integration (Titmuss, 1968, p. 131). Titmuss (1968, p. 133) argued that, for many of the consumers of social services, they represent not increments to welfare but partial compensation for social costs and social insecurities. The possibility that 'dis-welfares' or 'dis-services' may be one of the *intentional* consequences of social policy was not considered. In practice, the social-division-of-welfare thesis may conjure up the false image of social (i.e. public) welfare battling against inequalities forged in the fiscal and occupational sectors, or being undermined by them.

THE POLITICAL ECONOMY OF WELFARE

The social-division-of-welfare approach does not provide a framework in which to relate social development to the structure of social relations and the distribution of power. The production of social problems and the responses by the state in the form of redistribution must be examined in relation to the dominant interests at various levels of the policy system. Thus, the social division of welfare itself may be seen to reflect the dominance of certain values in social organization, and the social creation of various needs and their subsequent legitimation and socialization by the state. It also reflects the social relationship between the state and the dominant class interests in society, which in turn underpin the development of the division of labour. Undoubtedly, as Titmuss argued, the division of labour creates interdependencies, and it is the precise social formation and distribution of these that must be analysed and explained: the way that certain social groups control and use such developments in their own interest. An important part of this inquiry concerns the role that social policy and social services play in creating or enhancing inequalities and dependencies, in reinforcing certain values and in reproducing and controlling behaviour.

The clients' view of welfare

During the 1960s and 1970s the inadequacy of traditional conceptions of social policy and welfare were exposed by the growing realization that many of the institutions thought to hold the key to welfare were at the same time, in important respects, operating as means of social control (Fox Piven and Cloward, 1972). The crude social construction of the welfare state as the font of welfare was dismantled gradually by the constant feedback from clients of the welfare state, chiefly through the Community Development Projects (CDPs) and welfare rights movement, reporting that their experience of welfare institutions was often closer to repression than welfare. At best, welfare services, particularly in social security and housing, seemed to impose nearly as many sanctions as benefits. The clients of the welfare state, and indeed many of those working within these services, are therefore confronted with an apparently confusing situation (London Edinburgh Weekend Return Group, 1979, p. 8):

> The ways in which we interact with the state are contradictory — they leave many people confused. We seem to need things from the state, such as child care, houses, medical treatment. But what we are given is often shoddy or penny-pinching, and besides, it comes to us in a way that seems to limit our freedom, reduce the control we have over our lives.

Seen in this light, it is not surprising that, in a period of cuts in social expenditure during the late 1970s and early 1980s, the clients of the welfare state have not been among its staunchest defenders (A. Walker, 1982b, p. 15).

The liberal social construction of the welfare state has been subject to close criticism by students of social policy from the standpoints of both Fabian socialism and Marxist political economy. The former have demonstrated that the redistributive impact of the welfare state has been massively overestimated (see for example Townsend and Bosanquet, 1972; LeGrand, 1978, 1982; Townsend, 1979, pp. 116—76). Following from this sort of analysis, Marxists have shown that the welfare state is an integral part of the fabric of modern capitalist societies (see for example Miliband, 1969; Westergaard and Resler, 1975; Corrigan and Leonard, 1978; Gough, 1979). Both have provided important insights into the nature of welfare and the welfare state. These insights enable us to make the transition from an empirically based social policy to a normative one, from description to prescription. In particular, there is, on the one hand, the fact that distribution is at the heart of social policy (Donnison, 1975; A. Walker, 1981a), and on the other the fact that the institutions of the welfare state embody and therefore reflect the values and contradictions of the societies in which they are constructed (Gough, 1979; Ginsburg, 1979).

The dual functions of state welfare

Approaches to social policy based on Marxist political economy take as their starting point the fact that the welfare state, like the state itself, reflects the fundamental 'contradiction' of capitalist societies between the forces of production and the relations of production. This is the contradiction between the tendency of the capitalist mode of production to increase the potential for human freedom and development, and the tendency for the institutions and social relations that arise out of that mode of production to reduce freedom and increase insecurity. Thus, according to Gough (1979, p. 12), the welfare state

> simultaneously embodies tendencies to enhance social welfare, to develop the powers of individuals, to exert social control over the blind play of market forces; and tendencies to repress and control people, to adapt them to the requirements of the capitalist economy.

Although there are undoubtedly problems associated with Marxist accounts of social policy (see for example Pemberton, 1983), recognition of this dualism does at least enable us to escape from the blind-alley that traditional approaches to social policy inevitably end up in when they assume that social services are based on alternative principles of distribution to those that are dominant in society as a whole. There is, in fact, an inherent paradox underlying these approaches. Social policy can operate within the confines of capitalism to meet some of the social costs of industrial production and to assist the market in matters such as training, rehabilitation and health care; but if social policies have genuine social welfare aims and are to be treated as serious attempts at allocating resources according to 'need' or other *non-market* principles, then clearly these aims are constantly frustrated by the market itself. As postwar experience in British and other capitalist countries shows, if concern with 'social' aspects is restricted to the public sector, this may result in the amelioration of some social problems, but it will not have much impact on the overall distribution of resources.

The false separation between the institutions of the welfare state and those of the rest of society rests in large part on the equally false presentation of the state as a separate and neutral agency counterposing the economic market (London Edinburgh Weekend Return Group, 1979, p. 52):

> It is common to think of the state as being set apart from the rest of society. People sometimes think of the state as compensating for the inequalities of capitalist society, as redressing the balance between rich and poor. Or, even, if the government is clearly not doing much for the poor at present, it is argued that its policies should be changed, that the state 'ought' to help redress the balance more.

This corresponds to a liberal view of state intervention, but also draws on the *laissez-faire* conception of the state as an independent arbiter or umpire (Friedman, 1962; George and Wilding, 1976, p. 33). Of course the state is nothing of the sort. Even if it is not accepted that the state is 'simply a committee for managing the common affairs of the bourgeoisie', and such a bald assertion is difficult to accept, the dominant interests in any society are disproportionately represented within the state apparatus. In a capitalist society, these interests are primarily those of the capitalist class (Miliband, 1969). Because the distribution of power and advantage is not equal in class societies such as Britain, the conflict between classes is not equal, and the outcome is not an equal balance between them. If any society is to survive in its current form, then the state must not simply embody the prevailing structure of social relations; it must also take measures to promote their *reproduction* (an important concept that I return to in chapter 9).

So the state has a dual character. On the one hand, it has provided the institutional framework within which the welfare of the working class has been extended. But on the other, it has ensured that these institutions enforce the central values of capitalism, which at times conflict with the welfare of the working class (Ginsburg, 1979, p. 19). It is from this that the element of dualism in the welfare state is derived. Thus, in addition to being a vehicle for social welfare, social policy is often in part an instrument of class domination, social reproduction and control. The primary values on which capitalist distribution is based are inequality, individualism, monetary incentives and the work ethic. The 'control' or reproduction functions that these values imply for the welfare state include the disciplining of the labour force, the reproduction of the labour force and the reproduction of capitalist social relations, including the sexual division of labour. For example, women's dependence on men is reinforced by the social services through administrative devices such as the combined assessment of a couple's income, the assumption that the male is the breadwinner, and the cohabitation rules in the provision of social security (Lister and Wilson, 1976); and, less directly, through the assumptions about the role of women in providing care to relatives in the provision of personal social services (Moroney, 1976; Land, 1978, 1980).

Fundamental to capitalist (and state socialist) society is the work ethic (or what should more properly be termed the 'paid-employment ethic'). Welfare services will not endanger this ethic to a significant extent and will positively promote adherence to it. This can be gauged from newspapers such as the *Daily Mail, Daily Express* and *Sun*, which explode periodically with stories about 'scroungers' and 'dole-dodgers' (see Golding and Middleton, 1982, pp. 112–53).

The implications of the dual role of some forms of welfare provision are felt most immediately by the clients of the welfare state, particularly the 'short-term' claimants of supplementary benefit (which still includes all unemployed people claiming supplementary benefit). Their benefit is set so low (about one-third of adult male net earnings) as to allow a bare subsistence minimum, and therefore to discourage claims and prevent inappropriate life-styles. And their family circumstances and relationships are closely scrutinized by officials to ensure correct behaviour while on benefit. Moreover, they are often badgered by unemployment review officers, regardless of whether or not there are any jobs available (Sinfield, 1981, p. 115).

The rationale for such disciplinary functions was spelt out at length by the Committee on Abuse of Social Security Benefits in its assessment of the value of unemployment review officers in times of high unemployment, or in areas of high unemployment such as Wales and the North East. The Committee (1973, p. 96) suggested that relieving the unemployed of pressure from unemployment review officers could lead to:

psychological damage to the individual of allowing him to recline on benefit and abandon the search of work; the general effect on public attitudes to work and self-help, and on the extent to which the whole notion of a social security system paid for out of contributions and/or taxes is called into question . . . . officials of the DE and DHSS . . . have told us of the views held by the regional controllers and those working under them, some in regions where unemployment is especially high. They believe that society does benefit from a continuance of the work of unemployment review officers and others in relation to the long-term unemployed even in times and in areas of high unemployment.

The significance of deterrence was put, more succinctly, by Beveridge (1909, p. 195): 'the decision of the workmen to work or not depends to some extent on what happens to those who do not work.'

Control functions of welfare

The literature on the operation of the welfare state is full of such instances of the divergence — if not contradiction — between the theory and practice of welfare provision. The aim of welfare is constantly frustrated by the desire to sustain and reproduce the dominant structure of social values and relations, even when these are the antithesis of social welfare. Beneath the velvet glove there is often the iron fist.

As a result, few aspects of the welfare state are uncontentious. But while the capitalist class may be more or less united in opposition to some, though by no means all, benefits and services, the allegiance or opposition of the working class is fragmented. This is due partly to the individualism of capitalist society (London Edinburgh Weekend Return Group, 1979, p. 57), one component of which is the role of social services in individualizing social problems and atomizing political action (Galper, 1978). But also there is the fact that the potential target for opposition is elusive. There is not a simple dichotomy between services that promote welfare and services that promote control; both functions are combined to a different degree, implicitly and explicitly, in most services. Control functions are aimed primarily at disciplining the workforce, while welfare functions may increase the welfare of the workforce or the reproduction of the workforce, or may facilitate a more flexible labour supply. In other words, those activities that promote welfare may also make an important contribution to capitalist and other development (Jones and Novak, 1980, p. 152).

To argue, however, that the control functions are the primary functions of the welfare state (Ginsburg, 1979, p. 2) is to make an assertion unsupported by the facts. For example, by far the largest component of social expenditure is social security, and well over half of that expenditure goes to those over retirement age (Bradshaw, 1982, p. 93). Moreover, this position closes the door to the development of socialist welfare policies under capitalism (see chapter 9). But the precise balance between welfare and control differs both between and within services. The control functions are easier to detect within social security than within the health service, and welfare functions are more apparent in the personal social services than in housing.

Many of the subtleties of this discipline and control are not apparent because of the ideological support provided by other institutions, such as the media. Thus, social services can enhance the welfare of some special minority groups without challenging the values of the majority. Only the more repressive aspects of the welfare state — the cohabitation rule, liable relatives officers, unemployment review officers and so on — are obvious to clients and claimants, and the response to these is individualized and therefore is not directed at the state. So claimants' anger is often vented on other claimants, DHSS staff, themselves or their families. Yosser and Chrissie portrayed the frustration, repression and self-criticism that are encouraged by welfare services in the outstanding series of television plays by Alan Bleasdale, *The Boys from the Black Stuff*.

Despite the twin critique, from the Fabian and Marxist schools of thought, of the social construction of the welfare state as being uniquely for the working class, the degree of consensus about the purpose of the welfare state is remarkable. Anti-collectivists who argue that the state should be drastically curtailed, liberals and social democrats who support the mixed economy of welfare, and some socialists who argue that state social services should be extended all agree that welfare services are beneficial to the working class. While this is undoubtedly true to some extent, the redistributory impact of the welfare state has been massively overestimated (see for example Townsend, 1979, pp. 964–79; LeGrand, 1982). Furthermore, the *potential* for significant redistribution within the existing institutions, and more importantly within the existing structure of social relations, has been similarly overestimated. The social construction of the welfare state has successfully disguised not only who benefits from its services, but also the degree of change necessary to deliver the promise of welfare.

Recent analyses of welfare from the perspective of Marxist political economy have provided some valuable insights into the dual nature of the state and public policy and the sometimes contradictory growth of social welfare provision in capitalist societies. But there are serious drawbacks in attempting to use this approach as the basis for the development of a theory of social policy and social planning.

These analyses focus narrowly on the state in capitalist societies. As a result there is a strong tendency to equate social policy with the welfare state, with all the resulting restrictions for the analysis of social welfare associated with more traditional social administration. Gough (1979, p. 4), for example, excludes occupational welfare in so far as it develops independently of the state. The difficulty is apparent when Marxists like Gough (1979, pp. 4–5) are forced into a position something like the convergence thesis held by civil servants quoted on p. 26 above. They tend to be over-deterministic, implying, for example, that repression and control are necessary features of all aspects of welfare under capitalism (Pemberton, 1983, p. 302). Furthermore, although this perspective has proved a fertile basis for several penetrating analyses of the welfare state, these have been entirely theoretical and have not been accompanied by a pragmatic and prescriptive element similar to that which has proved to be the main strength of traditional social administration. A fusion of elements of these two paradigms, of theory and praxis, might overcome the short-comings of both, and create a basis on which to plan social development.

FROM SOCIAL ADMINISTRATION TO SOCIAL POLICY

What is it then that distinguishes *social* policies from other forms of policy? Social policies cannot be distinguished on the basis of their expressed rationales alone, on the explicit functions enshrined in official legislation and other rules, since institutions may serve several functions. It is not possible to divide policies neatly into market and non-market, egoistic and altruistic, with the implication that one set is 'bad' and the other 'good'. The distinction is as false as that attempted between productive and unproductive labour, but reflects the same ideological stance that places 'business' decisions outside the realm of 'social' concern and the competence of democratic authorities.

The scope of social policy cannot rest on the identification of need or 'states of dependency' similar to those covered by the state, although they are an important part of the subject matter of social policy. If these criteria were employed, we might include pensions provided by private companies but not, for example, company cars and clothing allowances (Titmuss, 1968, p. 193). Moreover, social policy has not attempted a concerted study of wage policy, wage structure and pricing policy in private industry. Without a study of the social formation and distribution of original income, social policy will remain one-dimensional, passive and reactive.

Thus, the concern of social policy analysis is as much with the processes by which needs are defined and created, with the structure of inequality, as with the social services institutionalized by the state to meet them. These processes are governed by the structure of society, the dominant mode of production and the resulting social relations. So in a capitalist society such as Britain, the values of capitalism are uppermost in economic and social development.

Social policies cannot be distinguished on the basis of the institutional apparatus through which different forms of welfare may be provided: the supplementary benefits system, social service departments, schools, insurance companies. Nor is it the problems they represent: poverty, family violence, educational disadvantage. What distinguishes social policies is the *distributional* implications, or outcome of the policy or decision involved (Donnison, 1975, p. 26). This is to suggest a concern not merely with the distribution of income and wealth, but rather with the distribution of *social welfare* and *social resources*.

'Social welfare' consists of a state of individual health and well-being, and of social solidarity and co-operation, that is in large measure dependent on a more equal distribution of social resources, status and power — in short, on distributional justice. 'Social resources' include income, assets and property, but also health, education and environment, which may ultimately be differentially distributed according to need (Townsend, 1972).

'Social policy' might be defined, then, as *the rationale underlying the development and reproduction of social institutions that determine the distribution of resources, status and power between different groups in society.* Social policy determines the creation, distribution and reproduction of social welfare (and dis-welfare). This conception of social policy is derived chiefly from Townsend (1975, p. 6) and can be embraced by Ferge's (1979, p. 19) definition of 'societal policy' as deliberate social action in both the short and the long term.

Reconstructing social policy

This approach to social policy opens the door for a comparative analysis of such policies in different societies and demonstrates the basic dilemma of the welfare state in capitalist societies: the need to alter aspects of the structure and operation of the market in order to create welfare, and the impossibility of doing so. In Ferge's (1979, p. 55) words, 'there is a theoretical and practical incompatibility between the market economy based on private ownership and a real social policy.' Although significant advances are possible within the existing framework of social distribution in capitalist societies, the more equal distribution of these resources is dependent on the introduction of radically different forms of social organization (Mishra, 1975, pp. 288–9).

Once it is grasped that 'social welfare' depends on a wide range of 'social' policies, both in society and outside it, the concept of social policy becomes both exciting and daunting. The task of the social policy analyst is, therefore, to evaluate the distributional impact of existing policies on social welfare: their implicit and explicit rationales, their impact on social relations and the implications of policy proposals. And his or her concern will be less with the problems of individuals or clients than with the multi-faceted behaviour of organizations, professions and classes; and less with the consequences of an unequally shared welfare than with the social production of inequality. Many of the same policies will be of interest to both economists and social policy analysts (see chapter 3).

The development of the scope of social policy implied by this conceptualization has four main advantages, which in turn may liberate the study of social policy from its overriding concern with government action in the form of public welfare. First, social policies may have hidden, unintended effects, underlying values as well as explicit aims. Policies that maintain sexual divisions in social security and employment are rarely expressed openly. Second, social policies are the activities not only of government, but of all social institutions and groups that determine the distribution of resources and life chances. As Townsend (1975, p. 3) has noted, 'Government policy is no more synonymous with social policy than government behaviour is synonymous with social behaviour.' Third, this conceptualization of social policy focuses attention on differences of status, power and rewards between individuals and groups in society — broadly, on inequalities of condition and their sources — and thereby provides a framework for the study of social welfare within and also between societies. The main dimension for such comparisons will be social class, but other sources of division in society, such as sex and race, will also provide bases for comparative analyses of social inequality. These social divisions are more significant to social welfare than the institutional division of government intervention considered primarily by Titmuss. Fourth, this approach provides a framework within which to develop radical or 'structural' social policies (see chapter 4). In particular, it liberates the practice of social planning from its current bureau-incrementalist form.

This approach to social policy also questions other assumptions underlying some conventional approaches that were discussed earlier. For example, it cannot be assumed that all social policies have redistributive effects, or that their impact will be beneficial even to a majority, still less to everyone. Public welfare services benefiting predominantly those in the lowest social classes usually have stigmatizing side-effects. It cannot be assumed that all of the outcomes from social policies are planned and explicit; some may be at best implicit and at worst accidental. The increase in senior management staff in social service departments and senior nursing in hospitals may be seen as a largely unintended effect of the Seebohm Committee's (1968) proposals and community health policies. It cannot be assumed that the growth of social welfare and social policies is tied to economic growth, or that growth creates equality. In the recent period of wage restraint and low GNP growth, fringe benefits in the private sector have been increased and have counteracted the effects of overall restraint for some high-income groups. This approach to social policy therefore asks two fundamental questions: Who benefits from social policies? And who pays, in terms of freedom, independence and command over resources?

One of the practical implications of this approach is that institutions hitherto ignored by social policy analysts, such as private enterprise, trade unions, banks and insurance companies, must become part of their considerations. For example, policy analysis might encompass, for the first time, the pricing policies of industry, and in particular their differential impact on some social groups. Concern might turn to the pricing of certain commodities which form an important part of the expenditure of some groups of people, and therefore may significantly affect their purchasing power. The prices of basic commodities might be compared, for example, with those of luxury goods produced by the same or similar enterprises; the profit margins from different commodities might be contrasted.

Similarly, institutions and services hitherto considered to be central to the study of social policy might also be considered in a fresh light. For example, an analysis of residential care for the elderly would look beyond the institutional setting and its organization and the health status of residents. It might begin from an examination of the role of the elderly in society, with an examination of differentially applied social status as well as with individual need. It would be concerned with the experience of care by elderly people. It would analyse the distribution of a range of resources, including income and security, between the elderly and the rest of society, and among the elderly according to lifelong social status. It would include an analysis of the conflict between control and care, between institutionalization and dignity. It would encompass an examination of the interests of various groups involved in caring for the elderly, combined with an examination of the exercise of the caring function. Lastly, it would be interested in the 'benefit' of society of the increasing use of institutional care for the elderly and the costs borne by that group.

Potential weaknesses of the approach

While the chief strength of this conceptualization lies in the fact that it attempts to embrace all of those social institutions and groups that determine the nature and distribution of social welfare, this breadth is also its main practical weakness. It covers so many activities and institutions that it may be impossible to relate them in analysis. One of the reasons for this difficulty is the lack of data and especially data in a comparable form. The social division of welfare is mirrored, in turn, by a social division of statistics and of knowledge generally. It is even more difficult to make international comparisons. Yet it is only by attempting to encompass all those processes in different societies whereby resources and life chances are distributed that conclusions can be drawn about the true state of welfare in them.

In addition, rather than setting questions about issues such as inequalities in income beyond the scope of social policy (Marshall, 1975, p. 205), it is important to integrate the analysis of the distribution of resources in society and of the social division of life-chances firmly into the study of social welfare. For example, unemployment is imposed on some social groups, such as the semi- and unskilled, older workers and the disabled, more than on others. Unemployment may be used as a tool of economic management on the one hand; but public policy responses, on the other, deny the unemployed equal status with other welfare recipients. Both sets of policies are significant for the welfare of unemployed people. Therefore the study of social policy must move beyond the passive acceptance of social costs as being simply the basis for a public policy response, to an analysis of the *production* of these costs. According to Titmuss (1968, p. 133), 'Socially caused dis-welfares . . . are part of the price we pay to some people for bearing the costs of other people's progress.' *The social creation of dis-welfares is as much a part of the study of social policy as the price society pays for them.* And the central questions that now confront British society and social policy analysis concern the production and management of inequality, rather than the consequences of an unequally shared welfare.

There is a risk not only that boundaries will become too wide, but also that distinctions that deserve study in themselves, such as between state and other policies and between the intended and unintended consequences of policies, will become blurred. It is essential for policy analysis to maintain its commentary on the impact of the activities of the state on social welfare; but this should not be its exclusive concern. There is also a danger that individual problems will be overlooked in social policy analysis. To be effective, this conception of social policy must operate at various different levels, linking individual needs and problems to underlying social processes.

CONCLUSION

Social administrators have tended to treat 'social policy' as if it were synonymous with the welfare state, or with publicly defined state social services. Social policy is thereby conceived of as a largely passive response to the problems created by industrial societies, and as such is always *reacting* to the creation of social costs and dis-welfares, rather than occupying a more positive role *as a basis for social development*. Without a transformation of social policy and a reconstitution of the study of social administration, both will continue to be concerned with only one part (and currently a shrinking part) of the real world of social welfare. Moreover, unless the concept of social policy is recast, social planning is likely to remain underdeveloped and similarly circumscribed by the institutions of public administration. It is to the reconstitution of social policy that the next chapter is directed.

3

Economics and Social Policy

INTRODUCTION

This chapter examines the dominance of economic policy over social policy and suggests that it has stultified the development of both social policy and social planning, as well as limiting the potential for a unified social and economic policy. Both 'social' problems and social services are defined by the economic system. The boundaries of the subject of social policy have also been circumscribed by economics and economic policy. A key function of social policy has been the legitimation of the economic system and 'economic' values. It has been allocated a relatively minor role in the distribution of resources and life chances, and social priorities have been subordinated to economic priorities (Walker, Ormerod and Whitty, 1979; Walker, Winyard and Pond, 1983).

The interrelationship between economic and social policy until recently has been almost entirely overlooked in the belief that social relations could be divided simply into the economic and the non-economic. Until this assumption is overturned social policy will continue to be concerned, at best, with the social costs and consequences of economic changes and conventionally defined social services, rather than with the institutions of the management of the economy and the social *production* of inequality, dependence and deprivation. Without a radical transformation of the present scale of economic and social values, social policy will continue to be characterized as either the 'poor man's economic policy' or a 'public burden' (Miller and Rein, 1975; Titmuss, 1963, p. 35). Furthermore, without a reconstruction of the relationship between economic and social policy, any attempt to establish social welfare as a national priority will continue to be frustrated by dominant economic values, relations and policies.

THE DIFFERENTIATION OF ECONOMIC AND SOCIAL POLICY

The social division in thought and practice between economic policy and social policy is a phenomenon of relatively recent origin. Our social science forebears took for granted the integration of social and economic thought in the study of political economy. The separation of economics and other social sciences may be traced to Marx's critique of political economy (Gough, 1979, p. 6). The subsequent replacement of a more or less integrated political economy with separate fields of inquiry resulted in an increasingly rigid distinction between the analysis of the 'economic' relations of production and 'social' relations. This division, and the assumption of the greater importance of the former over the latter, reflected, and in turn reinforced, the predominance of the values of economic production and growth in the developing capitalist societies (Rubin, 1979, p. 381). Thus economics has developed consciously in isolation from an understanding of social relations and has left this field of knowledge and inquiry to sociology, psychology and political science (Gough, 1979, p. 6). The search for elaborate mathematical models took economics into an increasingly abstract and artificial world; into what Wootton (1955, p. 12) has called a 'fairyland'.

The emergent discipline of sociology accepted the division between the analysis of economic and social relations and therefore reinforced the 'theoretical apartheid'. It assumed, and continues to assume, that the concerns of economics are not central to the analysis of social order: 'sociology is a discipline which takes economics and economic assumptions as givens . . .' (Gouldner, 1970, p. 20). Furthermore, while economists turned away from a recognition of the social character of economics, sociologists failed to fill this vacuum. As Shaw (1972, p. 37) succinctly puts it, 'Sociology recognises the social character of production — but by denying that it is to do with production, which is a matter for "economics".' This failure is attributable in part to a development in sociology similar to that in economics, whereby pure theory was assigned pre-eminent status in relation to other branches of the discipline. As a result, social policy has been discussed traditionally as 'applied' knowledge and the fundamental importance of its development to sociology has yet to be fully appreciated (Townsend, 1975).

Not only did economics develop in isolation from other social sciences, and determine the sphere of its own competence; at the same time it defined the boundaries and subject matter of the 'non-economic' sphere (Donzelot, 1979). Problems that arose in the operation of the economic system were conveniently defined as 'social' problems, and therefore did not present a political challenge to the economic system. In other words, society's problems were seen by classical economists as 'social' rather than 'economic'. For example, at the turn of the century, unemployment was considered primarily a 'social' problem, which arose in spite of the normal workings of the economic system and which was due to factors unrelated to the functioning of that system (Winch, 1969, p. 47).

Social policy and the public sector

The resulting distinction between economic policy and social policy paved the way for the development of social administration. This was further encouraged by the Keynesian 'revolution' and the arrival of macroeconomic policy (Pinker, 1979, p. 112). Keynes's general theory also treated social factors as residual in the explanation of the level of prices, wages and employment (Halsey, 1981, p. 18). For example, he did not consider the wage bargaining process to be rational and therefore subject to economic theorizing. Similarly, although in opposition to Keynesian theory, monetarist theory is concerned with the technical relationship between inflation and the rate of growth of the money supply. But it was Keynes who provided the basis for the formal division between economic and social policy and the rise of both in the realm of public policy (Roll, 1968, p. 32).

The status of economic policy was enhanced by the success of Keynesian policies in the period of sustained growth in the immediate postwar years. They became the orthodoxy in most capitalist countries (Aaronovitch, et al., 1981, p. 17). Also, the status of social policy was increased because Keynes assigned a role for it in supporting the process of production and not simply in meeting its social costs — in spite of the fact that he was opposed to collectivism (Dillard, 1950, p. 322). Thus, economic and social policy are sometimes considered together quite legitimately, and are even co-ordinated to some extent if the goal is to make the economic system work more harmoniously, for example in the achievement of economic growth (OECD, 1981, p. 43; CPRS, 1975). (However, in these circumstances it is assumed invariably that the role of social policy is to contribute to economic goals. The equally reasonable view that the economy should be subordinate to social policy objectives is never given equal consideration, a point I return to later.)

Both economic and social policy have become closely associated with the policy apparatus of the state. Both leave the price mechanism unchallenged as the most efficient and equitable allocator of resources.* Both, in other words, make similar assumptions about the preservation of microeconomic and social relations, including for example the primacy of the market in economic relations and of the family in social relations.

So, not only did the establishment of public social policy follow from and share common assumptions with economic policy; its subject matter and sphere of competence were also determined by it. The definition of social policy rests on economics and economic policy. Economics is primarily concerned with private costs and benefits, but even the earlier classical economists recognized that certain essential functions would not be performed without collective state action. For example, Adam Smith (1937, p. 681) argued that the market could operate at its optimum capacity only if, in addition to free competition, 'sympathy' and 'moral sentiments' exerted some restraining influence over competitors and, second, if the government established certain 'public institutions' and 'public works', which,

> though they may be in the highest degree advantageous to a great society, are, however, of such a nature, that the profit could never repay the expense to any individual or small number of individuals, and which it, therefore, cannot be expected that any individual or small number of individuals, should erect or maintain.

Externalities and social costs

The advent of the Industrial Revolution quickly confirmed the importance of Smith's moral strictures, and many economists were forced to recognize that there were a large variety of instances in which the

---

* Although Keynes challenged the appropriateness of applying some aspects of individual market behaviour to macroeconomic questions, he believed that under conditions of full employment the neoclassical system would operate efficiently and equitably (Winch, 1969, p. 322).

actions of individuals or firms affect others directly. Industrial pollution of the air by smoke is the most commonly quoted example (see Kapp, 1978). Such 'externalities' arise 'because economic agents take into account only the direct effect upon themselves, not the effect on others' (Atkinson and Stiglitz, 1980, pp. 7–8); or, as Robinson (1962, p. 50) put it, 'one man's consumption may reduce the welfare of others.' Externalities or diseconomies were defined as 'social' costs, which did not require economic solutions or imply alterations in the economic system, but instead required collective social policies. It was assumed, therefore, that the normal operation of the economy, firm, business and individual economic agents was the subject matter not of social policy, but of economics and economic policy. Once the 'efficient' operation of the economic system was interrupted or threatened, social policy was considered to have a role to play.

The restricted construction of social policy as public policy, discussed in the previous chapter, stems in part from its assigned role as an adjunct to economic policy. Economists commonly define social policy in relation to the public sector, and the welfare state in relation to externalities (see for example Culyer, 1981, p. 181). For many years most sociologists and social administrators accepted this restricted role and defined their subject matter in relation to economics. For example, according to Marshall (1975, p. 15),

> social policy uses political power to supersede, supplement or modify operations of the economic system in order to achieve results which the economic system would not achieve on its own, and . . . in doing so it is guided by values other than those determined by open market forces.

Moreover, social policies were said to be concerned with individual welfare and economic policies with the 'common weal' (Marshall, 1975, p. 15). Others have made a similarly broad distinction between economic and social policies. For instance, according to Boulding there is the 'simple economic solution' to poverty of establishing a minimum income to which every citizen would have a right, and 'social' solutions such as payments in kind, workhouses and the administration of relief by social workers.

Questioning the division between economic and social policy

A challenge to this simple division between the economic and social aspects of government policy was made by few social scientists until the 1970s. Wootton and Titmuss were pioneers in this country. In her powerful critique of classical wage theory, Wootton attacked the traditional divisions between economic and social policy and the latter's concentration on the state. She argued, for example, that wage policy was 'only one item in the distributive chapters of social policy' (Wootton, 1955, p. 185). She demonstrated that one of the central features of economics, wage determination, is concerned as much with social policy was with economic policy (Wootton, 1955, p. 166). Similarly in her comments on the artificial division of national income by economic accounting: 'In practice the question of how much we can afford without running into inflation cannot be disassociated from the question of how any increases are to be distributed' (Wootton, 1955, p. 174).

In his seminal analysis of the social division of welfare, Titmuss argued that, apart from the public social services, social policy may be implemented through fiscal and occupational systems of welfare. He questioned, by implication, the traditional boundary between economic and social policy in the administrative operation of public policy. This analysis was not fully developed by Titmuss, though he did continue it to some extent (Titmuss, 1967). In later work however he actually *reinforced* the distinction between economics and social policy, that is, between exchange and gift (Titmuss, 1970).

Subsequently other radical critics of the welfare state have outlined a political economy of the welfare state (for example, Townsend, 1975; Kincaid, 1973; Gough, 1979). But this important development has not, as yet, resulted in a reformulation of the relationship between economic policy and social policy in academic thought, still less of public policy. Marxists, as Hill (1981, p. 7) points out, share with *laissez-faire* economists the view that social policy should be seen as dependent upon economic policy. The two are still treated as largely separate entities, the former resting on resources provided by the latter.

The recent growth of interest in the economics of social policy, or 'social economics', has similarly concentrated on the public sector and has continued to treat economic policy and social policy as predominantly separate (Culyer, 1974; LeGrand and Robinson, 1976; Sandford, 1977). There are, of course, exceptions to this generalization. Gordon

(1982, p. 91), for example, argues that 'the only way of fully under-standing the impact economic policy has on the social services is to have some idea of the rationale behind the economic policies them-selves.' But even this radical departure from microeconomic analyses of social services stops short of recognizing that the division between economic and social policy, as it is presently constituted, is spurious. So, despite recent progress towards establishing a political economy of the welfare state, and the growth of social economics, the focus of social policy inquiry and practice remains concerned primarily with the realm of state activity traditionally defined as non-economic.

ECONOMIC POLICY VERSUS SOCIAL POLICY

What are the main implications of the dependence of social policy on economic policy? In the first place, the scope of social policy is restric-ted and its potential in social and economic development is consistently underestimated. Second, economic priorities dominate social priorities in policy-making. Third, social planning is narrowly conceived and sub-ordinate to economic planning. At the same time, by implication, economic policy and planning have themselves been distorted and occupy an unnecessarily narrow role as financial planning. Each of these will be considered in turn.

Before doing so it is necessary to recognize that, of course, there is not a single theory in economics, any more than in other social sciences. But there is a dominant school of thought − neoclassical economics − encompassing economists as diverse as, for example, Keynes and Fried-man, which is (Aaronovitch, et al., 1981, p. 16):

> primarily concerned with the process by which the self-interest of individual economic agents − firms maximising profits and consumers│maximising utility − leads, through the operation of supply, demand, and exchange in a free market, to an equilibrium.

It is to this school that the following analysis is directed.

However, I am concerned not so much with 'economics' as an intel-lectual mode of thought or academic discipline as with its social construction, in the realm of public policy, as the pre-eminent source of knowledge in questions of resource allocation. Economics is the science of resource allocation choices in conditions of scarcity (Sandford, 1982, p. 10), and such choices will always be necessary where resources are limited and have alternative uses. But the precise definition of scarcity is not necessarily a technical, economic matter so much as a political one. Most resources are in short supply: so it is the exact level of scarcity, and more especially the social (including political) definition of that scarcity, that is crucial. In the public sector, resources are determined primarily by taxation, and there is considerable potential for variation in the level of resources raised, as well as in their use.

This can be illustrated by a single example. If the income of the top one-tenth of the population could have been reduced to 75 per cent of their share in 1980–1, and that of the next two-tenths to 90 per cent of what it was, a further £19,000 million would have been raised — a sum equivalent to the amount spent on the entire social security programme in that year (Townsend, 1981a). Despite this indication of flexibility, resources are considered automatically to be insufficient to meet need.

In its application to government policy-making, economics has been narrowly conceived as conservative financial planning and accounting, and the efficient allocation of resources has become synonymous with the *control* of resources. Thus narrowly defined economic objectives have been used as a scientific legitimation for policies of public (but not private) resource constraint and, more recently, privatization. This is not to deny the fundamental importance of economic considerations to policy or the economic evaluation of policy, both of which have received a good deal of attention in the social policy literature (see for example, Glennerster, 1975; Judge, 1978; Culyer, 1981; Gordon, 1982). Furthermore, this is not a specific critique of the economic policies of the Conservative government, which has simply reinforced these tendencies. Economics, like other social sciences, may be used to different ideological ends despite its scientized and value-free construction. In the words of the former Chief Secretary to the Treasury (Kay, 1982, p. 14),

It is not a question of saying how much social security, health or education the state should provide. . . . The real question is how much the state can *afford* to provide, free, and still leave the individual citizen with the incentive and ability on top of that . . . to provide for his *own* old age, his *own* health, and his *own* children's education, directly.

While not going this far, all other political parties accept the dominant role of economics in resource distribution. Regardless of political ideology, economic hegemony predominates in social policy. Even in the 'alternative' economic strategies of the labour movement, increased expenditure on social services is held to depend on the successful regeneration of the economy (see chapter 8).

THE SCOPE OF SOCIAL POLICY

Since its emergence as a clearly defined aspect of government activity social policy has been assigned, effectively, a subordinate role to economic policy, whether 'as a palliative or corrective instrument' (Ferge, 1979, p. 50) or in establishing necessary social conditions for the achievement of economic goals. It is assumed, therefore, that social policy intervenes in a natural order of economic relationships to modify their outcome in the interest of 'social' goals. According to this dominant view, social policy is effectively confined to a wholly *reactive* and supportive — or 'reluctant collectivist' — role, aimed at alleviating the effects of economic change, temporary economic aberrations or individual misfortune (George and Wilding, 1976, p. 42). Thus, the social services do not represent a challenge to the cash nexus and distribution of resources primarily through the private market; indeed, they support the system of incentives and rewards in the economic system (Room, 1979, p. 51). It is not surprising, therefore, that this has been described as the 'handmaiden model' of social policy (Titmuss, 1974, p. 31).

In Britain the postwar period saw the consummation of the dependent relationship between social policy and economic policy through, on the one hand, Keynesian economic policies and, on the other, liberal social welfare policies associated chiefly with Beveridge. The postwar settlement and the development of those social services now known collectively as the 'welfare state' took place within the framework of a conception of social policy as an adjunct to the economy (Titmuss, 1974; Mishra, 1981). Thus, for example, not only were the welfare plans contained in the Beveridge Report circumscribed by the dominant economic ideology, but they were also subject to direct scrutiny from the narrowest approach to economic policy, in the form of financial accounting, as embodied in Treasury officials at the time. 'Before the Beveridge Report was made public it had already been tailored down to meet the notions of financial soundness which prevailed in Treasury circles' (Kincaid, 1973, p. 44). Many of the assumptions that Beveridge brought to his study of social insurance, and which underpin his plan for its reorganization, were based not on a consideration of social welfare 'but on the prejudices of official economic opinion' (Kincaid, 1973, p. 43). In particular, the necessity to limit the Treasury contribution was crucial in the decision to set benefits at a low level (Beveridge, 1942, p. 177). Thirty-six years later, the second review of social assistance since the National Assistance Act (1948) was even more overshadowed by financial considerations (Lister, 1978, 1979; C. Walker, 1983). So the review was concerned primarily with administrative reorganization within the existing social security budget, rather than with the adequacy of supplementary benefits (DHSS, 1978a, para. 13.1):

A realistic approach to the problems of the scheme as a whole must try to maintain a balance between extra costs and savings and to avoid propositions that are clearly impractical in present conditions of economic constraint.

Similar examples could be adduced from other sectors of the welfare state to demonstrate that everywhere social policy is circumscribed by narrow economic considerations. As the DHSS (1980a, p. 2) argued in their response to the House of Commons Social Services Committee's critical comments on strategic policy-making at the DHSS, social objectives 'are subject to the overriding requirement of the Government's economic policy as a whole'.

The subordination of social policy to economic policy

So deeply ingrained is this scale of values in Britain and other capitalist societies that it is assumed that economic values and relationships are natural, while social values and institutions have to be imposed on them through 'interventionist' policies. The first practical implication of this acceptance of the restriction of the scope and utility of social policy is that it occupies a weak position in relation to economics. Narrowly defined 'economic' objectives such as profit maximization and economic growth are considered automatically to be legitimate, while 'social' objectives such as health and community care must secure legitimacy in the policy system, and what is more are believed to rest ultimately on economic policy for their achievement (Pinker, 1974, p. 9). It is assumed implicitly that the former are derived from scientific rationality while the latter involve value judgements and as a result are contentious. In bald terms, narrow 'economic' policies dealing with such matters as financial management are considered to be more important than 'social' policies dealing with the poverty, health and education of the population. This restricts the scope of economic as well as social policy, when for example social policy objectives such as full employment might be pursued through economic policies or an integrated form of both.

This ascendancy has provided a rationale for the development of an 'economic imperialism' whereby, apparently, any aspect of state activity is subject to economic considerations. 'If the government acts in any field *mainly* with an economic objective in mind, then that action could be counted as part of economic policy' (Blackaby, 1979, p. 2). (The examples of the introduction of earnings-related benefits and redundancy payments in 1966 give some indication of the difficulties created by this expansionism.) It is argued, moreover, that advances in economic theory have enabled the identification of mechanisms of state intervention to increase social welfare (Grant and Shaw, 1975, p. 31). This assurance stems in part from the greater consensus among economists, at least over microeconomic issues, than among sociologists, political scientists or policy analysts (Brittan, 1973). It has encouraged a second form of economic imperialism in the extension of economic analysis to other social sciences. The economic theory of democracy is one of the best known outcomes of this trend (Downs, 1957; Buchanan and Tullock, 1965).

The chief cause for concern here is not the relative status between two academic disciplines, but the fact that this scale of values has an important impact on both the range of policies considered legitimate in the policy-making process, and the public attitudes towards the welfare state. Thus it can be argued more easily by some economists that social welfare expenditure is unproductive and even counterproductive, and is parasitic on the industrial sector of the economy (Friedman, 1962; Bacon and Eltis, 1976). More commonly, it is held that resources for welfare are dependent on economic recovery or growth. These whole- and half-hearted variations of the 'public burden' model of welfare are supported by the crude division between economics and social policy and the presumption of supremacy of the one over the other. This lends support, in turn, to the equally crude separation between the productive and unproductive sectors of the economy. It similarly sustains the simplistic division between the public and private sectors – even when the 'private' sector receives massive subsidies and the 'public' sector charges for its services.

As the predominance of narrow economic values over social values and of economic policies over social policies was proselytized more forcefully over the course of the last decade, public opinion, not surprisingly, has reflected this pattern. Gallup public opinion polls between 1959 and 1978 show clearly that economic policy was consistently considered the most important national problem (Alt, 1979, p. 49). This bias is also revealed in the amount of time spent in Parliament on economic as opposed to social affairs (Coombes and Walkland, 1980). What is more, the scale of values that underpins the pre-eminence of economic policy means that economic decline itself contributes to a hardening of public attitudes against social expenditure and altruism (Alt, 1979, p. 258).

Second, it has been assumed that, within the confines of economic policy, social policy can operate in isolation and according to different principles to those governing the operation of 'non-social' institutions in society (hence 'social' administration rather than 'economic' or 'political' administration). The distinction made by Titmuss (1970) between altruistic social policies and selfish economic exchanges contributed to the strength of this school of thought. Now, as I showed in the previous chapter, there is an increasing realization that these 'social' institutions form an integral part of the apparatus of capitalist society and do not exist in a political, social or economic vacuum (Gough, 1979). Nevertheless, this false social construction of social policy has resulted in a great deal of mystification over the apparent 'contradictions' in the administration of the public social services. Moreover, it has diverted attention from the fact that social issues such as poverty, unemployment, ill-health and bad housing cannot be left for social policy alone to tackle, but require a combination of social and economic policies. In other words, it is falsely believed that social policy can 'modify the free play of market forces' and redistribute income through taxes, transfers and services (Marshall, 1975, p. 15) and, as a consequence, that there is no need to alter economic relations.

This polarization of systems of distribution, and the distortion of reality it entails, has contributed to the tendency to view social policy as a sort of 'poor person's economic policy'. However, as postwar experience in Britain and other capitalist countries shows, if policy is concentrated purely on 'social' intervention it will not have much impact on the distribution of resources between social classes (Westergaard and Resler, 1975; Townsend, 1979). As Miller and Rein (1975, p. 17) have argued, 'Effective redistribution policies must seek directly to alter original income differentials and asset accumulation as well as attempt to offset them.'

The strict separation between the economic and social, but also the public and private, sectors is false too because it ignores the role of state intervention through budgetary measures to alter supply and demand, wage and price controls and company taxation, all of which indirectly affect the distribution of income. In addition to budgetary intervention, the state plays a major role in the market at both national and international levels, for example as consumer of the products of 'private' enterprise and increasingly as an investor in 'private' industry (Miliband, 1969; Baran, 1973, pp. 246–7).

ECONOMIC AND SOCIAL PRIORITIES

The dependence of social policy on economic policy means that economic priorities predominate over social priorities in the policy-making process. But economic criteria are an inadequate basis for determining national priorities. Social priorities would be determined wholly or predominantly by the distributional effects of policies (A. Walker, 1982b). The more equitable the outcome of the policy, the more socially efficient is the policy. Economic priorities are based on the 'efficient' use of resources. Economic 'efficiency' is judged primarily in terms of cost effectiveness or its close relation, Pareto efficiency. Both concepts of economic efficiency tend to undervalue the contribution of social services to economic development and growth.

Economic efficiency

Economic efficiency is achieved 'when the value of what is produced by any set of resources exceeds by as much as possible the value of resources' (Haverman and Margolis, 1977, p. 10). This is the 'least-cost' notion of efficiency (Culyer, 1981, p. 22). Clearly, when market value is the main criterion of value, social services are not likely to be efficient. For example, the economic product derived from the provision of home help support to the elderly is, to say the least, difficult to measure and relate to national production. However, regardless of whether or not such gains exist, they are assumed not to by the restricted financial accounting that now dominates the application of economics in the public sector. Expenditure on those services that cannot be related directly to production is, therefore, undervalued.

The second and related concept, *Pareto efficiency*, hypothesizes that a policy change should be pursued by government only if at least one person judges himself to be better off, while no one is made worse off, by the change. A *Pareto improvement* occurs when at least one person's welfare is raised without a decrease in the welfare of anyone else. A situation is efficient or 'optimal' when no further Pareto improvements can be made. This Paretian criterion underpins both welfare economics (Marshall, 1980, pp. 16–22) and the economics of social policy (Culyer, 1981, p. 5).

Despite modifications (Atkinson and Stiglitz, 1980, pp. 337–41), the concept has been criticized on a number of important grounds (Mishan, 1967). It is anti-collectivist because it assumes that the state will not intervene unless the market fails and therefore that the role of the state should, ideally, be confined to dealing with 'externalities'. It is individualistic, assuming both that the market is politically neutral and that the distribution of original income is fair. Perhaps most significantly, its applicability has been called into question as it is difficult to imagine a decision in the real world that would not make at least one person worse off. For these reasons, in practice it is the *potential* Pareto criterion that is commonly used.

Underlying both concepts is the notion that the individual is the best judge of his own welfare and will act rationally to maximize that welfare. In the words of one economist, 'Our basic premise in welfare considerations is that the only meaningful concept of marginal utility is an individual one' (Peacock in: Grant and Shaw, 1975, p. 18). Thus the influential concept of marginal utility, or value, states that the price that the consumer is just willing to pay for an extra unit measures the extra satisfaction or marginal value of that unit to him. This widely held assertion may provide a useful basis on which to hypothesize the maximizing behaviour of rational consumers in the perfect marketplace, but it also assumes that there is a government 'utility function' or 'social welfare function' analogous to the individual utility function (Peacock, 1975, p. 2).

There are serious difficulties associated with the assumption that collective welfare will be maximized by the pursuit of individual welfare. In particular, there is the presumption 'that self-interested actions have socially benign results' (Hirsch, 1977, p. 119). This brings us back to the problems of 'externalities' raised earlier. Thus, the pursuit of individual economic goals often involves a local community or society as a whole in additional costs that are external to the individual, and that will, therefore, not be taken into account by those individuals. In short, the ordering of social priorities would involve a 'tyranny of small decisions' (Hirsch, 1977, p. 106).

Then there is the conflict between efficiency and distribution (Dobb, 1969). The government may pursue economic efficiency as a priority, but 'if the outcome is *efficient*, it is not necessarily *fair*' (Lecomber, 1979, p. 193). For example, those in a relatively weak position in the market, because of low skill, poor education or physical or mental infirmity, will be further disadvantaged by the operation of the market. The traditional answer is redistribution through taxation. Unfortunately, such measures interfere with the economic relations on which the assumption of efficiency is based, for example by providing an alternative source of rewards and incentives. As a result, economists frequently ignore questions of distribution in the discussion of efficiency. In this theoretical vacuum it is relatively easy to disassociate economic policies from their social effects. But in practice macroeconomic policies have important distributional consequences. Price and income policies have a differential impact on the existing income distribution. Similarly, changes in the level of aggregate demand may be achieved by different combinations of consumption and investment, and taxes, subsidies, monetary controls and public expenditure all have a direct impact on distribution.

The equation of national welfare with economic welfare

As a result of these deficiencies in crucial economic concepts of efficiency, and of the domination of economic over social priorities, our idea of national prosperity and well-being is narrowly conceived. Moreover, the concepts of social welfare and economic welfare are both similarly distorted. Gross national product (GNP) and its variant gross domestic product are the conventional measures of economic welfare. Those aspects of national activity not included in the GNP accounts are usually taken as a rule-of-thumb division between economic and social welfare (MacDougall, 1977, p. 193). So, not only is social welfare defined as those activities not concerned directly with production and consumption, but economic welfare is equally narrowly related to those productive activities represented by GNP. The activities of 'housewives', for instance, are neglected.

The equation of national welfare with economic welfare entails ignoring those crucial aspects of social welfare — such as the quality of the physical environment, the health of the population, the distribution of income and the relative position of different social classes — that are not marketed and therefore are excluded from GNP. Also, the social costs of production are not deducted from this published record of national prosperity. Furthermore, this approach distorts both the relationship between the public and private sectors and the order of priority given to activity and expenditure within each sector. Thus, according to accounting conventions, a switch in economic activity from the public to the private sector usually represents an unqualified improvement in economic welfare. But as Hirsch (1977, p. 93) points out, 'The crucial limitation in the conventional analysis is that it does not allow for a change in the nature of the product according to the method of provision.' There have been many objections to the use of conventional measures of real GNP (see for example, Prest and Coppock, 1980, p. 7), but 'They are not taken so seriously that an alternative measure of aggregate welfare is published by any major national government' (Preston, 1981, p. 101). It is worth remembering here, though, that GNP is simply the accounting convention of neoclassical and Keynesian economists, and that an alternative theoretical framework would be more 'realistic', or comprehensive, from the viewpoint of the necessary interrelationship of economic and social values.

Economic growth and social welfare

Because national prosperity is closely associated with economic welfare, it is also identified with economic growth. Economic growth is commonly described as the major goal not only of macroeconomic policy but of society as a whole. 'Economic growth is the grand objective. It is the aim of economic policy as a whole' (Lecomber, 1979, p. 23;

Caves and Krause, 1980). The proselytization of economic growth is one of the most remarkable aspects of the domination of economic over social priorities. Everybody is gripped, apparently, by 'growth-mania'. By comparison, alternative goals of macroeconomic policy, such as a more equitable distribution of national resources, hardly get a look-in. Even the goal of combating inflation is intended to pave the way for growth. The popularity of growth lies predominantly in the fact that it is considered to be a neutral and value-free goal. Its import-ance to capitalist enterprise is self-evident. Priority for growth implies that the present structure and distribution of resources is sufficient and acceptable.

It is assumed that growth is a necessary prerequisite for any increase in redistribution. Not only does this create a major barrier to social change, but, when the strategy fails (as it is bound to do), it encourages a fatalistic approach to policy-making: 'Fundamental to the failure of growth to eliminate society's economic problems is the recognised fact that human wants are insatiable' (Grant and Shaw, 1975, p. 11).

In fact, there is no firm basis for the belief that economic growth is a necessary or even desirable goal for policy, let alone an overriding priority. Mishan (1967, pp. 65, 151) argues that economic growth *per se* should be abandoned as an independent goal of policy if we are concerned with social welfare: 'it is just not possible for the economist to establish a positive relationship between economic growth and social welfare.' The main problems are that growth entails social costs, 'exter-nalities', dis-services or dis-welfares (Titmuss, 1968, pp. 155–7) and that it reinforces and enlarges inequalities.

The term 'social costs' 'refers to all those harmful consequences and damages which other persons or the community sustain as a result of productive processes, and for which private entrepreneurs are not held accountable' (Kapp, 1978, pp. 13–14). Such costs include the social consequences of rapid technological change, such as the obsolescence of workers, the effects of automation on employment and health, the impact of scientific discoveries on health and the spread of materialism. They are borne disproportionately by the working class (Black Com-mittee, 1980). Moreover, because growth has a differential impact on income and wealth, this group is further disadvantaged in relation to the middle and upper classes. Clearly, then, high economic growth may actually jeopardize the prospects for social welfare.

The subordination of social priorities to economic priorities, and in turn of economic to financial or production priorities, has restricted the concepts of national prosperity and social welfare. The range of individuals and groups said to be involved in the processes of social and economic expansion is also confined artificially to those taking part in production in the market. This is not only socially divisive, but reduces the potential of many people to contribute to national prosperity.

THE SUBORDINATION OF SOCIAL PLANNING

The subjugation of social planning to economic 'planning' follows from the dependence of social policy on economic policy. This helps to account for the underdevelopment of social planning. In addition, the narrow interpretation of economics and the precedence given to economic institutions means that today economic planning is little more than public expenditure planning or financial planning (see chapter 5).

Economic planning has had a chequered history. It reached its heyday under the Labour government between 1964 and 1966, when a separate Department of Economic Affairs was established (in 1965) and produced *The National Plan*, 'the most ambitious official planning document yet to appear in Britain' (Coombes and Walkland, 1980, p. 32). By 1969 the Department had been closed and the task of economic planning reverted back to the Treasury and to the National Economic Development Council (NEDC).

The division between these two signals the underdevelopment of economic as well as social planning in this country. The Treasury is concerned primarily with public expenditure management and control, and thus the Chancellor's Annual Financial Statement and Budget Report deals with mainly financial matters. The NEDC, formed in 1962, is outside direct parliamentary scrutiny and is used as an alternative forum to Parliament rather than an institution for planning (Coombes and Walkland, 1980, p. 32).

Treasury domination of social planning

Public expenditure planning is also the main form of social policy planning, and this process is dominated by the Treasury (see chapter 6). As a result, social planning is cost-oriented and not needs-oriented (Glennerster, 1975, 1979). The Public Expenditure Survey Committee (PESC) was introduced following the recommendations of the Plowden

Committee (1961) to ensure better *control* of public expenditure. Subsequent amendments, particularly the transition from volume to cash-based planning, which began with the introduction of cash limits in 1975, have simply reinforced the primacy of this role (A. Walker, 1982b, p. 187). Although the initiative lies with the spending authorities, the public expenditure process relies on Treasury indications of the level of available resources, and departmental estimates are framed within that context. Thus, social priority planning is always conducted within the framework of financial planning. The Treasury is the only central department with an overall view of expenditure, deciding what can be afforded and also how expenditure will be financed – and what the balance should be between taxation and borrowing. Although the Treasury plays a leading role in PESC, it does not attempt a comprehensive review of departmental programmes, concentrating rather on changes to existing programmes (Wright, 1979). The implications of the Treasury's dominance of public expenditure planning are considered at length in chapter 6.

Despite the inadequacies of the expenditure process (Wright, 1979), expenditure control and the imposition of cash limits dominate social planning. The role and scope of social planning is therefore severely limited both to short-term goals and to predominantly financial considerations. In the social services, for example, the needs of clients, however pressing, are for the most part second to the presumed availability of resources.

According to the DHSS (1976a, p. 78) the central purpose of its programme budget, an integral part of its planning system, 'is to enable the Department to cost policies for service development across the board so that priorities can be considered within realistic financial constraints'. Thus the consultative documents on health and personal social services, issued in 1976 and 1977, were a response not so much to the need to set priorities in meeting the demand for services but to the need to limit the supply of resources (DHSS, 1976a; 1977a; see chapter 7).

The Department of the Environment's Housing Investment Programmes have also been used as a mechanism for controlling expenditure rather than for determining priorities in the need for housing (Kilroy, 1982). At the local government level, corporate planning has been introduced primarily to facilitate greater control of the budget rather than to plan social priorities.

Given this narrow role of social planning, it is not surprising that, in a period of retrenchment and cuts in public expenditure, the expenditure process has been used to contain and cut spending despite the existence of planned priorities. As Glennerster (1981a, p. 47) points out, 'Social planning comes to be seen as the means for legitimising cuts in public expenditure.'

Restricted construction of social planning

In addition to being wholly cost-orientated, social planning is confined solely to the activities of the public sector. As a result, many absurd anomalies are created in social planning and policy-making. Douglas Jay, for example, has criticized the division between public and private spending: 'under this crazy doctrine, the building of houses for those who need them but cannot pay for them is extravagant, but the building of houses for those who can pay for them is a growth of national wealth' (quoted by Abel-Smith, 1967, p. 7). Yet, economic, tax and incentive grant policies, which partly shape private consumption, are at least as important in achieving social objectives as direct public expenditure on the social services.

Unlike environmental planning, there are no social planning controls on the activities of the private sector in, say, production and employment. This does not mean that the state has not intervened to regulate some forms of production, or to ensure minimal employment protection, but rather that the *planning* of production and employment is a private matter. The state plays a significant role in the provision of employment and training when the private sector fails to do so, but the dominant form of 'planning' is the market through the operation of demand and supply.

Finally, the potential for social planning is limited because there is insufficient information on which to plan social development. Social statistics are circumscribed by the same orthodox economic framework, and therefore do not provide an adequate basis for social planning (MacDougall, 1977, p. 193: A. Walker, 1982a, pp. 24–5). The problem was recognized in the United States by the US Department of Health, Education and Welfare (DHEW, 1970, p. xxxi) more than a decade ago: 'The Nation has no comprehensive set of statistics reflecting social progress or retrogression. There is no government procedure for periodic stocktaking of the health of the Nation.' Moreover, it was noted that these much-needed social statistics were not likely to be produced as a part of the state's normal accounting or administrative routine. A similar point was made recently in this country by the House of Commons Social Services Committee (1980, pp. x–xi; see also Social Services Committee, 1981, p. xiii) in their assessment of the annual public expenditure White Papers:

> in some senses the kind of information provided in the White Paper and subsequent DHSS evidence – setting out the number of patients treated, the number of prescriptions dispensed and so on – is largely meaningless. Such statistics measure activity, they give no indication of impact . . . . the input of resources does not necessarily tell us very much about the output of services to patients . . . .

Without basic information about social conditions, the task of social planning is hampered considerably. Indeed, the absence of these vital statistics further emphasizes the underdevelopment of social planning in Britain.

There is a conflict, then, between narrowly defined economic policy on the one hand and social policy and planned social development on the other. (Furthermore, it could also be argued that there is a similar conflict between economic policy and the narrow financial accounting that is characteristic of government economic and social policy-making.) *The aims of social policy and social planning are frustrated by narrow economic definitions and priorities.* These do not have to be imposed: they are usually implicit in the policy-making and planning process.

THE UNIFICATION OF ECONOMIC AND SOCIAL POLICY

It has been assumed for too long that there is a simple division between economic and social policy. Acceptance of this assumption has often involved overlooking the interrelationship between the two. This position, as we have seen, was assigned to social administration by economics, but it has been accepted, until recently, without much question.

In fact, the distinction between a wholly economic and wholly social policy is entirely false. All economic policies entail or imply social policies (Winch, 1969, p. 323):

Economic policies, including *laissez-faire*, are essentially discrimi-
natory; they discriminate between groups within the population
and between industries and economic regions.

For example,
A policy for faster growth which entails raising the level of investment must also decide, implicitly or explicitly, which savers and
investers to encourage, and whether the social rate of return is
higher on private or public investment.

The interconnections between politics, sociology and economics are
being recognized increasingly, but usually only to the extent that
economic events have an impact on social and political arrangements
(Peston, 1981, p. 100). These are still treated for the most part as
distinct entities. Economists have supported the division by their
distinction between 'welfarist' motives for intervention in the economy
and those dictated by the needs of overall economic management.

Although a gradual change in the balance between fiscal and monetary policy had been taking place since the mid-1970s (Wright, 1981),
it was the election of the Conservative government in 1979 and its
re-election in 1983 that presented the clearest challenge to the division
between economic and social policy (Walker, Winyard and Pond,
1983). Some of the social costs of the government's economic strategy
− increased insecurity, unemployment, falling living standards and,
perhaps, increased violence − have demonstrated that it was not only
an economic but, implicitly at least, also a social strategy. Moreover,
the statements of various government ministers − on for example
public expenditure, unemployment, 'scroungers', women and the
family − have made it abundantly clear that this economic management
has social intentions, including a reduction in the living standards of
some groups of people relative to others and the withdrawal of some
groups, notably married women, from the labour market. Monetarist
policies have demonstrated openly what was always the case under
previous Keynesian regimes; that economic policy is itself subordinate
to social or ideological objectives, to the support of particular interests
such as financial capital and high-income groups. It is the incompatibility between the goal of social welfare and the prevailing relationship
between economic and social policy that suggests the need for the
creation of an integrated social and economic policy.

Towards a structural social policy

Conservative policies have demonstrated more clearly than hitherto the interconnection between economic and social policy by directly confronting us with the social effects of economic policies. They have shown that economics is not something that exists purely in the abstract models of economists, but on the contrary is actually *experienced* by individuals — whether in work or out of work, as taxpayers, claimants, clients, consumers and so on — and therefore embodies social as much as economic relations.

At the heart of the case for a unified political economy, then, is the artificial division between economics and social policy and the current limitations of both orthodoxies in explaining and planning social development. On the part of economics, there is the pretence of value neutrality, the assumption of universal market rationality, the acceptance of the distribution of income as given, the legitimation of the status quo, and antipathy towards social welfare. On the part of social policy, there is its restricted scope and narrow focus on the activities of the state and the false social construction of the welfare state as necessarily beneficial.

Partly because of their close association with the growth of the modern capitalist state, both economics and social policy have concentrated on the description and analysis of society in its current form rather than examining the processes of and potential for change. Both, and especially economics, are in essence more static than dynamic subjects. Both, in other words, are trapped within the dominant institutions and structures of society, British capitalist society, and operate to *reproduce* the status quo. The absence of comparative analyses in social policy is well known, but the relative lack of comparative analyses of social planning is also not surprising.

There is a need, then, for a unified economic and social policy, or for what may be termed *structural social policy*, first, to signify that economics cannot be separated from the politics of the society in which it operates; second, to recognize not only that economic policies and economic management cannot be disassociated from their social effects, but also that they embody social objectives; third, to provide the basis for planned social development; and fourth, when coupled with socialist values, to realize the goal of socialist welfare. The aim of this integrated structural social policy is to make explicit the interdependence of the social, political and economic. Thus, according to Ferge (1979, p. 56), such a policy

> is neither economic nor non-economic; its target is to reintegrate the economic and the social sphere by putting an end to the almost complete hegemony of the economic interest which dominates capitalist society.

The implications of this approach are very far-reaching. It requires us to move beyond the view of the economy as simply a producer and allocator of scarce resources in order to ensure the maximization of profit or output, towards a reintegration of 'normative' and positive economics. Thus, explicit social objectives might be pursued through a unified social and economic policy. The role of social planning would similarly be transformed. The transition to need-based planning would transcend the restricted economic definition of scarcity and the order of priorities it entails, and begin to demonstrate that, although resources are restricted, there is considerable scope for redistribution without growth. Narrow economic constraints would be rejected and economic policies formulated within a broad social policy framework. Clearly, this would entail a reorientation of orthodox economic policy, along democratic lines (Frey, 1983), as well as social policy.

This approach also requires us to step beyond the boundaries of traditional social administration and to recognize the main lesson of the last 150 years for the student of social policy: a radical redistribution of resources is impossible without a radical restructuring of the economy and a shift in the purpose of productive capacity. The dilemma of traditional social policy − the necessity of having to interfere with the market and the impossibility of doing so within the framework of economic orthodoxy (Ferge, 1979, p. 55; A. Walker, 1981, p. 231) − can be positively resolved only by confronting the inescapable fact that a structural social policy with the aim of socialist welfare is incompatible with a predominantly market economy (see chapter 9).

CONCLUSION

Policies for the reorientation of sectors of distribution towards social rather than narrow economic aims, the reduction of poverty and inequality, rather than the pursuit of profit maximization and monetary incentives, require a change in the character of social policy. It would become 'more normative than corrective' (Ferge, 1979, p. 55). This, in turn, would provide the basis for social planning that entails the restructuring of economic values and basic social relations. Both economic policy and social policy would be geared towards social development and the achievement of social goals, such as equality.

4

Models of Social Planning

INTRODUCTION

Both the theory and practice of social planning are relatively under-developed. This stems in part from a limited conception and gross under-estimation of *need* in both capitalist and state socialist societies (see Townsend, 1979, pp. 31–60; and pp. 19–27 above). The recognition of social need and the pursuit of social planning, like social policy, have been restricted by narrow economic considerations. In Britain the imperative to control social expenditure has overridden the need to plan social development explicitly in conjunction with economic development (A. Walker, 1982b, pp. 12–15). In consequence, social planning has been dominated by one particular form: public expenditure planning. Again like social policy, social planning has been narrowly confined to central and local government departments, with the activities of 'private' institutions considered to be outside of its legitimate domain.

This chapter examines different approaches to social planning. The three following chapters present a more detailed discussion of social service planning and economic planning. Together they demonstrate the fragmentation and restricted administrative application of social planning in Britain.

Discussion about planning often revolves around the two ideal types or models of the theory and practice of planning – incremental planning and rational–comprehensive planning – which together have dominated the field of planning for more than 20 years. To a large extent this is a spurious dichotomy, but it does provide a helpful way of illustrating some of the differences between the two major schools of thought in the planning literature. In the following pages I will describe these two models and go on to propose a third concept, that of structural planning, as the counterpart to structural social policy. Each model is in turn underpinned by political theories and values concerning particularly the distribution of power and the role of the state. It is primarily through a demonstration of this link that deficiencies in the two major models can be most easily understood.

BUREAU-INCREMENTALISM *or disjointed- iner.*

According to the leading theorist of this approach to social planning, C.E. Lindblom (1959, p. 86),

> Policy is not made once and for all; it is made and re-made end-lessly. Policy-making is a process of successive approximation to some desired objectives in which what is desired itself continues to change under reconsideration.

Karl Popper (1961) similarly has rejected utopian societal change and argued instead for a piecemeal approach. This then is pragmatic, trial-and-error policy-making, 'muddling through' or, more elaborately, the method of 'successive limited comparisons'.

This approach starts from the twin assumptions that, in practice, policy-makers do *not* attempt to clarify objectives and values in advance of examining policies. This is not possible, it is suggested, because values and objectives often conflict, and therefore agreement cannot be secured across a broad spectrum. Moreover, values cannot usually be disassociated from particular policies. So a choice is made between policies and at the same time between the values implicit in them. The policy-maker is not concerned with values and objectives, except in so far as they are embodied in specific policies. Second, and related to this, the adminis-trator or policy-maker considers not global values or objectives, but marginal or incremental ones (Lindblom, 1959, p. 82). In other words, it is the marginal differences between policies on which the policy-maker bases his or her choice.

Together, these assumptions show that bureau-incrementalism is focused wholly on existing policy and practice and not on future goals, and on pragmatic change at the margins rather than radical overhauls or shifts in direction. As a result, it is argued, policy-making should be 'disjointed' and not necessarily connected progressively. This is, in essence, policy-making (and therefore research and evaluation) from the bureaucrats' perspective; it is administration — and not needs — orientated, hence 'bureau-incrementalism' (the label is adapted from 'bureau-professionalism'; see Parry and Parry, 1979, p. 43).

The process of bureau- or disjointed-incrementalism (Braybrooke and Lindblom, 1963) begins with the decision-maker finding a policy that approximates an objective and on which there is a wide measure of agreement. Subsequently the policy is adjusted incrementally in the light of experience and subject to continued agreement. The process is a continuous one, with policy choices following in a disjointed but chronological series. The outcome of each policy is never expected to be the final resolution of the problem. It proceeds like a TV soap opera, which goes on and on apparently without end, in a series of small incremental episodes which do not depart from the format established at the outset.

According to its proponents the advantages of this approach to policy-making are that, since it is fruitless to try to secure agreement on major objectives, it is more sensible to do so for small-scale changes. Because the steps taken are small ones, any mistakes made are also likely to be minor. There are bound to be unanticipated effects arising out of policies, and small-scale changes mean that the effects can be taken account of more quickly than if the policy took the form of a distinct departure from previous policy. The administrators' knowledge is based on a similar series of incremental steps, and so they are never expected to reach beyond their previous experience in predicting the outcome of policy. The method therefore provides built-in feedback and empirical testing of policy at each incremental stage before the series continues.

Critique of bureau-incrementalism

Criticisms of this approach to policy-making are widespread. A large proportion of them stem from the other major school of thought, rational–comprehensive planning. Indeed, the construction of rational techniques was a direct response to what was seen as a complete lack of rigour in the muddled world of decision-making. It is obvious that, unless the assumption of free competition in the political arena is accepted, the whole process of policy-making, being a constant series of compromises between different interests, could be dominated by powerful interests such as a ruling class or elite, while excluding other weaker groups. There is within the bureau-incrementalism approach no recognition of the impact of the operation of power in the policy-making process. The fact that 'compromises' may always be loaded does not impinge on what is essentially a *description* of administrative behaviour.

Second, it is assumed that all conflicts are capable of resolution and consensus. Of course, within a state bureaucracy such as the British civil service this is usually the case, because radical or challenging policies rarely reach the political agenda. Moreover, conflict resolution is institutionalized in bureaucratic organizations through bargaining, negotiation and commonly held assumptions and values (Salaman and Thompson, 1973, pp. 169–264; for an analysis of the British civil service see Heclo and Wildavsky, 1974, pp. 1–36). Thus, even if there is a potential 'winner-takes-all', or zero-sum, choice, a 'compromise' is usually reached. This situation occurs constantly in the annual public expenditure process. Here the Treasury usually secures the precise expenditure targets or cuts it requires, either by asking for more than is actually required or by *force majeure* (for an inside description of this process see Barnett, 1982).

Third, the approach is conservative, because it is concerned only with marginal adjustments to existing policy and practice, and therefore positively discourages innovation. According to Dror (1964, p. 157), disjointed–incrementalism reinforces inertia and justifies a policy of no effort. This means that the model provides no framework in which to tackle major social problems in large steps, if they are required. If the existing policy is effective or requires only minor adjustment to make it so, incrementalism may be the adequate vehicle to improve it.

But if the policy is ineffective and requires substantial change, or a sweeping away and replacement with something more radical, this is not possible within the existing framework. In Third World countries, for instance, where innovatory policies are often needed, this is an inappropriate model for planning (Conyers, 1982). Conversely, where problems themselves are changing, policy-making based on bureau-incrementalism will be slow to respond (Dror, 1964). Thus, for example, planning in the social services has been lagging far behind changes in the structure of population, and particularly behind the contraction in the size of the pool of potential informal careers (A. Walker, 1982d). Because this approach is primarily descriptive, though not necessarily accurately so, it does not enable us to *explain* innovation (see Hall, et al., 1975, pp. 475–509).

RATIONAL–COMPREHENSIVE PLANNING

This approach to planning may be seen as one response to the inadequacies of bureau-incrementalism as a basis for decision-making. In contrast to the previous model, therefore, rational–comprehensive planning is characterized by clarity of objectives, explicit evaluation and comprehensive overview. But also, this model fits more closely than bureau-incrementalism most common, as well as common-sense, definitions of planning as a process of rational decision-making, relating ends and means to available resources (see for example Scott, 1967; Rein, 1968).

This approach to planning assumes that policy goals are clearly defined and accepted and therefore that the comprehensive search for policies, and the ultimate choice between them, is primarily a technical matter of deciding on means (Rein, 1968, p. 143). It is a model of rationality derived chiefly from mathematics and systems theory that lies at the heart of this approach. Drawing on the work of Simon (1957), the rational model on which this perspective is based is usually characterized by the following five stages:

(1)   clarification of goals, values or objectives;
(2)   comprehensive survey of all possible policies through which this objective may be achieved;
(3)   investigation of the outcome of each option;
(4)   comparative evaluation of each policy with the goal;
(5)   selection of policy, or combination of policies, with consequences that come closest to achieving the stated goal (Lindblom, 1968, p. 12; Self, 1974, p. 194).

Critique of rational–comprehensive planning

This model has also been subject to a great deal of criticism, mainly from the incrementalists.

In the first place, it is argued that the ideal type of rationality implicit in this model of planning is unattainable. It is, at best, impractical to collect all the relevant data that have a bearing on a public policy choice and to order potential courses of action into priorities based on a precise measurement of benefits and costs. It is not possible to anticipate every effect of policy. Even in the age of microchip technology, it is impossible to forecast and evaluate the outcome of every possible policy option. And in any case, the costs of following such a course may far outweigh its benefits. This is not to say that systematic research is not of fundamental importance to the planning process, but simply that it should be employed in a selective, and not a blanket, fashion.

The label 'comprehensive' is also problematic. Like the ideal of rationality, it is impossible to be fully comprehensive in the assessment of options. Furthermore, the term 'comprehensive' does not necessarily imply that it is more radical than other forms of planning. It suggests a comprehensive survey of all possible options; but this does not *necessarily* imply a distinctly different policy outcome, and certainly not a more radical one.

Second, the rational—comprehensive model pays no attention to social factors such as power, ideology and values, or to established organizational custom and routines, which tend to dominate the official planning process. It is, in essence, a technical process that professes to be value-free. The realm of social policy is more commonly associated with value conflicts and outcomes that are not always entirely predictable or quantifiable in monetary terms. Thus it is argued that in planning it is more important to recognize conflicting policy goals than to search for abstract rationality. So, for example, because policy-making and planning rest on ideology and values, the situation never arises in which every possible option is considered in turn and accepted or rejected. Political parties consider a limited range of policy options in compiling their manifestos. In government, policy-making and planning are further limited by the pattern of existing practice, skills and experience. Political power is exercised, therefore, not only positively, in the *choice* of policies, but also negatively, in the exclusion of policies from the agenda (Bachrach and Baratz, 1970). The hypothetical world of economic rationality, which attempts to systematize every choice, is incompatible with the real world of political decision-making, in which options are restricted by values. It is not possible, in other words, rigidly to separate values and decisions and facts and values, as the rational—comprehensive model suggests (Hyderbrand, 1964). Thus, the bureau-incrementalist would argue, we will get nothing done if we have to wait to secure agreement on objectives, and so these are best approached through marginal policy choices.

Third, the model is biased by the premium it places on rationality, by no means a universally prized value (Smith and May, 1980, p. 149). It was constructed to further the efficiency of decision-making in bureaucratic organizations. It is not surprising, therefore, that this approach favours the management of organizations and organizational efficiency. Unfortunately, this is not necessarily the same as efficiency in the *outcomes* of policy, for example in meeting need. Participants in the public policy-making process may and usually do have different perceptions of the services they manage and the priorities they should pursue from the clients or claimants served by those organizations (see for example, Smith, 1980; Townsend, 1981b; Donnison, 1982).

THE INTRODUCTION OF MICROECONOMIC TECHNIQUES INTO PUBLIC POLICY PLANNING

The quest for rationality in decision-making, spurred on by the desire to economize in the public sector, resulted in the importation, in the late 1960s and early 1970s, of a range of functional techniques such as cost–benefit analysis and programme budgeting from the private sector. The most famous, the Planning–Programming–Budgeting System (PPBS), was introduced into the US government by President Johnson in 1965. 'PPBS is an attempt to improve the use of resources in the public sector by introducing *more rational criteria* for decisions on resource allocation' (Banks, 1979, p. 150; my italics). It was originated in the 1950s by the Rand Corporation to study the location of military bases, and subsequently applied to decision-making in the US Department of Defense. According to the President, the aims of this 'very new and revolutionary system' (Novick, 1965, p. 24) of programme budgeting were as follows (Townsend, 1975, p. 60): to

(i) identify our national goals with precision and on a continuing basis;
(ii) choose among those goals the ones that are most urgent;
(iii) search for alternative means of reaching those goals most effectively at least cost;
(iv) inform ourselves not merely on next year's costs – but on the second, and third, and subsequent year's costs – of our programmes;
(v) measure the performance of our programs to insure a dollar's worth of service for each dollar spent.

This system will improve ability to control our programs and our budgets rather than having them control us.

On the face of it, these are highly desirable aims for planning to pursue, but the federal PPBS system soon foundered in the United States and by 1971 was partly if not wholly shelved (Schick, 1973, p. 146). Outside of the Defense Department, PPBS was never integrated with the existing budget process. The Budget Bureau attempted to impose the Defense model on other departments, and the resulting struggles simply reinforced their suspicion of the PPBS. The result was predictable: 'Faced with an imposed system which they neither designed nor understood, many departments reacted by divorcing the PPB system from budgeting' (Schick, 1973, p. 150). To a large extent, departments must have been reacting to what they perceived as a lack of commitment to PPBS on the part of the Budget Bureau, which maintained a strict separation between its major budget review functions and its relatively small-scale PPBS work.

The failure of PPBS: lessons for planning

The demise of PPBS provides two important lessons for a discussion of the development of social planning. In the first place, new forms of planning machinery cannot be grafted on to a pre-existing system of administrative practices, values and traditions at short notice and without preparation. They must either supercede or be fully integrated with the existing processes. This means that the introduction of new planning methods must itself be carefully planned. The relative failure of the Central Policy Review Staff (CPRS) to influence the policy-making process on this side of the Atlantic, which is discussed in chapter 7, further demonstrates this point. PPBS was introduced hurriedly with inadequate support and back-up resources. Moreover, the lack of preparation meant that there simply was not enough skilled staff and good data available to fulfil its aims.

Second, if it is to be successful, any innovative system of priority planning must confront the antipathy of the budgetary process to analysis. Again, as with the experience of the CPRS in this country, PPBS found it impossible to penetrate the budgeting process (Schick, 1973, p. 153; Heclo and Wildavsky, 1974, p. 327).

Programme analysis and review

So there were many administrative, technical and political reasons why PPBS failed. (This is not to suggest that the system itself was not faulted in various respects, a point to which I return below.) As a result of this failure, the first steps in the development of PPBS techniques in this country were much more tentative. In order to avoid the difficulties encountered in the United States, the 1970 Conservative government decided to go for a different system: Programme Analysis and Review (PAR). These were (they were abolished in 1981) supposed to be in-depth reviews of the main government expenditure programmes, examining their objectives, alternative ways of achieving them and the cost of alternatives. The reviews were conducted by the Treasury in conjunction with the CPRS and civil service departments, but the actual analysis was done within individual departments.

PARs represented an advance on US experience in that some attempt was made to link them with the planning of public expenditure, but they were still separate from the PESC process. One of the major differences that confronts the student of social policy between the experience of the PPBS in the United States and PARs in this country is the excessive secrecy that surrounded the latter. In comparison with the wide range of analyses of PPBS on both sides of the Atlantic, the PAR cupboard is almost bare.

After initial uncertainty as to its correct place in the administrative structure, the PAR system was established under Treasury control. It had not, as Heclo and Wildavsky (1974, p. 280) lamented, 'fallen to a detached, independent group of long-term thinkers'. The final version of PAR was a much diluted version of the Central Capability Department and corporate planning apparatus originally envisaged by the government's industrial advisers. In fact, there was little if anything to distinguish PAR studies from those that had been conducted in Whitehall departments for years. As Heclo and Wildavsky (1974, p. 280) predicted, 'Location in the Treasury means that PAR is likely to exclude analyses of subjects lacking significant and immediate expenditure content.'

PAR analyses were said to consist of five stages. First, there were departmental assessments of the determinants of expenditure on their programmes. The department was then asked to look at the use of resources in carrying out the programme and at what determined their value. Next, the department was questioned on the composition and distribution of current expenditure. Fourth, the department was asked to assess the impact of the programme in achieving its aims and the relationship between supply and demand over five years. Finally, departments were asked to specify the alternative options available on different assumptions about need or combinations of supply and demand (Heclo and Wildavsky, 1974, p. 282). Suggestions for PAR studies usually originated with departments but could come from anywhere in the expenditure process. The precise format and subject of the analyses was, like most things in the British civil service, a matter for negotiation between the individual department and the Treasury.

PARs survived the 1970s largely through inertia, with no significant measure of departmental commitment. Furthermore, because departments treated them as mechanisms for projecting resource allocation in an attempt to gain commitment for expenditure, they conflicted in practice with the PESC system. So, as the PESC system was gradually transformed into a tighter and tighter control mechanism (see chapter 6), the role of PARs was diminished in the eyes of both Treasury and spending departments. To put it bluntly, a government and Treasury that are concerned primarily with reducing expenditure are not likely to be interested overly in individual departments' detailed cases for increasing resources. Moreover, in a departmentally based political system detailed studies of particular programmes do not attract much interest from other departments, especially when each is seeking to protect its own levels of spending. Most importantly, though, as Heclo and Wildavsky (1974, p. 302) point out, 'PAR must be looked upon as an instrument for the future', and a government that has no interest in the long-term planning of public sector programmes in relation to needs and objectives has little use for PARs.

While the across-the-board introduction of PPB was rejected, one department – the DHSS – swam against the tide and conducted a feasibility study in 1971. The study team proposed a programme structure and showed how it could be used in costing policies, considering priorities and in programme planning. The team was instructed to concentrate on proposals that could be implemented quickly (Banks, 1979, p. 155). The progress of programme budgeting, therefore, was not held up by the same lack of information and statistics that bedevilled PPBS in the United States. On the other hand, this approach meant that programme budgeting was likely to be much less challenging than its

US counterpart. Thus, 'the most fundamental limitation of the programme budget developed for health and personal social services is that
it does not provide the information needed to evaluate alternative
policies in depth' (Banks, 1979, p. 169).

Programme budgeting was introduced into the DHSS planning cycle
in 1973 (the whole planning system itself had been reorganized the
previous year), and by 1975 the programme budget and public expenditure survey were consolidated in one departmental branch. The first
stage of the programme budget team's work was the analysis of past
policy and expenditure trends and discussions with the policy branches
of the DHSS on the costs of policies. Expenditure was then projected,
according to the policy changes desired by the different branches, on
the basis of different time-scales. The outcome of this planning exercise
is considered in chapter 7.

Critique of microeconomic techniques

Both of these attempts to introduce rationality into social planning –
PPBS in the United States and programme budgeting in Britain – and
also the much wider range of systems analysis and cost–benefit techniques suffer from similar deficiencies.

They are concerned with economic or financial rationality and not
with social or political rationality. Apart from the well documented
practical difficulty of attempting to translate all policies and outcomes
into monetary units (see for example Wildavsky, 1966; Self, 1970; and,
for an economist's response, Williams, 1972), the assumption that it is
crucial to do so reflects and reinforces the ascendancy of narrow
economic criteria in the planning process.

These functional techniques are derived from the microeconomic
assumptions that the benefits of economic activity to individuals should
be maximized, and that the most efficient mechanism for doing so is
through free choice in the private market. The immediate problem in
extending this assumption to the public sector is the absence of free
choice and the inappropriateness of private market principles in the
provision of many public services that may have been established, in
part at least, to counteract deficiencies in the market. There are, for
example, the unconsidered 'externalities' discussed in the previous
chapter that only public policies may respond to, or the collective desire
to redistribute resources in order to correct market inequalities. Even

when it is recognized that social benefits cannot be valued in monetary terms, some analysts attempt to measure the amount of benefit provided by different services (patients treated, for example) in order to set alongside that the cost of that service. The aim is to compare different ways of achieving the objectives of policies in relation to their cost. This sort of 'cost effectiveness analysis' is again based on the assumption that cost is the most important evaluative dimension.

The *cost imperative* that underpins these functional techniques reinforces the central control of policies and resource distribution. According to Wildavsky (1966, p. 305), programme budgeting contains 'an extreme centralizing bias', and in practice this means control according to narrow economic criteria. These techniques, therefore, are primarily mechanisms for improving the 'efficiency' of administration in terms of its control over resources. From the outset, programme budgeting in Britain was concentrated on the provision of services and particularly the expenditure on them, rather than on 'outputs': the benefits of services to their clients or their efficacy in meeting need. So, rather than detailed studies of the *impact* of services, it has been concerned primarily with their implementation. This means that, if the policies themselves are deficient, programme budgeting will simply compound that deficiency: 'It provides a framework for deciding priorities in implementing policies, but there is no point in planning to implement policies which are themselves misconceived because they are not based on adequate thought, consultation and research' (Banks, 1979, p. 169).

All this is not to suggest that microeconomic techniques are not useful in policy-making, since there are plenty of examples of their successful application (see for example Gordon, 1982). But it is important, first, to recognize that the veil of scientific rationality that surrounds them disguises an individualistic political philosophy, including utility maximization and the assumption of market superiority. In fact, every key decision involved in using these techniques — which policies to include, which benefits to measure and how — rests on value choices. Second, while it is highly desirable to increase cost effectiveness in public policy and to reduce the wasteful use of resources, the problem arises when this is the *only* criterion used to evaluate policies. This, unfortunately, is the point that social planning in the social services in Britain has reached in the early 1980s, where the economic tail is wagging the political and social dog.

THE BUREAU-INCREMENTAL/RATIONAL–COMPREHENSIVE
DEBATE

Although the debate between the incremental and rational schools has occupied a prominent place in the social planning literature for more than 20 years, and still provides a useful illustration of some of the differences between the two dominant schools of thought in planning, it rests to some extent on a false dichotomy (Smith and May, 1980). There are two sets of factors to be considered.

It has already been hinted that, in discussing these two approaches to planning, we are not comparing like with like. Although they both profess to be explanatory *and* normative, it is not clear, as Smith and May (1980, p. 155) have pointed out, how they can serve both as descriptions of how things are done and also, as prescriptions of how they might be improved. In practice, bureau-incrementalism is a description of decision-making in complex organizations, whereas variants on the rational model are widely held to describe the way decision-making *should* operate (see Leach, 1982). Each is derived from a different approach to decision-making; descriptive theory is concerned with how decisions are made in practice, and normative decision theory with how a rational decision-maker should approach a problem (Castles, et al., 1978, p. 11).

The two models differ in another important respect. While the rational approach is a prescription of how bureaucratic decision-making and planning might be improved, bureau-incrementalism is not primarily a description of planning but of decision-making. The two concepts are frequently confused. A decision is a conscious choice between at least two possible courses of action (Castles, et al., 1978, p. 11). But while planning involves decision-making, it includes more – for example, the programming of policy changes and policy formulation (see pp. 3–4).

Economic theory of decision-making

Second, having pointed to some differences in approach between incrementalism and rational planning, the models show enough *similarities* to undermine the debate between them. Both are based on restricted conceptions of power. Taking bureau-incrementalism first, it is assumed that individual decision-makers have what amounts to a free choice between marginally different policies. The theory is that, confronted with two policies, X and Y, which offer equal amounts of objectives a, b and c, but where X promises more of d than does Y and Y promises more of e than does X, the decision-maker is concerned only with the difference between the marginal amount of d and e. The final choice between increments will take the form of a choice between policies X and Y. This logic should be familiar to readers of chapter 3 and those conversant with economic theories of democracy. As Lindblom (1959, p. 83) points out, this is simply an extension of the economic theory of consumer choice to public policy-making. Decision-makers, it is argued, like consumers, seek to satisfy utility in choosing between different policies (Downs, 1967, p. 168). At the same time, it is suggested that a wide range of different groups and interests is represented in the form of inputs or 'demands' in the decision-making process. The political system hypothesized here is pluralist, one in which individuals can combine in pressure groups and so influence policy. According to Lindblom (1959, p. 86), 'the incremental pattern of policy-making fits with the multiple pressure pattern.' He suggests that it is easier for pressure groups to gain access to an incrementalist decision-making process and to secure change. Because change is incremental, however, their impact on policy is likely to be slight.

Turning to rational—comprehensive planning, this approach owes much to the same heritage as the previous one. It derives from economic assumptions about behaviour in conditions of uncertainty and the work of Simon (1957), who is the leading proponent of the utility 'satisficing' theory from which disjointed-incrementalism stems. Thus, instead of the traditional theory of decision-making based on the *maximization* of utility (see p. 58), both of the approaches discussed so far hypothesize that decisions are made in a process of utility-*satisficing* (Downs, 1967, p. 168). The economic concept implied here is the potential Pareto criterion (see p. 58). It has been applied to decision-making and has achieved the status of a rule, which dictates that no action should be taken if at least one person would be made worse off. The concept has been applied to decision-making by pluralist political theorists. So the rational—comprehensive model, like its bureau-incrementalist counter-part, rests on a pluralist theory of power. The link between the two planning models is demonstrated clearly in the work of some of the leading proponents of economic theories of democracy such as Easton (1965), whose pluralist analysis is derived from systems theory. So, as

Donnison et al. (1975, p. 28), have noted, 'The two approaches have more in common than their most ardent advocates recognise.'

Pluralism

Since pluralist assumptions underpin both models of planning, it is important to examine the limitations of that political theory. Pluralism assumes that power is shared by different interest groups competing in the political arena. According to Lindblom (1959, p. 85), for example,

> Almost every interest has its watchdog. Without claiming that every interest has a sufficiently powerful watchdog, it can be argued that our system often can assure a more comprehensive regard for the values of the whole society than any attempt at intellectual comprehensiveness.

Thus it is argued that any legitimate group can make itself heard effectively at some stage in the decision-making process (Dahl, 1956, p. 150). Criticisms of pluralism are widespread. Most telling is its failure to recognize the structural differentiation of power between major social groups or classes and the covert exercise of power in the decision-making process. Although pluralist accounts may accurately reflect the process of interest group competition, they cannot explain the process by which certain interests *consistently* dominate in the political system. Nor can they explain the hidden or covert operation of power, or what has been termed the 'non-decision-making process' (Bachrach and Baratz, 1970). In other words, interest group competition may result in policy change, but such changes take place within strictly limited bounds (Hall et al., 1975, p. 151). These bounds are set, in turn, by dominant economic and ideological considerations.

The domination of consensus

The bureau-incremental and rational—comprehensive models are also similar in being organizationally orientated and unhistorical (Donnison et al., 1975, p. 27). Both are addressed to decision-making and management in organizations and are appropriate to decisions about problems that lie within the compass of the organization's influence. At the societal level, both approaches are inadequate bases for planning because not all problems are capable of resolution by bureaucratic or technical means. This deficiency arises in part from the fact that decisions are treated as discrete problems and are not considered in the context of longer-term societal development. In particular, the development of ideology and the crucial link between ideology, values and policy-making have no place in bureau-incremental and rational–comprehensive methods.

Both models reflect a consensus theory of society, which assumes general agreement on fundamental goals and values. This consensus may be possible within small-scale organizations, but not in whole societies. It is within this consensus framework that theories such as the 'end of ideology' and 'convergence' have been spawned (see p. 26). The influence of consensus theories of society on the two models of planning under consideration is obvious. Both take for granted the institutional framework of services and assume that, at best, they need improvement or reform. Unfortunately, consensus theories are inadequate as explanations of the growth and development of the welfare state (George and Wilding, 1976; Mishra, 1981; Gough, 1978), and as a result these models of planning are inadequate as prescriptions of how relations might be ordered to improve the welfare of citizens.

Bureau-incrementalism and rational–comprehensive planning might best be viewed as two sides of the same coin, the one a descriptive model of how decisions are taken in complex bureaucracies, and the other a prescriptive model of how that decision-making process could be systematized. Both are bureau-orientated, and none of the hybrid versions of them (Etzioni, 1967; Dror, 1964) has overcome that deficiency.

It is tempting to conclude that, rather than expending energy in constructing further *a priori* models of decision-making, effort should be put into observing and analysing actual practice and the subjective interpretation of the actors involved in the decision-making process (Smith and May, 1980, p. 158). In view of the long sterile debate between incrementalism and rationalism, this is a compelling argument, but it would be mistaken to apply it to the analysis of planning. The chief problem is that, in a field that is relatively underdeveloped, to devote all our time to studying the very limited planning activity in Western capitalist societies would be very restricting. What is required instead are more radical models of planning, which move beyond the discussion of bureaucratic decision-making towards structural planning. These models are not necessarily purely *a priori* because planning experience in other countries has important lessons for this country. Unfortunately, the study of comparative planning is even more underdeveloped than the study of comparative social policy.

STRUCTURAL PLANNING

The previous discussion shows that the dominant schools of thought in planning are not distinct alternatives, but rest on similar assumptions about the nature and distribution of power and on similar values. Their prominence and the often artificial debate between them has had the effect of trapping the development of planning in the restricted world of bureaucratic decision-making. Like social policy, social planning has been constructed as an adjunct to the state, and to the social services in particular. Models of planning tend, therefore, to be centralized, elitist and technical rather than devolved, democratic and normative. An alternative, which mirrors the difference between traditional social administration and structural social policy, is *structural social planning*. This conception of planning is based on quite different theories of society and power to those outlined so far.

In contrast to the pragmatic organizationally orientated approach of bureau-incrementalism, structural social planning is, in most capitalist societies, a normative conception (In chapter 8 planning in state socialist societies is discussed.) The essence of this approach is its transformative objectives. Change would be incremental, but it is not incrementalism as such that has been questioned, but rather the incrementalism of existing policies and institutions. *The main issue here is not the pace of change but the nature of change.* What I am discussing, therefore, is structural incrementalism. Structural social planning would be the vehicle for radical change in the distribution of resources and life chances between different groups in society. It is born out of the recognition that existing bureau-incremental planning is not likely to prove a helpful medium for the production of the major social changes necessary to transform social relations. Also, in direct contrast to the previous models, structural planning attempts to reverse the dominant relationship between economic and social values and priorities.

This approach recognizes that the practice of policy-making and planning is restricted by dominant ideology and values, which in capitalist societies are necessarily capitalist. Therefore it is not only the form of planning and the institutional structure within which it is conducted, but also the antithetical values of capitalism that will have to be changed if socialist goals are to be achieved. (This is, then, a very long-term form of planning.)

It is possible, of course, that structural social planning may be employed to change socialist or social democratic public institutions into private ones. In some cases this would mean simply extending or reinforcing, rather than transforming, basic values and structures. In other cases it would represent a radical change in objectives, for example if the national health service (NHS) were privatized. Thus, in a capitalist society structural social planning would be usually, though not necessarily, socialist in objectives. This model of planning is more explicitly ideological than the others.

The form of structural planning

What form would structural social planning take? There can be no definitive answer to that question because it would depend on the objectives of planning. In the socialist approach proposed in chapter 9, it is suggested that the process of planning itself should be democratic and diffuse and therefore that the exact path it takes cannot be predicted. Others might suggest a more centralized, imperative form of planning, along the lines of that conducted in state socialist societies.

In order to counter the conservative tendencies of bureau-incrementalism and to ensure the implementation of structural social policy, it is necessary to reassess both the role and the function of social services. The starting point for this reappraisal is the explicit statement of the goals and objectives of policy. Concentration on needs and objectives enables the social planner to transcend institutional forms and techniques of resource management. Thus, planning becomes the tasks of clarifying the courses available to achieve the stated goals of policy, and of mapping out the proposed development of social institutions and groups to achieve the goals of policy. While structural social policy is concerned with altering the production and distribution of social welfare, structural social planning is the twin process through which the central goals of policy are clarified and achieved.

Often, structural social planners will be concerned with 'Utopian' goals (Reddin, 1980). Indeed, it is arguable that such long-term goals are essential if the aims of structural social policy are to be achieved. In the first place, a vision of the future is essential both for the construction of plans and for democratic participation in the policy-making and planning process. Second, without this future vision historical fatalism will remain dominant (Reddin, 1980), and what has happened will go on happening. Of course, most policies and plans are based implicitly on a vision of the future, or at least on a vision of an alternative or ideal set of relationships. They are derived from assumptions and values concerning the necessity for change and the balance of responsibilities between individuals and the state. Even the ideal type of *laissez-faire* or anti-collectivist 'planning' – the free play of market forces – contains implicit assumptions about those groups and activities in society that should be valued (see chapter 3). It is only when these values and assumptions are made explicit that the task of providing a framework within which to achieve structural social planning, and particularly the democratic discussion of planning goals, can be set underway.

There are, of course, problems with this conception of structural social planning. These derive chiefly from the fact that it is almost entirely prescriptive and has not been tested fully in practice. On the face of it, though, there would obviously be a major political contra-diction between transformative planning aimed at promoting socialist welfare, and capitalist society and state. How can we hope to plan the development of socialist relations in a society dominated by capitalist values and institutions? One way towards the resolution of this paradox (discussed at length in chapter 9) entails long-term oppositional planning and consciousness-raising, in order to change existing social relations and so gradually to counteract those aspects of dominant ideology that inhibit radical change. Thus the aim of socialist social planning would be eventually to change the processes whereby social problems, inequalities and so on are *reproduced*.

But there are also practical difficulties in operating a planning system that is diffuse and democratic. For example, how can local community interests be reconciled effectively with national interests, unless, that is, the two are identical? Moreover, because planning is concentrated in the first instance on the grand level of values and goals, detailed plan-ning may be left mistakenly to the incrementalist perspective of the bureaucracy. This underlines the need for democratic safeguards and checks on the planning process, but precisely how this can be achieved must be discussed and tested in practice.

Structural conflict

The theory of society underlying structural social planning is based on conflict rather than consensus. It is recognized that power is concentrated. The dominant interests in public policy are primarily those of the ruling class or elite. Any institutions established within a society, including welfare services, must reflect in important respects that society's dominant values. In a capitalist society key social problems are the product of capitalism itself; therefore it is society that requires considerable transformation.

The socialist variant of structural social planning derives from the observation that the inequalities the welfare state has sought partly to redress are deeply rooted in the social structure and require radical policy and planning. This approach rests on the analysis of the structurally determined interests of all members of society. Classes are defined in the economic sphere through the ownership and control of the means of production and the subordination of other classes. This structured class conflict is complicated by the growth of other groups with a different power base — welfare state bureau-professionals, for example. But the fundamental point is that there is a conflict of interests between different groups on major issues such as the control of different resources and knowledge, rather than a consensus.

Moreover, as I argued in chapter 2, the welfare functions of the state include economic, ideological and repressive aspects (Miliband, 1969). In other words, they are concerned in part, though not in whole, with accumulation and legitimation (O'Connor, 1973), with economic growth and social investment on the one hand, and with the promotion of social harmony on the other. Once it is grasped that the welfare state entails control as well as welfare, the need for structural social policy and planning becomes more apparent.

THE PLANNING CONTINUUM

So far in this chapter I have outlined three models of social planning, two of which are to a large extent mirror-images of each other with the third being diametrically opposed. Table 1 summarizes this position and emphasizes the link between the models and different theories of society and power.

These models might be represented diagramatically on a continuum, stretching from bureau-incrementalism to structural planning. Different national and organizational methods of planning could then be compared with these ideal types. These approaches to planning should also be compared on another dimension: their degree of central control. The two main examples on this second continuum are imperative or command planning, characteristic of Soviet-type countries (see chapter 8), and central indicative or guideline planning, more characteristic of capitalist countries. The two dimensions – objectives and organization – together provide a comparative framework for evaluating different approaches to planning (see figure 1). Western capitalist societies tend to be grouped in the bottom left-hand segment of the quadrant towards the horizontal axis, and state socialist societies in the same segment towards the vertical axis. The approach outlined in chapter 9 is aimed at shifting planning in Britain from the bottom left-hand segment to the top right-hand one. Planning in state socialist societies is, with the main exception of China, centralized and imperative (see chapter 8). In capitalist societies it is usually centralized and indicative. In the case of Britain it has become more centralized in recent years, whereas in the case of France, for example, it has become more centralized and more technocratic (Green, 1981, p. 120).

The four possible models represented by the polar extremes of the two continuums of objectives and organization may also be shown diagrammatically, as in figure 2.

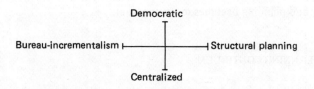

Figure 1 Dimensions of planning

Table 1 Models of planning

Criterion	Bureau-incremental	Rational–comprehensive	Structural (socialist variation)
Definition of objectives/values	Implicit in policies chosen	Explicitly defined and clarified	Explicitly defined as socialist, e.g. production for need
Evaluation of alternative policies	Only marginal changes to existing policies	Comprehensive, covering all relevant factors	Limited to range defined by values, e.g. would it meet social needs?
Basis of policy choice	Rests on consensus among policy-makers	Means to achieve objective	Means to achieve objective with democratic support
Measure of successful policy	Agreement achieved	Objective achieved	Objective achieved with continued support
Relationship between economic and social priorities	Economic goals predominate	Economic goals predominate	Social goals predominate
Theory of society	Consensus	Consensus	Conflict
Theory of power	Pluralist	Pluralist	Elite/class

Objectives of planning

	Bureau-incremental and democratic	Structural and democratic
Organization of planning	Bureau-incremental and centralized	Structural and centralized

Figure 2   Dimensions of planning: four possible models

CO-ORDINATED BUREAU-INCREMENTALISM

Having discussed in detail three main models of planning, it is important to note as a prelude to the next three chapters, which examine planning in practice, that ranged within the two continuums are various other types of planning. In Britain and the United States these are for the most part modifications of bureau-incrementalism.

The prime case, a number of examples of which are considered in chapter 7, is co-ordinated bureau-incrementalism. It is a matter for debate whether or not this is a distinct model of social planning. According to this perspective, planning is equated with co-ordination and reform. In the words of Myrdal (1960, p. 46), for instance, 'Co-ordination leads to planning or, rather, it *is* planning, as this term has come to be understood in the Western world.' The case for co-ordination is based on a belief that the institutional structure within which to realize welfare, the relief of poverty and so on has been created; all that is required is greater efficiency and co-ordination in their operation. In other words, social progress is equated with the better working and co-ordination of public services. Government research is also geared to these limited ends.

This 'agency deficiency' approach to social problems is a common one in capitalist societies and is most closely identified with liberal and social democratic ideology. Roy Jenkins (1972, p. 57), for example, while still a Labour politician, argued that 'Poverty can be eliminated only if we improve the standards of our social services generally, and change our priorities in them.' Similarly, in his analysis of the politics of poverty, Donnison (1982, p. 41) observed that 'Too often poor people were caught in the cross-fire of frontier warfare between bureaucracies, and ended up getting the wrong help or none at all.' Furthermore, 'Wherever you looked, there were no common principles or practices to protect poor people who were the bewildered victims of these frontier problems' (Donnison, 1982, p. 42). It is sometimes argued in a similar vein that the solution to poverty lies in the co-ordination of the tax and social security systems.

It has been assumed that co-ordination is equivalent to comprehensive or strategic social planning, and so it has been pursued as an end in itself. According to Kahn (1969), 'Co-ordination is an urgent motivation for planning on all levels; provision for co-ordination is a significant objective of planning; and co-ordination is an important outcome of planning.' Co-ordination has been pursued more thoroughly in the realm of economic planning, but the artificial separation of economic and social planning has meant that the potential for both has been limited.

Co-ordinated bureau-incrementalism shares common assumptions with the bureau-incrementalist perspective; in particular, there is a broadly consensus view of the world. Again, this is best expressed in the convergence thesis, implicit in this approach and so beloved of civil servants, which suggests that fine-tuning is all that is required to create welfare. It does recognize, however, that planning is necessary to improve the operation of institutions, and therefore represents a significant step from the 'non-planning' of bureau-incrementalism and its conservative acceptance of institutions and policies. At times social planning in Britain has been shifted significantly along the objectives continuum towards structural planning through measures such as joint planning between the health and personal social services. Myrdal (1960, p. 46) goes further, and argues that there is a positive trend from intervention to co-ordination and on to planning in Western societies:

> Co-ordination of measures of intervention implies a reconsideration of them all from the point of view of how they combine to serve the development goals of the entire national community, as these goals become determined by the political process that provides the basis for power. . . . This co-ordination of policies . . . does not take the shape of a rigid, all-embracing plan. Nevertheless, it constitutes a steadily developing approach to planning, which tends to become firmer and more embracing as present tendencies work themselves out.

Whether or not this prediction proves true is a matter for observation. For the present, it is reasonable to say that there are no signs as yet of this progressive development of planning in Britain. Co-ordination between services has not been achieved, let alone collaboration (Booth, 1981, p. 25). For the most part, efforts to co-ordinate services and planning have been very limited and have not as yet approached the comprehensive reassessment suggested by Myrdal. Moreover, in recent years the Conservative government has been positively opposed to planning. It has abolished PAR and the CPRS and has restricted the freedom of local authorities to plan independently (see chapter 6). Planning in Britain in the early 1980s, therefore, has been shifted back towards a strict centralized bureau-incrementalist position.

CONCLUSION

This chapter has outlined three main models of social planning, two of which combine, as mirror-images, into a bureau-incrementalist perspective. In contrast, structural social planning, the counterpart to the integrated social and economic policy outlined in chapter 3, is a normative and transformative concept. It is discussed in greater detail in Part III below. There, planning in state socialist and Third World societies are examined to see how far they fit the structural model, and to determine what lessons planning in those societies holds for this country. In the next Part, however, we are concerned with the actual practice of social planning.

PART II: Social Planning in Practice

5

Planning the Economy

INTRODUCTION

In the next three chapters attention switches from the mainly theoretical concerns of the last section to the actual practice of planning. The division between the subject matter of this chapter and chapter 6 and that of chapter 7 is between those aspects of planning that are primarily labelled 'economic' (chapters 5 and 6) and those that are primarily labelled 'social'. The wholly artificial nature of this division will soon become apparent.

The Department of Health and Social Security (DHSS), along with every other Whitehall department, is subservient to the Treasury. The organization and operation of social services planning reflects this: it is concerned overwhelmingly with resource inputs rather than with need. Treasury ministers and officials determine both the overall level of public expenditure and the distribution of expenditure between different programmes. The main mechanism for imposing their will throughout Whitehall is the Public Expenditure Survey Committee (PESC). The PESC machinery was developed specifically to ensure Treasury control over the growth and pattern of expenditure. It is within the public expenditure process that most of the key decisions are taken about what resources will be devoted to the different programmes, including social spending (A. Walker, 1982b). Treasury control extends to local government through the rate support grant.

In practice, therefore, public expenditure planning is the most important form of social planning in Britain (Townsend, 1980, p. 8). At the same time, however, public expenditure is a key instrument of macroeconomic policy and, specifically, of demand management. This emphasizes the point, made in chapter 3, that in its present narrow form social planning is vulnerable to changes in economic policy and management. Since the mid-1970s, for example, economic policies have resulted in greater emphasis on the control of central and local government expenditure and less on the planning or programming of expenditure. Economic policy overrides social policy and social planning.

This chapter concentrates on the role of the Treasury in planning the development of the economy. Economic policy and planning sets the context for social planning in Whitehall and, increasingly, in local authorities. Chapter 6 considers the primary means by which the Treasury controls social planning, the public expenditure process. It is this process that determines the level of resources in central departments and, to a large extent, also in local ones. Here we examine economic planning, the critical role of the Treasury in national life, and the impact of recent changes in economic policy on the planning process.

ECONOMIC PLANNING

Although economic planning takes place at all levels of the economy – by households, firms and government – here I am interested primarily in the role of the latter. Economic planning, like social planning, is divided administratively between different organizations and groups, both between the public and private sectors and within the apparatus of the state. The first division is bound to occur in a market economy. But even in command economies there is an organizational division of labour within the state's planning machinery (see Ellman, 1979, pp. 19–20). As with the social division of welfare, the administrative division of planning is unimportant unless it creates or masks inequalities, colours social perceptions, duplicates effort or frustrates the intentions of policies. Economic planning by the state is less strictly divided administratively than is social services planning. This is because the Treasury is the main economic planning department, whereas social services are divided into four departments.

The Treasury

The Treasury is the central finance ministry and controls the expenditure process throughout Whitehall. The Treasury exists 'to manage the economy of the United Kingdom so as to achieve the economic objectives laid down by Ministers and approved by Parliament', and to advise the Chancellor on all aspects of economic policy (Committee on Policy Optimisation, 1978, p. 20). The most influential department in both economic and social policy, it controls the day-to-day expenditure of government, scrutinizes all new policies entailing expenditure and manages the economy. Its influence is exerted in the formal machinery of the expenditure process (see p. 123) but also through the norms it imposes informally on Whitehall departments. For example, for the new recruit to the Treasury, 'One of the first and most obvious things learned is that the Treasury's business is to save money, not to spend it' (Heclo and Wildavsky, 1974, p. 41). In negotiations with individual departments the role of the Treasury is to question all proposals that involve expenditure. But Treasury officials are not merely professional sceptics; their role is to be 'energetically critical' (Heclo and Wildavsky, 1974, p. 45).

Following a management review completed in 1975, the Treasury is organized in the five main sections shown in figure 3. Three of them are headed currently by a second permanent secretary or, in the case of the Chief Economic Advisor, someone of equal status. The Public Service Sector covers public expenditure and associated topics; the Overseas Finance Sector, the management of sterling and international financial and monetary relations; the Domestic Economy Sector, fiscal policy, domestic monetary policy, incomes policy and industrial policy, including the nationalized industries; and the Chief Economic Adviser's Sector, economic advice for the other sectors and responsibility for the macroeconomic model and for forecasts and policy analysis. In each of these sectors there are one or more deputy secretaries reporting to their own second permanent secretaries, except in the Domestic Economy Sector, where they report directly to the permanent secretary. Under them the work of the Treasury is in the hands of under-secretaries heading different sub-groups, such as the social services, fiscal policy, macroeconomic policy and forecasting groups.

Policy discussions are centred on the Policy Co-ordinating Committee, which is chaired by the permanent secretary and consists of all permanent secretary and deputy secretary level officials. It draws together all aspects of the Treasury's work in order to provide co-ordinated advice to ministers. The Secretariat of this Committee is provided by the Central Support Unit. This small division is headed by an under-secretary.

Figure 3 Organization of HM Treasury (February 1983)

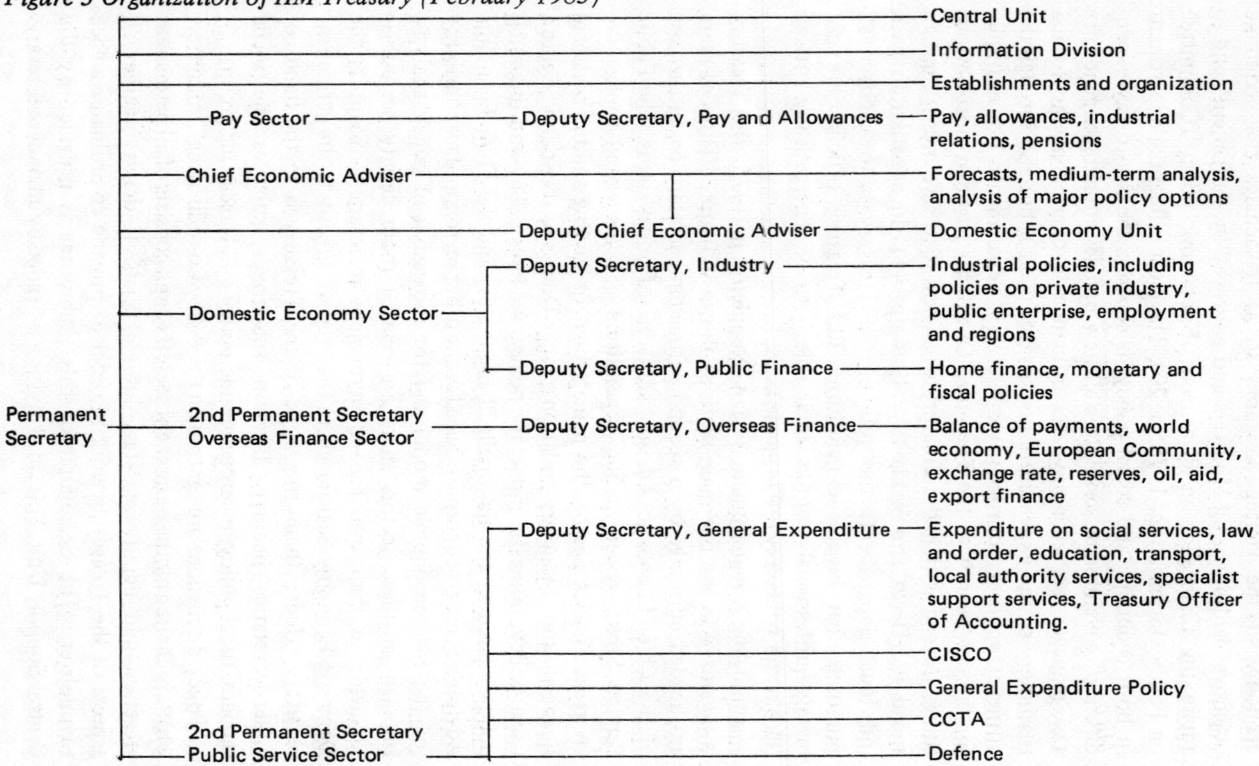

```
Permanent
Secretary

         Pay Sector ──────────── Deputy Secretary, Pay and Allowances ──── Central Unit
                                                                           Information Division
                                                                           Establishments and organization
                                                                           Pay, allowances, industrial
                                                                             relations, pensions

         Chief Economic Adviser ───── Deputy Chief Economic Adviser ──── Forecasts, medium-term analysis,
                                                                             analysis of major policy options
                                                                           Domestic Economy Unit

         Domestic Economy Sector ──── Deputy Secretary, Industry ──────── Industrial policies, including
                                                                             policies on private industry,
                                                                             public enterprise, employment
                                                                             and regions

                                       Deputy Secretary, Public Finance ── Home finance, monetary and
                                                                             fiscal policies

2nd Permanent Secretary
Overseas Finance Sector ──────────── Deputy Secretary, Overseas Finance ── Balance of payments, world
                                                                             economy, European Community,
                                                                             exchange rate, reserves, oil, aid,
                                                                             export finance

                                       Deputy Secretary, General Expenditure ── Expenditure on social services, law
                                                                             and order, education, transport,
                                                                             local authority services, specialist
                                                                             support services, Treasury Officer
                                                                             of Accounting.
                                                                           CISCO
                                                                           General Expenditure Policy
                                                                           CCTA
2nd Permanent Secretary                                                    Defence
Public Service Sector
```

Source: HM Treasury.

Its other tasks are to ensure that policy advice is co-ordinated by ensuring the interrelationship of policies in different sectors, and to take the lead in suggesting major policy options.

Micro- and macroeconomic planning

Government economic planning takes two main forms. Microeconomic planning is concerned with interventions in individual industries or firms. This includes the nationalization of industries, such as energy and the railways, and the subsequent planning of their development. More often, though, economic planning takes the form of intervention in macroeconomics; that is, in the aggregation of all firms, industries and consumers (for a detailed discussion of the distinction between micro- and macroeconomics see Lipsey, 1979, pp. 453–5).

A clear distinction between the two forms of intervention is not always easy to sustain. So, for example, when the government manipulates energy prices it is dealing with the aggregate price or prices because the gas, electricity and coal industries are monopolies. Moreover, the simple theoretical picture of the state intervening in the free competition between businesses in order to regulate operations or prices becomes much more complicated in the real world.

There are, for example, huge transnational corporations which often have a higher financial turnover than small nation-states. What companies such as Exxon, ITT, BP and ICI plan by the way of investment, employment and location can have major repercussions for the economic fortunes of the countries, including the most advanced capitalist countries, in which they are situated. Within individual countries, the rationalization plans of transnational companies can have devastating effects on small local communities, such as North Tyneside (CDP, 1977; Foster, 1982).

In addition to major transnational conglomerates, there are many large private corporations that have a close and to some extent dependent relationship with the state. Thus Galbraith (1975, p. 60) has drawn a distinction between the 'market system' and the 'planning system' in capitalist economies. The former resembles more closely than the latter the neoclassical model of competition, where the individual small firm has no control over prices and production. The two systems approximate to the distinction made by O'Connor (1973, p. 30) between the 'competitive sector' — the *petit bourgeoisie* — and the 'monopoly sector' – the complex, large-scale capitalist enterprises (see also Judge, 1982, pp. 32–4).

The planning system consists of large firms, which are also relatively large in the markets they supply, that have sought and gained control over their markets and prices. Unlike the millions of small firms and businesses in the market sector, large companies can control their prices and outputs because they are large. But, and this is the most important aspect of the planning system for our purposes, it seeks to exercise control over its economic environment, including its consumers, and enlists the help of the state, and the bureaucracy in particular, to achieve it. In effect, corporations in the planning system seek to render the future less unpredictable by manipulating market demand and co-opting government agencies. In contrast to the neoclassical model of the market, in the planning sector the purposes of the producer are dominant. 'The planning system pursues its own purposes and accommodates the public thereto. . . . What serves the planning system becomes sound public policy' (Galbraith, 1975, p. 259).

At the core of this relationship between corporations and state is the large expenditure by the government on their products (Galbraith, 1975, p. 171). The purchase of armaments from companies such as Vickers and Marconi are obvious examples. But in addition, the planning system relies on the state for direct investment and for indirect investment in education, transport and so on. It also requires a continual public belief in the importance of its goods and services, and the state, like advertising, plays an important role in commodity conscious-ness. Mrs Thatcher at the wheel of the latest BL model is one small, and generally atypical, example of this. More usually, state sponsorship takes a less overt or promotional form. The state, as well as private enterprise, contributes towards the 'excessive creation and absorption of commodities', or commodity fetishism, in advanced capitalist societies (Hirsch, 1977, p. 84). The media too are dominated by corporations in the planning system, not only by means of direct ownership, but also through the identification of the needs of the planning system with the national interest (Galbraith, 1975, p. 175). The planning system, then, is an important aspect of the environment within which the market system operates.

Not surprisingly, the chief source of criticism of Galbraith's theory of advanced capitalist development comes from neoclassical economic theorists. They stress, for example, the plurality of interests impinging on the state and large corporations. They concentrate too on the effects of advertising rather than on the more covert or subliminal influences on the general shape of consumer preferences, or the simple absence of alternatives when one or two corporations dominate a market. So for these economists the key issue is whether or not consumers buy a particular brand of, say, cars. The more significant question for political economy and social policy is whether or not they buy cars at all, and in preference to what (see Lipsey, 1979, pp. 335–8).

State intervention in the economy, therefore, takes the form of expenditure on investment and consumption – or what O'Connor (1973, p. 30) calls social capital – as well as of regulation. The first form of intervention is legitimate and indeed essential for the reproduction of capital, but the second form is sanctioned and particularly so by firms in the market sector. State intervention in the planning sector is justified if it conforms to the needs of that sector.

As well as direct microeconomic intervention in individual firms and industries, the state is expected to regulate the economy as a whole so as to provide a favourable climate for accumulation within the planning sector. This includes, on the one hand, support for consumption by means of social and economic policies, and for consumerism in the face of ever more dispensible and frivolous goods (Galbraith, 1975, p. 174; Hirsch, 1977, p. 84). On the other hand, there are macroeconomic policies designed to promote growth, inspire confidence and sustain the status quo in economic and social relations. Macroeconomic policies are subject not only to the requirements of the planning or monopoly sector but also to international regulatory bodies such as the European Economic Community (EEC) or the International Monetary Fund (IMF). These may impose, by law in the case of the EEC, economic policies such as import tariffs, or may oppose the introduction of other policies such as import controls.

KEYNESIAN DEMAND MANAGEMENT AND BEYOND

Apart from the nationalization of some primary industries, the main form of economic planning since the Second World War has been Keynesian-style demand management. And the main instruments of policy have been public expenditure and taxation, or fiscal policy (see Prest and Coppock, 1980, pp. 25–37). We saw in chapter 3 that Keynes's theories had a major impact on both economic thinking and public policy.

In opposition to the neoclassical economic theories, held most notably by the Treasury in the 1920s and early 1930s, Keynes argued that the market alone could not produce an optimum, equilibrium level of output and employment. In particular, he concentrated on aggregate or macroeconomic indicators and on the level of total demand in the economy, which he believed to be insufficient to regenerate growth and employment. Keynes drew attention to the central role that the state had to play in the management of aggregate demand, chiefly by means of fiscal policy, in order to maintain the economy at 'full employment' (for a full discussion of this concept and Keynesian unemployment theory see Showler, 1980, pp. 35–9; for a detailed account of Keynes's work and its impact on economics and government see Dillard, 1950; Winch, 1969; Stewart, 1972). The orthodox Keynesian view, then, according to Cross (1982, p. 130), is

> that governments can achieve objectives such as avoiding depressions, reducing the size of business cycle fluctuations and, most of all, 'full' employment, by managing aggregate demand by way of government expenditure and taxation policy: government expenditure policies have direct effects on aggregate demand; and taxation policies affect aggregate demand indirectly by changing private sector income or expenditure.

This approach to macroeconomic policy, and neo-Keynesian variations on it, dominated official thinking in the 1940s, 1950s and 1960s, and proved remarkably successful in maintaining growth and prosperity. Its hold was particularly strong on Treasury officials, who, as the following quotation from Lord Armstrong, a former permanent secretary, shows, set the framework in which political decisions were taken (cited in Benn, 1980, p. 67):

> Obviously I had a great deal of influence. The biggest and most pervasive influence is in setting the framework within which questions of policy are raised. We, while I was at the Treasury, had a framework of the economy, basically neo-Keynesian. We set the questions which we asked Ministers to decide arising

out of that framework, and it would have been enormously difficult for any minister to change the framework, so to that extent we had great power.

Treasury civil servants were seeking to promote stable economic conditions within which business enterprise could prosper, and in doing so were also meeting the needs of the planning sector.

Keynesian orthodoxy was modified primarily in response to two problems: (1) low investment and relatively poor economic performance in the 1950s, and (2) escalating wage demands (Robinson 1966, 1971; Hicks, 1974; Blackaby, 1979). A third factor that precipitated the introduction of planning in the early 1960s was exasperation with yet another balance of payments crisis in 1961, which had been deliberately generated by policy in 1958 (Opie 1972, p. 159). In looking for a better way to manage the economy, planning was the chief candidate. In response to these problems, the state intervened on a far wider scale than Keynes had ever intended, even on the supply side of the economy in the form of wage controls. Governments of both parties, but first a Conservative government, began in the 1960s to introduce limited forms of economic planning.

Planning and corporatism

Why was planning chosen as the response to Britain's economic problems, especially since less than ten years earlier it had been considered a dirty word? In the first place, it was popularly believed that economic success in France was based on indicative planning. Directive planning along the lines of state socialist countries was considered unacceptable, but French experience was seen to show that planning could work in a mixed economy. Second, there was a 'remarkable' conversion to planning among employers (Opie, 1972, p. 159). More remarkable perhaps is that the potential of planning for growth was not seen by employers much earlier. By 'planning' they meant consultation. Thus it was the Federation of British Industry (as the CBI was then called) that urged the government, and more particularly the Treasury, to set up machinery for consultation with employers and trade unions about policies to stimulate growth and stabilize prices. Third, politicians too were converted to planning, or at least to a brief flirtation with the idea of planning (Opie, 1972,

p. 171). The 1964 Labour Party election manifesto asserted that 'at the root of the Tories' failure lies an outdated philosophy — their nostalgic belief that it is possible in the second half of the 20th century to hark back to the 19th century free enterprise economy and a 19th century unplanned economy.'

The growth of state intervention in the economy and of limited forms of planning have led to accusations, particularly under Labour governments (because the Labour Party has close links with the trade unions), that we have a corporate state. The essential features of corporatism are (Taylor-Goody and Dale, 1981, p. 250):

> an economy based primarily on private ownership, but where there is considerable state control over prices, wages and investment decisions, combined with a political structure which incorporates the trade unions and business organisations in national planning.

(See also Winkler, 1976; Crouch, 1979.)

Although the Conservative government elected in 1979 set about reducing the role of the state and dismantling QUANGOs, developments over the previous two decades, such as the National Economic Development Council (NEDC) and incomes policies, were in the direction of corporatism. Although there was a broad consensus that economic planning had a role to play, it would be mistaken to conclude that developments under governments of different parties were entirely similar. Certainly their intentions were different. They meant different things by the term 'planning'. It was the Conservatives who took up 'indicative planning' and incomes policy in the early 1960s, whereas the Labour Party differed in both the objectives it saw for planning and the extent to which it thought planning should be used (Beckerman, 1972, p. 49). So, for example, the Labour Party (1969, p. 6) criticized earlier Conservative attempts at planning:

> Very belatedly the Macmillan Government had paid lip-service to the widespread demand for planning — but it was a timid empty gesture. The National Economic Development Council, which was established as the new planning instrument, was right outside the ambit of Government policy making and remained so throughout the Tory years.

The objectives of Labour's planning − the ending of economic privilege, the abolition of poverty and the creation of real equality of opportunity − set out in the 1964 election manifesto, were very different to those of the Conservatives. There is a danger, of course, of confusing rhetoric with action. But in practice the Labour government of the mid-1960s went further than previous Conservative governments − and, indeed, subsequent Conservative and Labour ones − in the introduction of economic planning. The most famous example was the National Plan and the machinery set up to develop it.

THE NATIONAL PLAN

The remarkable consensus on economic planning (remarkable, that is, in relation to the disenchantment with planning in the mid- and late 1950s) resulted in the setting up of the NEDC in 1962. It was at once christened 'Neddy', some argue to symbolize its ineffectiveness (Horne, 1970, p. 229). The Conservative government had been urged by both employers and unions to establish a tripartite forum to discuss broad economic and social problems. The NEDC carried out exercises in 'planning' and in forecasting future growth rates, and prepared outlines of policies that would achieve specified rates of economic growth (Robinson, 1972, p. 301). The role of the National Economic Development Council was set out in the NEDC plan 1963: to examine the future potential performance of the British economy, point out the obstacles to more rapid economic growth and seek agreement on ways to remove these obstacles. The only power at the NEDC's command was persuasion (Opie, 1972, p. 162). Despite this, but more likely because of it, the NEDC secured a wide measure of collaboration in exploring solutions to the problem of slow growth (Balogh, 1965). Thus, according to Opie (1972, p. 164), 'the NEDC was a milestone along the road from total disillusionment with the whole theory and practice of planning in the UK towards a new willingness to experiment with some form of indicative planning.'

The NEDC plan of 1963 involved no formal commitment from government, employers or unions (see NEDC, 1963). This first official flirtation with indicative planning since the early 1950s coincided with an important shift of Treasury policy, away from the mainly financial control of public spending and towards a greater concern with the real level of resources used (see p. 125 below). The medium-term plan set a target growth rate of 4 per cent per annum to 1966.

A major boost to economic planning was given by the election of Harold Wilson's Labour government in 1964. The planning machinery was brought inside Whitehall and established within a new Department of Economic Affairs. George Brown was the first Secretary of State for Economic Affairs. The Department's job was to co-ordinate micro- and macroeconomic policy within Whitehall. But − and herein lay the main seed of the DEA's destruction − the Treasury retained firm authority over short-term demand management. Thus economic planning, ironically, was more deeply divided in Whitehall then than it had been before the creation of the new department. Much of the DEA's and Secretary of State's time was spent in discussion and argument with the Treasury. In addition, during its first year the DEA produced a Declaration of Intent, which formed the basis of the voluntary prices and incomes policy in force until 1966, and drew up the National Plan.

This 500-page document, produced with remarkable speed, if not undue haste, was 'the high water-mark of the planning movement in the 1960s' (Opie, 1972, p. 165). It was drawn up on the assumption that the government had a responsibility both to use its considerable economic authority, as the major investor and purchaser in the country, and to intervene in other spheres of the market to correct the deficiencies of competition. So (Department of Economic Affairs, 1965, p. 2),

> Most manufacturing industry and commerce is, and will continue to be, largely governed by the market economy. But this does not necessarily, and without active Government influence, bring about the results which the nation needs − for example, sufficient exports to pay for our imports and other overseas expenditure. Also, the forces of competition often operate too slowly. Then again, where productive units are large and investment decisions have to be taken two to five years ahead, competing companies tend to bunch their investment, holding back and moving forward together.

This restatement of the liberal case for government regulation and intervention in a mixed economy was clear about the limits to the role of the state in planning (DEA, 1965, p. 3):

Care will be taken not to destroy the complex mechanisms on which the market economy is based. The end product of both co-operative planning and the market economy is an internationally competitive industry; and in securing this aim they complement each other.

The Plan contained growth targets for the economy; a detailed 'action programme' including industrial policy, manufacturing investment, regional policy and labour market policies; detailed proposals on manpower, industrial efficiency, investment, prices and incomes and the balance of payments; analysis and plans for the different industrial sectors; and consideration of the 'use of resources' through, for example, consumer's expenditure, housing, defence, health and welfare services and education. Its main medium-term purpose was to secure faster economic growth (DEA, 1965, p. 2). It proposed an increase in national output of 25 per cent between 1964 and 1970, an annual average of 3.8 per cent. This goal was tempered in the short term, or so it was hoped, by worries about the huge external trade deficit: 'An essential part of the Plan is a solution to Britain's balance of payments problem: for growth cannot be maintained unless we pay our way in the world' (DEA, 1965, p. 1).

The Plan was drawn up by the DEA in conjunction with the NEDC and the extended system of Economic Development Committees (EDCs), or 'little Neddies', which covered individual industries or activities under the NEDC. The EDCs together with firms, research organizations, trade associations and production ministries, conducted the industrial inquiry part of the plan. The economic model-building sections were done by the staff of the DEA and NEDC.

The demise of the National Plan

By July 1966 growth and full employment had been sacrificed in order to sustain the existing exchange rate. The deflationary measures introduced in that month, including a statutory wage and price freeze, meant that the National Plan was effectively abandoned. The DEA had predictably lost its battle with the Treasury. Opie (1972, p. 170) describes the life-cycle of the Plan as: 'conceived October 1964, born September 1965, died (possibly murdered) July 1966'.

Why was the Plan abandoned so swiftly? Its future, as for all economic planning, rested on political and not economic decisions. But of course it is not quite that simple. Political decisions rest on the balance of power and influence, and within Whitehall the Treasury is the most powerful force. So, had the Treasury constructed the Plan, it could have *imposed* its will on Whitehall. But paradoxically, the Treasury has always had an institutional dislike of economic growth: 'It is not growth but the limit on national resources that is the staple of Treasury doctrine' (Heclo and Wildavsky, 1974, p. 49). Therefore, 'politically and psychologically, it was impossible to allow or invite the Treasury to produce a Plan for more rapid growth' (Opie, 1972, p. 171). Instead, a new department was given the impossible task of swimming against the Treasury tide.

Second, there was the continuing balance of payments crisis. But again, it was a political decision to give this precedence over economic growth and full employment. Devaluation was the obvious answer to reconcile both goals, but the Treasury took the view that the existing exchange rate was sacrosanct (a decision taken, incidentally, before the Plan was even started).

Third, the Plan itself was weak and lacked teeth. It had no formal power to direct investment, production or expenditure, because the DEA had no such powers. Micro- and macroeconomic policies were not linked to the Plan. For example, participation in the prices and incomes policy was voluntary, and investment was not at all selective in supporting those industries or services considered essential for growth. The statistics on which the Plan was based were out of date and crude (Opie, 1972, p. 173). Many of the technical deficiencies of the Plan derive from its hasty preparation.

Together these factors indicate that, despite all of the rhetoric about planning and the introduction and extension of planning machinery, planning was not taken seriously as a part of the policy process. The conception of planning underlying the National Plan was narrow and stultifying.

In particular, social planning was treated as an appendage to economic planning, and therefore social priorities were poorly formulated (Townsend, 1972, p. 290). This reflects the familiar theory of growth lead redistribution (see p. 60). For example, the Plan was crudely divided between sections on the *generation* of resources — output productivity and investment — and on the *use* of resources — including expenditure on the health and social services and social security.

Having said that, at least the National Plan considered both economic and social policies in the same planning exercise. When the Plan died, the main form of central social planning was the public expenditure process, to which I return later. Economic objectives had been paramount. The planning process had remained centralized, and therefore remote from the everyday concerns of citizens and communities. The National Plan was not a people's plan but an economists' and politicians' plan. Because of this, the crucial links between social development and economic development had been consistently overlooked.

For example, the incomes policy lacked explicit social objectives such as justice and greater equality; it was concerned primarily with controlling wage increases. The social implications of taxation were not considered, and expenditure was regarded as a matter of Treasury financial policy rather than social policy. The Plan did not examine the relationship between public expenditure and private consumption (Townsend, 1972, p. 294); so (for example) the government planned a smaller growth in social services in 1970 than the previous Conservative administration had achieved between 1959 and 1964.

Finally, the Treasury and some other Whitehall departments were diverted from the strategic planning of the growth of services in relation to need, into experiments with cost-benefit and analysis and other microeconomic techniques in order to control resources more effectively (see p. 76).

OBJECTIVES OF ECONOMIC PLANNING

The aims of economic policy and planning have been altered considerably by governments over the postwar period (the impact of these changes on social planning is considered in the second half of this chapter). According to the Radcliffe Committee (1959), which was set up to examine the working of the monetary and credit system, the five aims of economic policy were: full employment, reasonably stable prices, steady growth, a balance of payments margin to help overseas development, and a strengthening of reserves. For a relatively brief period in the late 1950s and early 1960s planning was not a dirty word. The deflationary measures adopted in July 1966 to deal with the balance of payments crisis spelt the end not only of the

National Plan but also of economic growth and full employment as the objectives of economic policy and planning – and, indeed, of the very notion of planning for growth. 'The passage from panacea through bitter experience to music-hall joke which had been planning's fate in the first decade after the Second World War was repeated fifteen years later' (Opie, 1972, p. 177). The only other document to emerge from the DEA, on economic assessment in 1972, was not a plan; it was carefully emphasized, but it was a planning document.

The main purpose of the Plan was economic growth. But the intervention of the government, or rather its central role in the promotion of growth represented a major departure from previous *laisses-faire* theories.

A similar sea-change in economic theory and the goals of economic policy occurred with the rise of monetarism in the early 1970s. Just as the Keynesian revolution was born out of the failure of classical theory to prescribe for mass unemployment, so the monetarist 'counter-revolution' arose from the failure of Keynesian orthodoxy to counteract what has come to be considered officially as a major social problem – inflation (Johnson, 1971, p. 7; Showler, 1980, p. 39). The abandonment of full employment and economic growth 'required the public to be persuaded of greater evils. Inflation has been the central one' (Hirsch, 1977, p. 278). In place of full employment, monetarist theory assumes a 'natural rate' of unemployment. In effect, economic policy has turned full circle, with the natural rate theory of unemployment being the contemporary version of the classical theory that Keynes opposed (Tobin, 1972, p. 2).

The full importance and influence of this change on policy can be gauged by substituting 'monetarism' for 'neo-Keynesian' in the quotation by Lord Armstrong on p. 102. Economic policy-making and economic management in the Treasury are now dominated by supply-side assumptions. Since indicative planning in the medium term was discredited along with the National Plan, there is very little official information published on the possible evolution of the economy (Blackaby, 1979, p. 434). With the advent of full-blown monetarism or new classical macroeconomics in 1979 (Cross, 1982, p. 2), tripartite discussions ceased to have any official importance and interventions in the economy became less explicit. A belief in the free play of market forces militates against open intervention and planning.

The new economic strategy was based on four principles (Treasury, 1979, p. 1):

first, the strengthening of incentives, particularly through tax cuts, allowing people to keep more of their earnings in their own hands, so that hard work, ability and success are rewarded; second, greater freedom of choice by reducing the state's role and enlarging that of the individual; third, the reduction of the borrowing requirement of the public sector to a level which leaves room for the rest of the economy to prosper; and fourth, through firm monetary and fiscal discipline, bringing inflation under control and ensuring that those taking part in collective bargaining are obliged to live with the consequences of their actions.

Demand management policies that characterized macroeconomic policy and planning until the mid-1970s were abandoned in favour of restrictive fiscal and monetary policies. In particular, public spending has not been used in its familiar role as the chief instrument of demand management, at least not in reflation.

PUBLIC EXPENDITURE AND ECONOMIC MANAGEMENT

Public expenditure is a key element in both economic and social planning. Fiscal policy — control of the level, composition or timing of government expenditure or taxation — was the main instrument used by governments to manage the level of aggregate demand in the economy throughout the 1940s, 1950s and 1960s. The 1944 White Paper on Employment Policy, in which the government pledged itself to maintain full employment after the war, represented 'the final recognition of the principles of the Keynesian revolution in Britain' (Winch, 1969, p. 269). (In the light of the current officially constructed pessimism, which asserts that 'there is no alternative', it is worth recalling that for nigh on two decades up to 1939 unemployment had averaged 10 per cent or more; see Stewart, 1972, p. 185).

Public expenditure was used to compensate for shortfalls in other forms of spending — private consumption, investment by firms or foreign expenditure on British exports — to maintain a desired level of total spending (Else and Marshall, 1979, p. 24). Although Keynesian policies granted an independent role for public expenditure, for example on the welfare state, its primary role was that of a stabilizing agent.

The aims of public spending included, of course, the important social goal of full employment. But the precise nature and distribution of expenditure was seen as secondary to its macroeconomic functions. Thus, ironically, as we saw in chapter 3, Keynesian policies, which formed the basis for the expansion of the postwar welfare state, also contained the seeds of the attack on social spending in the late 1970s and early 1980s. If the primary justification for public expenditure is demand management, then when assumptions about macroeconomic policy change some part of the rationale for that spending may disappear.

The reaction against the deficit financing that characterized Keynesian demand management came in the early 1970s with the rise in inflation following the Yom Kippur War and the subsequent oil price increases. Deficit financing is the term used for the government's borrowing on the financial markets to fund the deficit between its expenditure and taxation; the Public Sector Borrowing Requirement (PSBR) is the total amount of borrowing by the public sector. The rise in the PSBR in the mid-1970s, from a negative value in 1970 to nearly 10 per cent of GDP in 1975/76, rested on the combination of four factors. There was the decline in economic growth (Rose and Peters, 1979) from nearly 6 per cent in 1973 to negative figures in 1974 and 1975. Second, the rise in inflation, which peaked at 27 per cent in 1975, contributed to increased demands for public resources. Moreover, the prices of public sector goods and services rose faster than those in other sectors of the economy (Judge, 1982, pp. 44–5). Third, unemployment began to rise dramatically in the mid-1970s, from 2.8 per cent of the UK workforce at the end of 1974 to 5.1 per cent by the end of the following year. This not only cut government tax revenue but also increased the need for spending, primarily on social security.

Fourth, partly as a result of government policy, the balance of taxation shifted significantly from taxes on consumption and capital to taxes on income. For example, the relative contribution of companies to national taxation fell from 37 per cent in 1952–3 to 14 per cent in 1973. Moreover, measures introduced in the mid-1970s, such as 'temporary' stock relief, further reduced the tax contribution of companies (Pond, 1982, p. 51). As a result, governments found even greater than usual resistance to increases in personal taxation.

So in the mid-1970s, rising demand for public spending, caused chiefly by the slump in growth, the rise in inflation and increasing need resulting primarily from unemployment, combined with political resistance to increases in taxation (for a fuller discussion of these factors see A. Walker, 1982b, pp. 7–10). In other words, at this time there was a *structural gap* between state expenditures and revenues (O'Connor, 1973; for a summary see Judge, 1982, pp. 32–5). The proclivity of Keynesian economic policy-makers was to use public borrowing to fill this gap as well as to encourage reflation. The resulting 'fiscal crisis' paved the way for the transition from the Keynesian era of demand management to the monetarist period of control over the money supply and PSBR.

Monetarism

The monetarists, or new classical macroeconomic, position is that persistent budget deficits are the major source of the growth of the money supply, and that rapid monetary expansion results in price inflation (for a full discussion of differences between Keynesians and monetarists on deficit financing see Else and Marshall, 1979, pp. 24–38). The change in the balance between fiscal and monetary policy began in the mid-1970s under the Labour government and was completed with the election of the Conservative government in 1979.

The Labour administration's response to the fiscal crisis was to concentrate on reducing public expenditure and controlling the growth of the money supply and the PSBR, which had not previously been under the direct control of government. In 1976 a series of important changes were introduced, including the monitoring of money supply, the setting of targets for M3 (the broader definition of money supply, which includes bank deposit accounts as well as notes and coin in circulation and bank current accounts) and the PSBR, and the imposition of cash limits (discussed in the next chapter) on a large proportion of expenditure by central and local authorities (Wright, 1980). In his 'Letter of Intent' to the IMF in 1976, the Chancellor of the Exchequer wrote that 'an essential element of the government's strategy will be a continued and substantial reduction over the next few years in the share of resources required for the public sector' (Healey, 1976).

As the quotation on p. 111 shows, the election of the Conservative government in 1979 led to the adoption of a fully fledged monetarist strategy based on the steady reduction of the PSBR and the size of the public sector and the tight control of the money supply. In his 1979 Budget Statement the Chancellor stated (House of Commons, 1979, cols 241–2):

> It is crucially important to re-establish sound money. We intend to achieve this through firm discipline and fiscal policies consistent with that, including strict control over public expenditure . . . . We are committed to the progressive reduction of the rate of growth of the money supply.

The achievement of price stability at a low rate of inflation and budgetary balance have been the twin macroeconomic policies since 1979. At the same time, full employment and economic growth as objectives of government policy were formally abandoned. Public expenditure is no longer an instrument of demand management, but it does occupy a central role in the monetarist strategy. The first sentence of the Conservative government's first White Paper on public expenditure stated that 'Public expenditure is at the heart of Britain's present economic difficulties' (Treasury, 1979, p. 1).

The government has attempted to reduce public spending in order to allow the private sector to grow and to reduce taxation and the PSBR. Although it has not been successful in this policy – total public expenditure was 41 per cent of GDP in 1978/79 and 44 per cent in 1982/83 (Treasury, 1983, p. 9) – there have been significant cuts in some programmes, and spending has not risen as fast as might have been expected in response to low growth and mass unemployment. (The impact of the Conservative government's policies on social spending and social priorities is reviewed in Walker, Ormerod and Whitty, 1979; A. Walker, 1982b; Walker, Winyard and Pond, 1983.) Public expenditure has been used, effectively, as an instrument of deflation. The idea of large-scale reflation along Keynesian lines is out of the question in this strategy. Moreover, because of the successful proselytization of monetarist dogma by the government ('there is no alternative'), it is widely believed that such reflation would be disastrous (see Golding, 1983).

THE TREASURY MODEL

Economic 'planning' today consists primarily of forecasting. The formal machinery of macroeconomic forecasting and analysis is based on the Treasury's econometric model of the UK economy. Like all economic models, it is 'a collection of mathematical formulae, based on statistical data, which define relationships in numerical terms between such quantities as the levels of employment, incomes, taxes, government expenditure, interest rates, prices etc.' (Committee on Policy Optimisation, 1978, p. 22). The model consists of 1,000 variables and 700 equations (Treasury, 1982, p. 14). It includes simple mathematical relationships, such as 'personal disposable income equals gross personal income minus taxes', and more complex relationships based on economic theory. Thus, the model is changed to reflect prevailing economic assumptions in the Treasury. For example, between May 1980 and December 1981 three key relationships were replaced, including that dealing with the growth in earnings, so that the 'natural' rate of unemployment could be determined (Treasury, 1982, p. 51). However, it remains weak in its treatment of the supply side of the economy, primarily because it developed out of an orthodox Keynesian framework.

The primary use of the model within the Treasury is to produce a forecast of the development of the economy. There are two main short-term forecasting rounds per year, one in January for the pre-Budget forecast, and the other in the early autumn. They each take about six weeks. The forecasting round begins with the setting of policy assumptions and the collection and entry on to the model of the latest economic data (Committee on Policy Optimisation, 1978, p. 25). The initial policy assumptions have to be approved by the Policy Co-ordinating Committee. The forecast then passes through a rigid procedure, including a two-day seminar-discussion, after which the forecast is redrafted. The final forecast is circulated to Treasury ministers.

Within the Treasury, the next phase is a consideration of the policy implications of the forecast by the Policy Analysis Division, together with the Central Unit. They work with the Policy Co-ordinating Committee, and the Macro-Economic Group also plays a co-ordinating role in relation to macroeconomic policy. In the light of these discussions, the Central Unit prepares a draft paper for the Chancellor. This is discussed again by the Policy Co-ordinating Committee before it goes to the Chancellor. Although the paper may express doubts about the contents of the forecast, 'the important point is that the forecast, once composed and approved by the Forecast Group Under-Secretary, stands as one of the main bases for decision-making, albeit only one of them' (Committee on Policy Optimisation, 1978, p. 28). In the pre-Budget round the forecasts are updated to include any new information since the January forecast. After the Budget, a post-Budget forecast is prepared by the Forecast Group. A summary of this updated forecast appears in papers published with the Budget.

In addition to the production of short-term forecasts, the Treasury model is used to prepare medium-term assessments. A similar format is followed, but here the objective is to explore a range of possible outcomes given different assumptions about policy and other changes in the relationships in the model.

The Treasury model, like any other economic model, can only attempt to approximate reality. It is a model of how the economy *should* work, in theory. Much of the discredit for what is seen in some quarters as the failure of demand management has fallen on economic forecasts: 'The Treasury got it wrong again.' Equally, however, under the regime of monetarism economic modelling, and especially its inadequate application, has been criticized heavily. For example, the Treasury and Civil Service Committee (1981, p. xcvii) stated: 'We are not satisfied that present arrangements produce the most useful model-based evidence for the Committee, for Parliament, or for the public.'

Despite such criticism, the Treasury model is an important tool in decision-making, though certainly less so since 1979 than before, because the economic framework within which policies are made differs substantially from the Keynesian basis of the model. Criticisms may be made of the use to which the model has been put, and of its inadequacy as a basis for social planning and as an economic tool.

Problems with the Treasury model

Like all such models, the Treasury model is used to support the ideas and prescriptions favoured by the Treasury at a particular time. When the model fits in with prevailing economic assumptions, contra-

opinions are filtered out; when the model is at variance with current assumptions, its results are suppressed. The choice of policy options is a political matter, regardless of whether they are derived from Treasury officials or ministers. These options are filtered through prevailing economic theories, and, again, the choice of those is a political rather than a purely economic matter. Thus, if options are not considered practical or feasible by the Treasury simulators they do not get into the model's analysis. There is a 'house view' about policy options, and 'any new proposals have to run the gauntlet of informed scepticism' (Committee on Policy Optimisation, 1978, p. 31). This scepticism or 'energetic criticism' is, in other words, resistance to change. It is the Treasury brand of bureau-incrementalism, whereby Treasury economists set the agenda of policy options they consider to be important. And, because of the power of the Treasury, it is vital in sustaining bureau-incrementalism throughout Whitehall.

When the basis for economic management changes, as in the late 1970s and more thoroughly after the election of the Conservative government in 1979, the Treasury model is either adapted or ignored in the determination and analysis of key policies. For example, when a government does *not* believe, in the words of the former Chief Secretary to the Treasury, Leon Brittan (1982, p. 15), 'that spending money on public works is in any sense an engine of sustained growth', it clearly presents a challenge to the basically Keynesian ideas underlying the model. Thus, as I pointed out earlier, the Treasury model has been modified; it is, again in Leon Brittan's unfortunate words, a 'much raped maiden'. When the Treasury's analyses still do not produce the desired result, they are not published (Treasury and Civil Service Committee, 1981, p. xiii):

It is one thing to attempt to pursue monetary policies without a model of the economy sufficient for the purpose. It is another thing to pursue monetary policies while in possession of a model which is indicating the other implications of those policies and not publishing the indications — if necessary, with suitable qualifications.

Monetarists have argued that econometric models have such large forecasting errors that they should be abandoned in favour of control of the money supply, with other aspects of the economy being left to regulate themselves (Treasury and Civil Service Committee, 1981, p. ci). To some extent this is what has happened in the last four years, at least as far as the central economic policy objectives of the government are concerned.

The Treasury model is a totally inadequate base for social policy-making and planning. There should be no doubt that, in so far as it is an important adjunct to economic planning, it is also instrumental in setting the framework for social planning. 'When we are formulating economic policy we are planning for a number of years ahead' (Committee on Policy Optimisation, 1978, p. 54).

Deficiencies arise more from what is *excluded* from the model than from what is actually included. We have seen that monetary variables are inadequately represented. But more importantly, the distribution of income and wealth is assumed to be constant in the model's operation. There is no quality of life index, no calculation of the environmental impact of different policies, and no assessment of social as opposed to narrow economic needs. In short, the model pays no attention to social development (Committee on Policy Optimisation, 1978, pp. 68–9). It reflects the narrow financial concerns of the Treasury, and when it is used in economic forecasting and analysis, the social consequences of economic policies and plans are overlooked.

In addition to being an inadequate basis for social policy-making and planning, the Treasury model is flawed as an economic tool. In the first place, there are disagreements between economists about how the economy actually functioned in the past (Committee on Policy Optimisation, 1978, p. 36). This creates difficulties for a model, the predictive capacity of which is based on past experience. In part this is due to the inadequacy of the data on which the model is based, which creates uncertainty about current events as well as about the past outturn of events (Committee on Policy Optimisation, 1978, pp. 38–9).

Second, even greater problems arise when economic assumptions are changed, as in 1979, so that past experience does not cover current policy directions. This is brought out in the following passage from the Treasury and Civil Service Committee's examination of the government's monetary policy, in which Terence Higgins, MP, questions Mr P. Middleton, Deputy Secretary in the Domestic Economy Sector of the Treasury:

.... you have a Treasury model which is based on a vast mass of past empirical data .... You are saying in fact that that model was not compatible with the views which Ministers have recently been expressing, because their view depends on changes in expectations as a result of the monetary targets and so on .... There is not any past empirical data on which to justify, if you like, ministerial views as to what will happen in the light of the policy they are now pursuing, because it has not been tried before.

Mr Middleton: What I was seeking to say there was I do not think you can expect any model to incorporate the structural changes in behaviour which the Government are trying to bring about. If you have a major change in policy your model is never going to be able to tell you how people will react in the changed situation. So, one would not use the Treasury model, and the Government did not, of course, to decide that one wanted to get the inflation rate down by pursuing a particular set of monetary policies. The model is primarily used for forecasting purposes, as you know, in the short term and for simulations of fairly small changes .... It seems to me the Treasury model would get into the most curious state if it had to have to justify almost any policy that any Government pursues.

Mr Higgins: We are nonetheless agreed that the policy which the Government is now pursuing does not have any past empirical basis because it has not been tried before, and the model to that extent is irrelevant.

Mr Middleton: No, I did not say that. I was talking about the Treasury model and its relationship to expectations and the adjustment of expectations. You only have to read through the mass of evidence which has been submitted to this Committee to see there is a very considerable body of empirical data on which one can base these policies, data relating the rate of inflation, to the rate of monetary growth and that sort of thing. I think the Chancellor has promised you a letter in which he will set some of this out .... A large number of people pursuing monetary targets at the moment do not have models of any description, and it is not reasonable to tell them, 'You cannot pursue monetary policies if you do not have a model.'

Third, relationships built into the model may change over time. The problem here is not that the model is organic, but that it is often difficult to say when a particular relationship no longer holds. The original relationship may have been based on inadequate data, or there may be an unpredictable behavioural change.

Fourth, there are more technical criticisms of the Treasury model. In particular, it is suggested that the model is too large and contains too many unknown variables, and that the possible errors in the model have been insufficiently studied and taken into account (Committee on Policy Optimisation, 1978, pp. 48–9).

These four criticisms may be applied with equal force to all large-scale econometric models (such as those of the London Business School and National Institute for Social and Economic Research), but they are particularly important when applied to the Treasury model because it plays an important role in the policy-making process.

The main answer by economists to criticisms of the model has been the concept of policy optimization, or the construction of an optimum path for policy between competing objectives (Committee on Policy Optimisation, 1978; Treasury and Civil Service Committee, 1981, pp. ci–cix). The chief problem with optimal control theory and any similar device is that it is limited by the assumptions made in constructing the economic model on which it is based, including assumptions about the operation of the economy and the policy instrument considered appropriate. It does not overcome the fundamental deficiencies we have considered above. Thus, the 'best' policy that emerges is conditional on the limitations of the economic model. So, for example (Committee on Policy Optimisation, 1978, p. 68),

> even if the chosen optimality criterion favoured a more equal distribution of wealth, no policy could be derived to achieve greater equality unless the process of wealth creation and distribution were to be included in the econometric model.

As with other variants of systems theory considered in chapter 4, the application of optimal control theory to social planning and social development is severely limited. As the Committee on Policy Optimisation (1978, p. 69) recognized, 'for those . . . who feel that the quality of life is the only appropriate measure of social welfare, applying optimal control theory to the present Treasury model would be irrelevant.' Unfortunately, if optimal control theory is used to improve the effectiveness of economic forecasts, it will also confirm the Treasury bias against social needs. Labelling macroeconomic policies constructed with the aid of the Treasury model as 'optimal' or 'best' will further disguise the inadequate assumptions on which they are based.

CONCLUSION

The Treasury dominates economic policy and planning. It is primarily responsible for managing the economy and achieving central economic objectives. In the early 1960s there was a brief flirtation with collaborative economic planning and, to some limited extent, with co-ordinated economic and social planning. Recent changes in macroeconomic policy have created a forceful opposition to long-term economic planning. Policy has taken a more *laissez-faire* stance, and explicit economic planning has been all but abandoned. The replacement of the goals of Keynesian demand management with those of monetarism has had a major impact on social planning, and it is to a consideration of this that the next chapter is directed.

6

The Treasury and Social Planning

INTRODUCTION

Although individual Whitehall departments have introduced machinery to plan the development of social services (those used by the DHSS to plan the health and personal social services are discussed in the next chapter), by far the most important mechanism of central social planning is the public expenditure process (Glennerster, 1975, p. 254).

The Treasury dominates social planning through the control it exerts over public expenditure (Townsend, 1980, pp. 8–9):

> Despite protestations from some government departments, like the DHSS, that their planning is 'needs'-conscious, the fact is that the exigencies of the economy, as decided by the Treasury, have led to the adoption of public expenditure control as the dominant form of planning approved by the Cabinet and imposed by Whitehall.

The Treasury also dominates local social planning through the control it exerts over the allocation of resources to local authorities. Since the mid-1970s central government has imposed increasingly rigid controls on local authority expenditure (Greenwood, 1979, p. 79). Local authority finance officers are in a similarly powerful position to that of Treasury officials in deciding the distribution of resources between different departments.

THE PUBLIC EXPENDITURE SURVEY COMMITTEE

Before examining the impact on social planning of the changes in macro-economic policy outlined in the previous chapter, it is necessary to describe the main mechanism of central social planning.

The Public Expenditure Survey Committee (PESC) consists of the finance officers from the different Whitehall departments and Treasury officials, and is chaired by a Treasury Deputy Secretary (see figure 3 on p. 98). The annual PESC planning cycle begins in November or December, when the Treasury sends to Whitehall departments the operating assumptions on which to prepare their spending forecasts. By the end of February the spending departments submit preliminary returns to the Treasury, showing their projections over three years of expenditure on existing policies (four years until 1981). Between March and May the Treasury scrutinizes these figures and holds discussions with spending departments in order to reach agreement, if possible, on what existing policies are and what their future cost will be. The PESC meets in May and writes a report projecting the cost of current policies and specifying any areas of disagreement. This goes to the Chancellor and all departments in June. The Treasury then assesses the economic prospects and decides whether or not the expenditure forecasts are too large (Heclo and Wildavsky, 1974, p. 171).

The Cabinet discusses these spending forecasts for the first time in June or July, together with any 'bids' from departments for extra spending. Between June and November there are usually several such Cabinet meetings. These are interspersed with regular discussions between Treasury officials and officials in the spending departments and 'bilateral meetings' between the minister in charge of public expenditure, the Chief Secretary to the Treasury, and individual spending ministers (see Barnett, 1982, pp. 46–7). The results of these decisions are published in the annual White Paper on public expenditure in February or March (see for example Treasury, 1983). These annual reports are among the most important documents on social policy and social planning (A. Walker, 1982a).

The Plowden Committee

The PESC system was established in 1961 following recommendations of the Plowden Committee (for a full account see Clarke, 1978, pp. 51–2). The Plowden Committee was set up in 1959, after the Select Committee on Estimates (1958) had concluded a study of the Treasury's control of expenditure with the recommendation that a small independent committee should be appointed to examine the matter further.

Prior to 1961 the management and control of public expenditure was diffuse and decentralized. To paraphrase the Estimates Committee, it had grown like a tree, unplanned, over the centuries (Clarke, 1978, p. 3). The 'system' was *ad hoc*, with little or no forward planning of expenditure or the implications of spending, and it was concentrated on a single financial year. The departments' spending proposals were considered 'on their merits', each being added up in January (on 'Judgement Day') to see whether or not economy measures were necessary in the light of the Budget forecast. There was no overall view or plan of public expenditure; indeed, the concept of public expenditure as a whole was not yet operational: 'there was no process of reasoned judgement of the scale of aggregate acceptable expenditure, or its implications for taxes, or its allocation between the departments and services' (Clarke, 1978, p. 3; see also pp. 4—5 for a full account of the pre-Plowden system).

The appointment of the Plowden Committee signalled a return to favour of economic planning. Its report coincided with the chancellorship of Selwyn Lloyd, who was 'probably unique' among postwar Chancellors in that he had formed his own ideas about how to manage public expenditure prior to taking office (Clarke, 1978, p. 50). Lloyd favoured the long-term planning of public expenditure and so did Plowden. (It was Selwyn Lloyd too who established, in 1962, the NEDC.)

The Plowden Committee (1961, p. 7) laid down four principles:

(1) regular surveys of public expenditure as a whole over a period of years ahead, and in relation to prospective resources, with decisions involving substantial future expenditure to be taken in the light of these surveys;

(2) the greatest practicable stability of decisions on public expenditure when taken, so that the long-term economy and efficiency throughout the public sector have the best opportunity to develop;

(3) improvements in the tools for measuring and handling public expenditure problems, including major simplifications in the form of the estimates, modernization and clarification of the Exchequer accounts, and more widespread use of quantitative methods in dealing with these problems throughout the public sector: these should serve both to improve the work inside the government machine, and to contribute to a better understanding by Parliament and the public;

(4) more effective machinery for the taking of collective responsibility by Ministers on matters of public expenditure.

(In fact, the Plowden Report was only the published summary of the advice given to the Chancellor. In the original version there were three principles, (1), (2) and (4) above, and 'collective responsibility of ministers' was put first; see Clarke, 1978, pp. 25–6.)

Annual public expenditure surveys have been conducted since 1961. All such programmes are considered together: central and local government and the capital expenditure of nationalized industries. Originally the surveys covered a five-year period and were concerned primarily with the end of that period – with the level of expenditure in five years'time. Subsequently the focus of the surveys has switched at different times to the beginning, the end and the middle of this period, and the period itself has been cut. The first White Paper was published in 1963, another in 1966, and from 1969 they have appeared annually.

In order to enable comparisons between successive years in the actual volume of goods and services – that is, in the number of nurses, teachers, social workers, home helps, aids and adaptations for the disabled and so on – used by or transferred by the public sector, plans were formulated in 'constant-price' terms. Constant prices, or 'survey prices', show the expected level of expenditure in future years if prices remained the same as they were at the time of the original survey. Figures in the White Papers up to 1981 were expressed in this form. Thus, when allowance was made for inflation there was always a divergence between what was planned and what was actually spent. Nevertheless, the operation of PESC remained broadly as established in 1961 until 1976.

Problems with the PESC system

How successful was the PESC system in its first 15 years in achieving the principles laid down by Plowden? The first innovation – classifying all expenditure as one entity divided into different programmes – enabled ministers to discuss the relationship between different programmes and to judge more easily the overall growth of expenditure. What was left out consistently from the consideration of public expenditure was tax expenditure. Thus, whereas public expenditure was subject to scrutiny, and in recent years to strict control, tax expenditures were allowed to rise unchecked (see Pond, 1982). The first of the annual public expenditure White Papers contained information on tax and other receipts, but this information did not appear subsequently (Treasury, 1969a; see also Treasury, 1969b). Since 1979 the White Papers have contained details of the main tax allowances, but these are not subject to the same control procedure as decisions about public expenditure. The fiscal welfare state is still divided administratively from the conventional welfare state (Titmuss, 1968), and the Plowden Committee did not consider the impact of that artificial separation.

The second innovation – collective decisions by ministers on public expenditure and resource allocation – was a limited one. The Cabinet discusses the final shape of public expenditure programmes and makes decisions. But the PESC system has strengthened the hand of the Treasury and Chancellor (as indeed it was intended to do). The majority of the detailed decisions about public expenditure on different programmes are taken in the PESC process *before* the Committee's report reaches the Cabinet, or in subsequent bilaterals, and the Cabinet rubber-stamps them.

Moreover, ministers may be prevented from speaking in Cabinet. For example, David Ennals, as Secretary of State for Health and Social Services in 1979, was prevented from arguing against a cut in his programme and the fixing of priorities by cash limits because Jim Callaghan, the Prime Minister, 'was annoyed with the way the Health Service dispute had been handled' (Barnett, 1982, pp. 59–60). PESC has signally failed to provide ministers with a detailed comparison of different expenditures and decisions: it does not force ministers to weigh proposals against each other (Heclo and Wildavsky, 1974, p. 227).

The third innovation was the longer-term planning and control of public expenditure. Regular surveys have been made of projected expenditure, but each survey has revealed a divergence between actual and planned expenditure, at constant prices (i.e., not arising because of differences in the rate of inflation). In general, expenditure has risen faster than plans. The fact that much of this difference is accounted for by policy changes subsequent to the original plan (Else and Marshall, 1979, pp. 56–7) suggests that expenditure planning has been neither comprehensive nor forward-looking. Large differences between planned and outturn expenditure over the five-year planning period, sometimes of more than 20 per cent, cast doubt upon the usefulness of the fourth and fifth years of the plans.

The fourth innovation brought by PESC was the alignment of future expenditure to future resources. There is no doubt that 'aligned with' (economic growth) meant 'equated with' or 'slower than' (Glennerster, 1975, p. 132). On this count PESC has completely failed. Part of the problem was the difficulty, which also bedevilled the National Plan, of forecasting future rates of growth and the temptation to overestimate it. But there was also the tendency to underestimate the calls of the public sector for resources. This arose because many of the policy decisions taken to commit resources were not part of the PESC process. Prior to the imposition of cash limits in 1976, spending programmes were to some extent open-ended, varying according to the judgement of those in a position to make spending decisions, such as doctors in deciding how many patients to treat in hospital and what drugs to use, or teachers deciding which books to purchase (Goldman, 1973).

As a result of these two factors, the policy of aligning expenditure and resources was not successful in the early years of PESC. Between 1963 and 1967 the public sector's share of GDP increased by 4 per cent (Price, 1979, p. 81). Following the devaluation crisis of 1968, growth paths of public expenditure were specified annually in an attempt to stabilize the growth of expenditure. Also, emphasis was put on the third year of the survey rather than the fifth. Neither of these changes achieved its objective. Despite more radical changes to the PESC system in the mid-1970s, expenditure and growth have been no more successfully aligned: the ratio of public expenditure to GDP rose from 31 per cent in 1971/2 to 44 per cent in 1982/3 (though a range of other factors have come into play – see Judge, 1982).

In sum, the PESC system represented a considerable advance on the previous arrangements for the planning and control of public expenditure. But the PESC innovations – classification of expenditure, collective ministerial decisions, the use of time as a dimension in public expenditure policy, and the relationship of future resources to future expenditure – were very limited steps in the direction of national social planning. They were concerned primarily with strengthening Treasury control over expenditure. The first task of PESC was to reduce the overall level of expenditure, and in that it has failed – although it was successful in reinforcing bureau-incrementalism in Whitehall, which itself acts as a control on spending.

THE TRANSITION FROM PLANNING TO CONTROL

The first reaction to the fiscal crisis of the mid-1970s, and to the monetarist rationale that was beginning to hold sway in economic

policy-making, was felt by the PESC system and the expenditure programmes, and in turn by the millions of workers, clients and claimants
who are dependent on the public sector. The year 1975 was the turning
point for PESC, for it was then that the Treasury acknowledged implicitly that it could not control the monetary costs of public expenditure (Wright, 1979, p. 43). In 1975 the House of Commons Expenditure
Committee commented that: 'The Treasury's present methods of controlling public expenditure are inadequate in the sense that money can
be spent on a scale which was not contemplated when the relevant
policies were decided upon' (Expenditure Committee, 1975, p. 1). The
Committee drew attention to the divergence between planned and
actual expenditure in 1974/5. This was due in large measure to the
higher than predicted inflation, exacerbated by the relative price effect
(see Judge, 1982, pp. 44–5).

The government's response was to change the whole basis of the
PESC system and turn it into a more effective control mechanism
(Wright, 1980). The medium-term planning of public expenditure that
Plowden had created was, effectively, abandoned. The most important
measure was the setting of 'cash limits' or ceilings on the actual amount
of cash that could be spent, as opposed to the volume of goods that
could be bought.

Cash planning

The introduction of cash limits in 1975 was innocuous enough, but
they were soon to become more important than the volume figures in
the White Papers because they took precedence over the achievement
of plans (Wright, 1981, p. 23). The Chief Secretary to the Treasury at
the time, Joel Barnett, recalls: 'I got Cabinet approval rather more
easily than would have been the case if they had fully comprehended
the consequences that would inevitably flow from the decision in later
years' (Barnett, 1982, p. 78).

The cash limits were first applied to some central and local government building programmes in response to higher than average inflation
in building costs. In 1976, following the 'IMF crisis' and the acceptance
of PSBR limits agreed with the IMF, cash limits were extended to cover
40 per cent of central government expenditure, local government capital
expenditure, the rate support grant and the borrowing of nationalized
industries.

Cash limits were an immediate success: in 1977/8 expenditure *fell short* of cash limits by more than £4,000 million (Jutsum and Walker, 1979, p. 2). The main areas not covered by cash limits were the 'demand-determined' aspects of public expenditure, that is, where there is a commitment to meet the claims of all those who qualify for benefits or services. The main expenditures exempt from cash limits therefore are those of social security and general practitioner services. Cash limits were used effectively to cut expenditure by being set below the level of inflation (Barnett, 1982, pp. 181–2). For example, in 1979/80 a 'planned' increase in real resources was turned into a £200 million cut (Social Services Committee, 1980, p. vi).

Following the introduction of cash limits, the PESC system was modified from an instrument of planning to one of control (Expenditure Committee, 1976). Emphasis was placed on the second year of the survey, the next year ahead, and figures for that year were to be regarded as firm. Any variation was to be met from the 'contingency reserve'. The figures for years 3–4 were provisional (Else and Marshall, 1979, p. 63). The volume figures were linked to cash limits in order to control expenditure more effectively. Also, the development of actual expenditure in any year was monitored much more closely, in relation to the cash limits, by the new financial information system (FIS) introduced by the Treasury in 1975 (Wright, 1979, p. 46). Non-cash-limited expenditure was also monitored in order to provide the government with an early warning of any divergence between outturn and planned expenditure.

Further indications of the reduced emphasis on planning were provided by presentational changes in the 1977 White Paper, including an omission of the analysis of economic prospects over the whole survey period, which had appeared in previous White Papers, and reduced prominence given to the estimates of expenditure in cost terms (Else and Marshall, 1979, pp. 64–5). These changes were repeated in the White Papers of 1978 and 1979.

The Conservative Party came to power in 1979, committed, as we have seen, to the reduction of public expenditure. Measures were soon to follow that finally buried public expenditure planning. The system of Policy Analysis and Review (see p. 78), the main mechanism for monitoring expenditure programmes, was abandoned in 1979. The planning period in the PESC survey was cut from four years to three in 1981. The most important change, however, was announced in the 1981

Budget. For the first time, cash limits and broad cash totals for 1981/2 were to be included in the White Paper. But in planning expenditure for 1982/3 discussions were to be conducted *from the outset* in cash terms. So, from 1982, public expenditure White Papers have contained cash figures throughout rather than survey prices. At the same time, no information has been provided about the inflation assumptions used to adjust volume plans to cash terms; it is not possible, therefore, to calculate the exact *impact* of expenditure plans on different programmes.

Also in 1981, the powers of the Treasury to control spending and influence policy-making in other departments were extended and strengthened. It is the duty of the Treasury and the Civil Service Department (CSD) to define the essential elements of a system to monitor and control the use of resources allocated to departments and to verify that such systems are in operation (Treasury, 1981, p. 2). The responsibilities of the principal finance officer, who it will be recalled represents each department on the PESC, and the principal establishment officer, the chief adviser to the permanent head of each department on the provision of manpower and staff-related resources, were spelt out in detail. For example, principal finance officers were reminded of their duty to ensure that spending proposals are fully appraised and costed. They were also told of their duty to co-operate closely with the Treasury (Treasury, 1981, para. 8):

> You . . . have a responsibility to co-operate fully with the Treasury and CSD, in particular in keeping with the planned limits, and to provide them with information they need for their tasks of allocation and control.

PUBLIC EXPENDITURE 'PLANNING' IN THE 1980s

Where do these changes leave public expenditure planning, and in particular the PESC system — currently the main mechanism of social planning? The PESC system was always an uneven compromise between control and its junior partner, planning. Following recent changes in economic policy and the marked shift towards control, the last vestiges of planning have been removed. Now PESC is not only a wholly inadequate basis on which to plan social priorities and social development, but is positively antagonistic to these aims.

The Treasury and social spending

In the first place, Treasury control and influence over planning and policy-making throughout Whitehall is now stronger than ever. As I argued in chapter 3, the Treasury is concerned wholly with narrow economic, that is financial, policy-making. Thus, Treasury control of the PESC system institutionalizes the subordination of social policy and planning to economic policy-making. In the words of the Treasury, 'finance must determine expenditure, not expenditure determine finance' (Treasury and Civil Service Committee, 1982, p. 5). Public expenditure planning is, therefore, cost-orientated rather than needs-orientated. And because Treasury control and influence extends to all central departments, planning in individual departments reflects this same bias. For example, the DHSS's programme budget is linked to the PESC system.

Since the Treasury is primarily responsible for economic management, it is natural that it should regard public expenditure from that perspective. This would not be harmful to the planning of social priorities if there were countervailing forces to the Treasury in the expenditure process, successfully putting an alternative case to the Treasury's assessment of the economic implications of expenditure. Unfortunately there is no such force. Treasury control of expenditure and of the PESC means, in practice, the domination of narrow economic priorities. So, for example, the PESC system underemphasizes questions of distribution and redistribution. 'Since no one is in a position to refer to the distributive or other social effects of various forms of public expenditure, economic perspectives are likely to be the most predominant' (Heclo and Wildavsky, 1974, p. 356; see also Glennerster, 1979, p. 33).

Because the Treasury controls expenditure planning, it is also in a position to impose its or the government's will on departments. Therefore, when coupled with economic theories such as those of monetarism, which are positively antagonistic to the public sector and to some aspects of the welfare state, the Treasury becomes the vehicle for substantial attacks on social spending. The figures in table 2 demonstrate the selective impact of cuts in expenditure since the mid-1970s (see also A. Walker, 1982a; Walker, Winyard and Pond, 1983; for an account of the impact of recent economic policies on social services spending see Glennerster, 1981b).

Of course, Treasury antagonism to social spending did not start with

Table 2 *Changes in public expenditure, 1973/4–1984/5*

Programme	1973/4 (£m)	Labour growth* (%)	1978/9 (£m)	1978/9 (£m)	Conservative growth† (%)	1984/5 (£m)
Defence	7,764	−3.4	7,502	9,026	+30.1	11,799
Industry‡	4,674	−54.4	2,133	2,293	+5.0	2,408
Roads and transport	3,343	−11.0	2,975	2,915	−2.8	2,834
Law and order	2,023	+15.1	2,329	2,596	+23.5	3,206
Social security	13,399	+36.3	18,266	18,644	+29.5	24,139
Housing	4,897	+7.3	5,256	4,728	−69.8	1,430
Education	9,569	−0.6	9,516	9,171	−11.0	8,158
Health	6,885	+7.0	7,370	7,653	+6.6	8,160
Personal social services	1,152	+15.9	1,335	1,320	+10.9	8,160
Employment and training	403	+165.5	1,070	1,237	+102.9	2,510
Total social expenditure§	36,305	+17.9	42,813	42,753	+7.3	45,861
Total public expenditure	65,890	+9.4	72,106	77,951	+3.0	80,302

* Based on 1979 survey prices, revalued on the basis of information contained in Cmnd 7841, p. 178.
† Based on 1980 survey prices; cash amounts revalued on the basis of information contained in Cmnd 8484-II, pp. 97, 103, 109.
‡ Excludes lending to nationalized industries and employment and training (latter included in social expenditure).
§ Social security, housing, education, health, personal social services, employment and training.
Sources: Treasury (1980, 1982, 1983); format derived from Judge (1982, pp. 40–1).

the election of the Conservative government in 1979, or even with the adoption of some monetarist policies in the mid-1970s. It has a long history. (For example, the Treasury watered down several of the Beveridge reforms in 1942 – see p. 53.) The difference is that now improvements in the mechanisms of Treasury control of planning and policy-making have been coupled with (and stem from) the adoption of economic policies that are more openly opposed than previously in the postwar period to the public sector.

The Conservative government's first public expenditure White Paper asserted that 'higher public expenditure cannot any longer be allowed to precede, *and thus prevent*, growth in the private sector' (Treasury, 1979, p. 2). The assumptions underlying this 'public burden model of welfare' (see p. 28) have exerted a powerful influence on both official and public attitudes to the welfare state over the last 30 years. Economists in the monetarist school have been influential in sustaining and popularizing the thesis that the public sector is a burden on the economy, or that it 'crowds out' private investment (see Bacon and Eltis, 1976). It is linked to 'anti-collectivist' critiques of the welfare state (see for example, Friedman, 1962; and George and Wilding, 1976). This thesis has been accepted by the Treasury and, as far as possible, built into its model of the economy. It is reflected, and reinforced by, the statistical conventions in the collection and presentation of the national income accounts, which measure public services only by their inputs or costs and not by their outputs (Glennerster, 1976; Hall, 1983).

Thus, because of the domination of narrow economic criteria which exalt the private market in capitalist society, we have a restricted and 'unreal' concept of public expenditure (Townsend, 1975, p. 62). This is assumed *by definition* to be a non-productive burden on the 'productive' sector. It excludes tax expenditures – which embody the Treasury's own 'social policy' (Townsend, 1980, p. 11); it is never related to the growth in private consumption (Townsend, 1972, p. 294). Faced with these restrictions, the planning of priorities is equally limited to only one part of official expenditure, and to an even smaller part of total national expenditure which has some bearing on social welfare.

Behind closed doors

The second major inadequacy of PESC, its excessive centralization and secretiveness, is reinforced by Treasury dominance (CPSA, 1979).

Parliament is unable to exercise any effective influence over the expenditure process (Heclo and Wildavsky, 1974, pp. 242–63). It does not even control the auditing of the public expenditure that it formally votes (Committee of Public Accounts, 1981). The Cabinet discusses the programme of expenditure only after most of the key decisions have been made. This means that there is no opportunity publicly to debate spending priorities before resources have been allocated. Those who pay for and receive public services have no say in the relative priorities of governments between elections.

Moreover, because planning is centralized, the government controls information about spending. It is able, therefore, to obscure the precise implications of its spending plans, for example by not publishing figures that may be compared with previous years, or by not publishing statistics at all, as the Conservative government refused to publish figures annually on the numbers of people in poverty since 1979. The centralized power that the Treasury has been granted and now wields poses a greater threat to democracy than the much criticized corporatist tendencies of planning in the 1970s.

Bureau-incrementalism and social priorities

Third, the PESC system militates against radical changes in the distribution of resources between programmes. It developed as a bargaining system with some medium-term interests, an institutionalized system of competition over incremental resources (Wright, 1979, pp. 27–8). In Heclo and Wildavsky's (1974, p. 238) words, 'PESC has enshrined incrementalism with a vengeance. It is incrementalism to the nth power.' In its pre-cash control days PESC insured that, once a department had won a slice of the Budget, the *volume* of resources agreed in the PESC round would be maintained despite price increases (Glennerster, 1975; Wright, 1979, pp. 34–6). With the advent of cash control, however, departments could no longer guarantee the maintenance of resources in volume terms. But this did not liberate planning from bureau-incrementalism or -decrementalism and, in fact, made it more difficult to plan social priorities. Cash-based planning is not, in itself, opposed to the considered planning of priorities. The problems arise when cash limits are the only form of planning, and when cash expenditure figures are set *below* the level of the rise in relative prices. This is precisely what has happened since the introduction of cash limits in 1975. The use of over-optimistic inflation assumptions by the Treasury to cut the volume of expenditure resulted in an average reduction of just over 2 per cent per annum in the real level of expenditure between 1976 and 1981 (Treasury and Civil Service Committee, 1982, p. xxvii).

Cash limits and cash planning are blunt instruments, intended to reduce the *overall* level of expenditure. They tend to be counter-productive to the consideration of social priorities because they entail rough justice or crude across-the-board cuts and encourage protective reactions from ministers, officials and professionals (Glennerster, 1981a, pp. 181–93). Again, planning is discouraged because cash figures obscure the implications of spending plans: will there be more doctors in 1984/5 than 1983/4? Will health care standards be reduced, main-tained or increased? (Kay, 1982, pp. 100–1). Departments are unsure as to what their cash allocation will actually buy in future years. More-over, cash limits do not necessarily confront the issues of performance and efficiency in public sector services and may positively work against their achievement (Glennerster, 1981a). As the House of Commons Social Services Committee (1980, p. ix) pointed out, cash limits blur responsibility and accountability by passing responsibility for the service cuts that result from the implementation of cash limits to the operational level. Changes in volume figures were explicit, but cash figures hide policy assumptions (Treasury and Civil Service Committee, 1982, p. xxiii).

LOCAL AUTHORITY EXPENDITURE

In addition to officials from Whitehall departments, since 1975 the PESC system has included the representatives of local government. The Consultative Council on Local Government Finance is chaired by the Secretary of State for the Environment and includes ministers, civil servants, representatives of local authority associations and local govern-ment officers. The Council negotiates annually the share of resources to be allocated to local authorities. As the PESC system was transformed into a control mechanism, so local authorities were brought more fully into it (Wright, 1979, p. 37). Since 1979 even more stringent controls have been exerted over local authority expenditure, to the extent that already limited local democracy has been substantially eroded.

Just over one-quarter of total public expenditure is spent by local authorities — some £31,000 million in 1983/4. By far the biggest single programme is education, which accounts for one-third of the total. A long way behind come transport, housing and environmental services, law and order, personal social services and social security (principally the housing benefit scheme). In 1983/4 just over one half (55 per cent) of local authority expenditure considered 'relevant' for central funding purposes (85 per cent of their total expenditure) was funded by central government in the form of direct grants. Negotiations about the annual total expenditure considered to be relevant for grant purposes takes place on the Consultative Council on Local Government Finance between the representatives of government and local authorities. The lower the proportion agreed upon — that is, the lower the proportion of relevant expenditure the government agree to pay — the higher will be the major source of locally raised funds, the rates. In 1976/7 the proportion of local authority expenditure funded by central government was 65 per cent. So while central control of local expenditure has increased, the proportion the government contributes has fallen.

The Rate Support Grant

The main form of central government funding is the Rate Support Grant (RSG), which was introduced in 1967 as a temporary measure. It relates to three factors: domestic rates, resources and needs. The *domestic element*, the largest of the three, was designed to limit the rise in domestic rates as compared with industrial and commercial rates in a period of rising prices. The *resources element* was designed to compensate for differences between authorities in rateable values per head of population. The *needs element* attempted to equalize differences between the demographic, geographic and social characteristics of authorities. Multiple regression analysis was used to identify those factors that have a statistically significant correlation with variations in authorities' previous expenditure and to calculate the importance of each factor in explaining variations. Spending 'need' was measured by the strength of the relationship between the factors, such as the proportion of the population over the age of 65 and the level of unemployment, and the expenditure of authorities. (For a penetrating critique of the calculations that underpin the RSG, see Burgess and Travers, 1982, pp. 45–64).

Centre–local relations

Since the Second World War, local authority expenditure, especially capital spending, has been used in exactly the same way as central expenditure, as an instrument of demand management to counter-balance fluctuations in the private sector (Layfield Committee, 1976, p. 56). The same arguments that have already been advanced in this chapter and in chapter 3 concerning the direct and indirect use of public expenditure in demand management apply with equal force to local authority expenditure. The major difference is that, in the case of the latter, there are democratically elected representatives with responsibilities for local spending. Increasing central control over local authorities, therefore, involves challenging local democracy.

The Whitehall view of centre–local relations was set out in the Green Paper that contained the last Labour government's response to the report of the Layfield Committee's inquiry into local government finance (DoE, 1977, p. 3):

> Parliament has entrusted the running of many important social and other services to democratically elected local bodies. The dilemma which faces central government is to secure and promote an effective local democracy with genuine political choice and at the same time fulfil their responsibilities for the management of the economy and for the standards of public services.

The relationship between central and local government, assumed to be natural and constitutionally inviolable, is just one model among many possible ones. This point can be underlined easily by suggesting an alternative model (see Burgess and Travers, 1982, pp. 83–4). For example, local authorities might be responsible for raising all of their own revenue. Central government might manage the economy independently of local government spending, rather than using it as a tool of economic management or policy. Even if this model were introduced, however, there would still be the issue of the standards of services between different authorities. Again, a number of approaches are possible, ranging from central direction of services to complete local autonomy in service provision.

Until 1979, at least, governments chose to attempt to standardize the provision of services between areas with different populations and needs (hence, for example, the needs element in the RSG); they had gone some way towards promoting 'territorial justice' (Davies, 1968). One important aim of the planning initiatives in the personal social services, reviewed in the next chapter, was to correct major inequities in the distribution of services (see, for example, DHSS, 1976a, pp. 8–9). None of them has achieved a great measure of success in ensuring a more just distribution of services between local authorities (Davies, 1971, 1972; Shearer, 1981, p. 71). In an effort to respect local autonomy, but also to avoid the financial implications of bringing sub-standard services up to a national norm, plans have been indicative. It has been suggested by Davies (quoted in Judge, 1979, p. 74), after reviewing the admittedly unsatisfactory evidence, that local authorities are not, in fact, particularly responsive to local needs, a fact that perhaps owes more to the inadequacy of central compensation for local variations in need than to local authority malfeasance. This does not mean, however, that local autonomy is not an important political objective; and any serious proposal for planning social services must recognize the need to reconcile territorial justice and local autonomy (see chapter 9).

Controlling local expenditure

Prior to 1980, government exerted influence over local authority expenditure through the RSG and other grants, control of loan sanctions for capital projects, policy advice, and regulations and control over the use of charges (Hepworth, 1976; Judge, 1979). The government's control over capital projects was the most effective mechanism for regulating the *content* of local authority services as well as their expenditure (CPRS, 1979; Judge, 1978).

From 1974 authorities began to receive a series of circulars urging them to reduce their expenditure in the interests of centrally determined economic goals (DoE, 1974). 'Stand-still' or 'zero growth' were the targets. Greater central control over the RSG was achieved by the establishment of the Consultative Council on Local Government Finance and strict control of borrowing for capital projects. But PESC was still unable to ensure that local authorities kept within planned expenditure. The turning point came in 1976, when cash limits were extended to local finance. The Labour Secretary of State for the Environment in 1976, Anthony Crosland, told local authorities that 'the party's over'. Remarkably, the increase in local authority expenditure was brought under immediate control in the mid-1970s and thereafter was cut back gradually, yet at the same time there was an *increase* in central government spending. Between 1975/6 and 1980/1 local authority spending fell by 17.0 per cent compared with a rise of 7.5 per cent in central government spending (Treasury, 1979, p. 15; 1981, p. 24). Because of the prior commitment of increases in expenditure on, for example, debt charges, running expenses and the financial implications of recent legislation, zero growth means a reduction in previous expenditure (see Greenwood, 1979, p. 79; Webb and Wistow, 1982).

Despite this success in reducing local authority expenditure, the Conservative government elected in 1979 sought additional powers over authorities' budgets. Its desire to reduce local spending further was combined with the longstanding critique of the RSG for inadequately compensating authorities for differences in local needs. There were other disadvantages of the RSG from the perspective of the Conservative government. The resources element operated to allocate more money to high-spending authorities and less to low-spending ones, which was a complete reversal of the rewards and penalties the government wished to impose. Second, the government could cut the total amount of the RSG if it wanted to; but to do so would penalize those authorities that *had* cut their spending as well as those that had not. Since Labour authorities were, in general, the main recalcitrants, the government sought a measure that would enable it to control individual councils' spending. Consideration of alternative systems of finance did not dwell on more significant, that is less party-political, criticisms of the RSG, such as its complexity, doubts about the use of regression analysis, objections to the concept of spending need, and especially questions about rateable values and rates themselves (see Burgess and Travers, 1982, pp. 60–5).

The block grant

The major step in the Conservative government's extension of control over local authority spending came in 1980 with the passage of the Local Government Planning and Land (No. 2) Act. This introduced the block grant in place of the needs and resources elements of the RSG. It is similar to the unitary grant proposed by the previous government (DoE, 1977). In the same way that changes to the PESC system centralized power in the hands of the Treasury and departmental planning was undermined by cash control, so the block grant has increased the power of the Treasury over individual authorities and has undermined local responsibility and accountability. It has threatened the long tradition of local responsibility and accountability in Britain (Burgess and Travers, 1982, p. 154):

> The new grant system is avowedly designed by the Government to make it difficult, if not impossible, for authorities to over-spend, and to apply for the first time explicit government judge-ment about what authorities should spend on each service and in total . . . . It will end the English tradition of responsible local government.

The block grant became operational in 1981/2. In one important respect it attempts to achieve the same goal as the RSG: to allow all authorities to provide a comparable standard of service by levying the same rate poundage (Lansley, 1980, p. 510). It works as follows. The government decides the amount that each of the 467 local authorities in England and Wales ought to spend in order to provide the same standard of service as the other authorities, taking on board their differ-ent needs. This is the grant-related expenditure (GRE) (DoE, 1980). A grant-related poundage is then calculated for each authority on the basis of the relationship between its actual expenditure and the GRE. (The 'rate poundage' is the number of pence in the pound that occupiers pay on the rateable value of their properties.) The block grant is the difference between what the authority spends and the notional income produced by the grant-related poundage and local rateable value. The exception is that, where an authority spends significantly more than what is centrally advocated, it will receive a declining rate of grant and so have to raise more from ratepayers.

The method of calculating the GRE is as complicated as that for the needs element of the RSG. It is based on the same assumptions as the RSG that Whitehall civil servants can and should determine local needs for spending. The first calculations of the GRE formulae produced some bizarre patterns, whereby some authorities were faced with a considerable incentive to spend, while others were faced with a dis-incentive to spend, or were even encouraged to underspend their GREs. This suggests that the system is 'even more complex and arbitrary than its predecessor' (Travers, 1981, p. 8).

Along with the block grant system, the Local Government Planning and Land (No. 2) Act introduced several other control measures. In the first place, the Environment Secretary was given new powers to penalize 'high'-spending authorities in the transitional year before the block grant became operational. Second, the Act replaced existing controls over borrowing for capital projects with controls on spending. The freedom of councils to increase capital expenditure by using revenue finance was stopped by this measure. Now authorities are informed each year how much they can spend on housing, social services, education, transport and other services. Third, urban development corporations (UDCs) were introduced, in the first instance in London and Merseyside. These have wide powers to take over the planning and housing functions of the local authority as well as public land. They are not elected, but are appointed by the Secretary of the State. Fourth, the Environment Secretary was given the power to order the disposal of public land under terms and conditions determined by him. Fifth, the Act requires local authorities to publish any information about their activities that is requested by the Secretary of State. Finally, the government has reduced the role of planning and also public participation in urban districts.

The wide discretionary powers given by the Act to the Secretary of State for the Environment, coupled with the firm control over local spending that the block grant gives the DoE and Treasury, raise fundamental questions about the ability of local authorities to determine and meet local needs and also about the viability of local democracy. The subsequent creation of the Audit Commission to take over the book-keeping work of the District Audit Service and to conduct efficiency studies of local authority services, and the intention of the government to limit, or 'cap', the rates levied by some authorities, underlines these questions.

Distribution of expenditure within authorities

Increased central controls over local authorities have reduced the authorities' freedom and scope to distribute resources between programmes. All local authorities have an annual policy planning and budgetary process through which decisions about resource distribution are made, although there are wide differences between them in the form they take (Greenwood, 1979, pp. 84–90). Unlike the PESC system, the main constraint on expenditure comes externally, from central government.

In the late 1960s and early 1970s some local authorities followed central departments in experimenting with the PPBS methodology (see p. 76). Some, notably Greenwich and Lambeth, employed management consultants and developed corporate, community or programme planning systems (Skelcher, 1982, p. 36). As central financial control over local authority finances has tightened, local authorities have turned to new mechanisms for controlling their own expenditure and resource distribution. The main form has been corporate planning (Stewart, 1971; Eddison, 1973; Greenwood and Stewart, 1974), and its development mirrors the move towards increasing centralization and tighter Treasury control over the PESC system.

The main impetus to corporate management and planning was given by the Bains Committee (1972) on management in local government in England and Wales (and the Paterson Committee, 1973, for Scotland). It proposed the appointment of a chief executive to manage the whole authority, together with a management team of the heads of departments. On the member side, a policy and resource committee was proposed to decide major policy questions. Bains, like the Maud Committee (1967) before it and indeed the Fulton Committee (1968) on the civil service, was cast in the same managerial and national decision-making mould that led to the consideration of PPBS in central government. There was, on the other hand, dissatisfaction with the existing organizational and management structures, and on the other a belief in the importance of corporate rather than narrow departmental objectives and the need for a new organizational structure that would enable these objectives to be achieved. Local government reorganization in 1974 provided the opportunity to adopt the new committee structures proposed by Bains, and most authorities did so (Greenwood, et al., 1975).

Corporate management and planning is aimed at relating resource allocation decisions and the policy planning process across the whole local authority, thus enabling authority-wide decisions to be made in relation to needs and priorities. But the main motivating force for the adoption of corporate planning was the series of restraints on local authority expenditure that started in 1974. Corporate planning provided the means to assess priorities across all departments but also to strengthen financial control (Bennington, 1976; Cockburn, 1977). Thus, since the imposition of strict cash control on local authorities, most of them have sought more 'rational' methods for assessing priorities and allocating resources on an interdepartmental basis (Skelcher, 1982, pp. 41–2). At the same time, they have begun to question some aspects of their existing expenditure.

Although a firm conclusion must rest on detailed evidence from different authorities, there are signs that, in contrast to central government, local authorities are becoming slightly less bureau-incremental (Greenwood, 1979, p. 95). Some authorities too have begun to extend their planning horizons and have adopted strategic and not simply the usual short-term operational planning. For example, Coventry produces a ten-year City Policy Guide, which is updated every year in the February–November period of the annual planning cycle (Skelcher, 1982, p. 45). Cambridgeshire has recently introduced a three-year rolling plan. Again, this trend is the reverse of that taking place in central government, although it must be emphasized that, as a general rule, local authorities rarely consider future options or debate explicitly the sort of community they would like to create.

The annual policy planning and budgetary process commences in April, when the party in control gives an indication of the total level of expenditure that will be allowed. Then individual committees, but primarily the chief officers and their committee chairpersons, prepare draft estimates and options for the development of their programmes. These are completed and presented to the Policy Finance and Resources Committee in September or October.

These first two stages are common to most authorities, although some of those that have adopted corporate planning would begin with a series of position statements from committees (Skelcher, 1982, p. 40). The third stage may take one of three forms, or contain elements of all three (Greenwood, 1979). Between November and January a simple percentage allocation may be made across all departments. Alternatively, private meetings take place between the leader of the controlling party, the treasurer and the chief executive to decide the share of expenditure or cuts to be borne by each department. Increasingly common however is the third (corporate) approach, whereby the programme option statements that are prepared are linked with position statements and set out different priorities and the finance and manpower implications of each option. Decisions are taken in the Policy Finance and Resources Committee, and the rate is declared in February.

Throughout this process the main actors are the chief officers, including the treasurer and chief executive, and the committee chairmen. The Department of Finance is usually crucial. It services the other departments, especially in the preparation of draft estimates, and is in a strong position to influence the shape of the estimates (Greenwood, 1979, p. 83).

One of the main problems with the development of corporate planning and budgeting is that it has reinforced the centralist tendencies of local authorities. Indeed, that was one of its main purposes, in common with the introduction and elaboration of PESC. Power has been centralized in two respects (Skelcher, 1982, p. 46):

> *horizontally*, in the sense that the traditionally autonomous service departments have become subject to increasing direction by the policy and resources committee, and *vertically* as the hierarchy of decision-making is reinforced through the leader–chief executive nexus.

Like the PESC, the policy planning and budgetary process is a closed system. Some authorities are attempting to temper this centralization by providing some opportunities for policy debate. Councillors, field-workers and the public have been encouraged, in various initiatives throughout the country, to take part in discussions about council policies and priorities. Some authorities have attempted to overcome centralism by introducing decentralized area-based planning inputs. For example, Middlesborough has a system of permanent district policy committees comprising ward representatives, minority party members and other members. Some authorities, such as Walsall, have decentralized the management of some of their services.

Although these initiatives may make service providers more responsive to client needs, an important goal, they do not challenge the power, which corporate planning strengthens, of the chief executive, treasurer, leader and chief officers. There is no evidence, moreover, that corporate planning has improved the effectiveness of priority planning and service provision. This rests partly on the almost complete lack of research on, or monitoring of, the outcome of local services. But there is undeniably the fact that proponents of the corporate approach have overlooked this aspect of planning, and have concentrated instead on 'ideal' structures. Yet, as Barras and Geary (1979, p. 40) point out, 'policy effectiveness should be the main criteria against which the utility of the planning process should be judged.'

THE NEED FOR PLANNING

To all intents and purposes, public expenditure planning has been abandoned, yet the need for planning is greater than ever. Regardless of whether or not resources are expanding or contracting, policy decisions are being made that entail the commitment of resources. It is necessary to plan the allocation of resources for the implementation of policies. This is particularly the case for capital investment projects − the building of schools, hospitals and so on − where decisions may take many years to come to fruition and incur current expenditure. Social service planners need to know the number of teachers, doctors, nurses and other staff that can be employed in those buildings when they are completed. In turn, education and training authorities would, ideally, like some indication of the future demand for different specialist skills so that they can plan their intakes accordingly.

Second, planning is required to enable social priorities between different programmes and items of expenditure to be assessed and weighed against each other. The PESC system has never approached an assessment of social priorities; it has always been a vehicle for bureau-incrementalism and political expediency. In times of retrenchment, the consideration of priorities between programmes is even more urgent than before. In this respect most other Western industrial societies allow more parliamentary time to discuss tax and spending proposals, and provide more information on which to assess plans, than does Britain (Treasury and Civil Service Committee, 1982, p. xxxiii).

Third, there is a need to ensure greater stability in the development of public expenditure programmes so that short-term economic criteria do not override long-term social needs. This requires not only planning, but also a new role for social planning in conjunction to economic policy. This means that the power of the Treasury over economic and social policy must be challenged.

Fourth, planning is required to give those who work in or are clients of public services influence over the pattern and development of those services. Of course, the administrative and elitist PESC system was never intended to do this: the clients of public services have no say in how they are managed and run. As was argued in chapter 2, this is an important factor in the widespread disaffection of claimants and clients from the welfare state. If this is to be reversed and services are to become more responsive to the needs of those they serve, then more open planning is essential.

The fifth argument for public expenditure planning rests on the sheer size and importance of the public sector in relation to the economy. Planning is required to manage those resources and to ensure that future expenditure is consistent with economic and social priorities. Because of its importance, successive governments have used public spending to vary the overall level of demand in the economy. If this intervention is not planned it can disrupt programmes and cut across the allocation of priorities. For this reason, in the mid-1970s there was a shift away from the use of public spending in short-term demand management (see Expenditure Committee, 1974).

Finally, regardless of whether or not resources are expanding or contracting, society itself is changing. For example, there is the changing structure of the population, and in particular the increasing numbers of very elderly people. Planning is required to ensure that resources are allocated in line with population and other changes. Planning conducted by individual departments to this end is not likely to be successful unless the overall distribution of resources is planned accordingly.

Contrary, then, to the Treasury and Conservative government's approach, the effectiveness and efficiency of public expenditure programmes rests on careful planning. In the words of the Treasury and Civil Service Committee (1982, p. xxv), 'In order to ensure the highest degree of efficiency and effectiveness in a programme it is necessary for it to be properly planned, carefully managed and, we consider, subjected periodically to a fundamental review.'

CONCLUSION

The PESC system was introduced primarily to curb the rise of public expenditure in relation to national income. It was always an uneasy compromise between planning and control. With the demise of Keynesian demand management and the rise of monetarism, the emphasis of the PESC system has been shifted, essentially in two major steps in 1975 and 1981, from medium-term planning to short-term control. Increased control has also been exerted on local authorities, damaging local autonomy and responsibility.

The Conservative government that completed the shift has been no more successful than its predecessors in controlling the *overall* growth of central government expenditure — the greatest success was achieved by the Labour government in the mid-1970s — but they have cut back the growth of social spending and particularly the non-demand-determined programmes. Moreover, in abolishing PARs and reducing the scope and effectiveness of the government's statistical services, it has also made it much more difficult to assess the social consequences of these policies. In 1984, then, there is no central form of social planning that determines social priorities within and between public expenditure programmes.

7

Planning the Social Services

INTRODUCTION

Social services planning is often equated erroneously with social planning. This is as narrow and misleading as the even more common tendency to equate social policy with the welfare activities of the state. The two observations, of course, are closely related: when it is assumed that the state has a monopoly in social policy, then it is likely that it will have a similar monopoly in social planning.

The purpose of this chapter is to examine the conduct of planning within the social services, as one important part of the field of social planning. Because of the limitation of space, attention is concentrated on planning conducted, wholly or partly, by the DHSS. Even with this restriction we are concerned with services that currently spend some £47,000 million (£14,000 million on health and personal social services and £33,000 million on social security) or two-fifths of total public expenditure (Treasury, 1983, p. 13). The DHSS, therefore, could reasonably claim to be the central focus of government social policy and planning.

STRATEGIC PLANNING IN THE DHSS

Planning remains a fragmented and often *ad hoc* activity in the DHSS. It is divided principally along the lines of the Department's tripartite responsibilities and reflects the different organization of these functions. In the field of health, delegated responsibility is coupled with the central control of financial resources; the personal social services are primarily a local authority responsibility; and in social security the Department directs both policy and operations. ·Strategic planning is usually concentrated on specific policies, such as the promotion of community care, joint financing or changes in the structure of the supplementary benefits scheme, rather than being a continuous, progressive and comprehensive activity (for a definition of 'strategic planning' see p. 10).

Moreover, until recently there has been very little public information on the organization of planning in the DHSS. That there is now more to go on is due to the persistence of the House of Commons Social Services Committee, which since 1980 has been questioning the Department closely about its planning machinery (see Social Services Committee, 1980, 1981, 1982 and DHSS, 1980a). Each report has been highly critical of DHSS planning and policy-making. For example (Social Services Committee, 1980, p. viii):

> On the basis of the evidence we have heard, we are struck by the apparent lack of strategic policy-making at the DHSS: the failure to examine the overall impact of changes in expenditure levels and changes in the social environment across the various services and programmes for which the Department is responsible. ... At this point, the Committee wishes to record its disappointment − and dismay − at the continuing failure of the DHSS to adopt a coherent policy strategy across the administrative boundaries of individual services and programmes.

Penetrating criticism such as this has produced not only information but also changes in the planning machinery.

Planning at the centre is conducted through the various policy divisions of the DHSS that are responsible for strategic policy analysis and the identification of research priorities. This departmental planning system was established in June 1973, following a review of the DHSS's organization and methods of working on the health and personal social services side, in the light of the reorganized NHS and personal social services. In the previous year the Department was reorganized and policy branches were created to deal with the elderly and physically handicapped, the mentally handicapped, the mentally ill and children. The planning system entails the production of planning statements by the policy branches covering primarily the present pattern of services, the use of resources and desired future changes (Banks, 1979, p. 165). These statements are translated into submissions to ministers which review policies and propose options. The programme budget that was added to this structure in October 1973 is the mechanism through which the policy statements are costed.

A management review conducted in 1978 recommended improvements in the co-ordination of the different divisions. As a result, two strategy committees were established to cover the health and personal social services on the one hand and social security on the other. These are supported in turn by a cross-sector policy group, which examines the interaction of national policies across programme boundaries, and a research strategy committee, which is responsible for co-ordinating the development of research across the whole field of the Department's activities (DHSS, 1980a, pp. 3—4).

The strategy committees are divided primarily in line with ministerial responsibilities. Under the secretary of state, two ministers of state are responsible respectively for health and personal social services and social security (although the latter also includes issues relating to disability). The health and personal social services strategy committee is chaired by the Department's first permanent secretary and includes chief professional officers and other senior staff at deputy secretary level in the health and personal social services field. The social security strategy committee is composed of the second permanent secretary and administrative and professional staff at and above under-secretary level working in the social security field. The deputy secretaries for finance and administration attend both committees. Papers for the committees are seen by ministers (Social Services Committee, 1981, p. 2).

The cross-sector policy review group is chaired by the chief social work officer and includes senior administrative and professional staff from the two sides of the Department. It has two primary roles. First, it reviews the Department's cross-sector policy and wider social policy work and reports to the strategy committees on priorities with regard to government policies, the potential social benefit, the impact on resources and the implications for staffing. Second, it makes proposals for reviewing cross-sector or wider social policy issues not already under study. Following the Social Services Committee's first report, the membership of the cross-sector policy review group was extended in order to strengthen its contribution to strategic planning. Similarly, the research strategy committee was placed under the chairmanship of the second permanent secretary and given wider terms of reference, including the close scrutiny of the usefulness and value for money of DHSS research (Social Services Committee, 1981, p. 2).

In addition to the two strategy committees, until 1981 a policy and planning unit had the task of reviewing existing policies and undertaking longer-term strategic thinking primarily in the fields of health and personal social services. Following DHSS recognition of the force of the Social Services Committee's criticism of the lack of strategic planning across the whole range of the Department's activities (DHSS, 1980, p. 3), the policy planning unit was replaced by the policy strategy unit (PSU). This comprises an assistant secretary at its head, three full-time principals and three part-time professional staff. According to the DHSS, the unit is 'charged to maintain an overview of policy work in all parts of the Department, preparing a periodic review of policy initiatives and identifying any apparent gaps (particularly of a cross-sector character)' (Social Services Committee, 1981, p. 2). In addition, the unit has to comment on all major policy reviews within or involving the Department from a strategic long-term perspective. It has also carried out specific policy studies or reviews.

The policy strategy unit differs from the policy planning unit it replaced in that it covers the whole range of DHSS activities and not just the health and personal social services. Second, its officials now work full-time on the studies. Third, it has direct access to ministers and may report directly to them (Social Services Committee, 1981, p. 72). So far the unit's studies have covered, for example, prescription charges, benefits for the unemployed, elderly people, ethnic minorities, unemployment and health, benefits and services for disabled people, NHS residential accommodation and benefits and services for poor families with children (Social Services Committee, 1982, p. 15). Only one report by the PSU has been published (on alcoholism and voluntary organizations), despite the recommendation two years running by the Social Services Committee that there should be a strong presumption in favour of publishing them and, more importantly, professed ministerial acceptance of the principle (Social Services Committee, 1982, pp. xx, 211).

Despite recent attempts to overcome some of the fragmentation of social planning in the DHSS, it is still conducted separately in each of the three sectors of the Department. Because of this administrative division of planning, it is necessary to consider each of the three sectors separately.

PLANNING SOCIAL SECURITY

For most of the postwar period, social security was administered by a separate Ministry of Pensions and National Insurance (from 1948 to 1966) and then by the Ministry of Social Security until 1968, when it was amalgamated with health and personal social services in the new DHSS. Until 1980 supplementary benefits were administered separately from the DHSS by the Supplementary Benefits Commission (SBC), although supplementary benefit officers in local offices were in fact employed by the DHSS. This distinction was removed by the abolition of the SBC. At the same time its advisory role was taken over, along with that of the National Insurance Advisory Committee (NIAC), by a newly created, independent, Social Security Advisory Committee (SSAC). In addition to the advisory responsibilities of the SBC and NIAC, the Social Security Act (1980) made the SSAC similarly responsible for child benefit and family income supplement (SSAC, 1982, p. 1). Its advisory remit covers, therefore, virtually the whole of the social security system. The exceptions are the industrial injuries and occupational pensions fields, which have their own advisory bodies.

Social security differs from other social services in its highly centralized planning and control, the large degree to which operational roles are circumscribed by legal rules and entitlements, its demand-lead expenditure and its very low level of capital expenditure. These distinctive features indicate why there is no permanent machinery for the strategic planning and review of social security equivalent to that in the NHS and other centrally administered services. The two main reasons may be spelt out.

Social security expenditure fluctuates according to demand, and once legal entitlements are established it is not possible to control access to benefits, and therefore expenditure, with total confidence. Information may be inadequate, may have restricted circulation, or both. Benefit officers and those administering the system may be more or less offputting; but these are less successful and predictable methods of rationing resources than the cash limits applied to other social services. Expenditure control and rationing have been the main motivating forces behind the planning of other social services, but in the case of social security control has had to be secured directly through the manipulation of eligibility for benefits (the total population who are entitled to benefits) and the level of benefits (the total sum that might be paid out to the eligible population). Thus the rationing and control of social security expenditure bypasses the social planning process, including the public expenditure planning process.

Second, as a result of this unique legal and financial structure, the administration of social security is highly centralized and tightly controlled at the top. Unlike other social services, such as education and the personal social services, there is very little local autonomy in the distribution of benefits and, with one exception, no local authority responsibility (unlike the poor law system) (the exception being the housing benefit introduced in November 1982). Similarly, unlike the health service, there is no powerful professional group that can determine access to resources, and therefore create a differential pattern of access across the country. Thus, the other main incentives to planning in the British social services − the co-ordination and standardization of local provision − are absent in the social security system. Again, much of the need for this form of planning has been overriden by rhe creation of a unified legal structure.

Unlike the health and personal social services side of its work, the DHSS directly administers the social security schemes. This function occupies 90 per cent of the Department's staff. Most of these are dispersed in some 540 local and regional offices in Great Britain and in two large central offices in Newcastle and North Fylde. As a result of this massive administrative responsibility, operational matters are much more prominent in the planning of social security than in other social services. Strategic 'planning' is confined to programming expenditure in line with projected changes in economic and social policies and the periodic piecemeal review of different parts of the system. In fact, operational issues are so dominant in the central Department that what is in any case a rough-and-ready distinction between operational and strategic planning breaks down completely in the social security field. In the absence of explicit strategic plans, they are often contained implicitly in the operational planning process.

Recent developments: from strategic to operational planning

There have been several far-reaching changes in social security in recent years, including the replacement of family allowances and child tax allowances with child benefits, the extension of benefits for people with disabilities, and the reform of the supplementary benefits system.

But there is no evidence whatsoever of a coherent strategy for planning the development of social security as a whole in relation to need, let alone between social security and other social services. For nearly 20 years social security planning was concentrated almost entirely on devising and then charting the transition to the new pension scheme. Both Labour and Conservative schemes proposed in the 1959 election involved long-term planning, over a 40-year period. The enormity and complexity of the task led to the creation of a special policy planning unit in the mid-1960s (Glennerster, 1975, p. 155). This unit was strengthened following the election of the Conservative government in 1970, and also took on the policy analysis work under the newly established PAR system. As a result of economic changes and the resource constraints placed on the public sector (see p. 130), the mid-1970s marked the start of an increasingly intensive review, first of social security policy and subsequently of operational organization and management.

The first was the review of social security provision for people with disabilities, published in 1974, which proposed a range of new non-contributory benefits for this group (DHSS, 1974; A. Walker, 1976). Then there was the culmination of policy-making in the pensions field: the introduction of the new pensions scheme. This was heralded by the White Paper *Better Pensions* (DHSS, 1974b) and enacted in 1975, although it does not come fully into operation until 1999. This period of planning in relation to need was followed by one in which operational issues were uppermost. It saw the production of a major review of the supplementary benefits system conducted between 1976 and 1979, the main recommendations of which were enacted in 1980 (Bull, 1979; C. Walker, 1982, 1983). During 1979 and 1980 the newly elected Conservative government initiated reviews of the industrial injuries scheme, the benefit payment systems, the position of the self-employed in the national insurance scheme, and sickness benefit. Also in 1980, the operational strategy steering group was established, primarily to develop studies of the computerization of benefits which had already been in train for three years.

The operational strategy

This last named initiative illustrates the shortcomings of recent planning on the social security side of the Department. In particular, it shows how far planning is dominated by operational issues and at the same time how these disguise strategic choices.

The Social Security Strategy Study began in 1977. Its overall aim was to review the operational methods in use for the administration of social security benefits, and to make proposals for increasing the efficiency and cost of administration through the use of computer and telecommunications technology (DHSS, 1980b, p. 1). The specific objectives identified by the first report from the study group may be summarized as follows: (1) to improve operational efficiency, reduce administrative costs and increase the flexibility of the operational system; (2) to improve the quality of service to the public by treating claimants in a less compartmentalized benefit-by-benefit manner and more as 'whole persons'; and (3) to modernize and improve the work of social security staff. A special branch, MSC6, was formed to work full-time on the study.

The second report on the study recommended the following long-term strategy: (1) that the administration of social security benefits should be viewed as a single operational entity with movement towards the whole-person concept, and in particular towards the unification of the administration of unemployment and supplementary benefits for the unemployed; (2) that computer and communications technology should be used to cut administrative costs, including the widespread use of computer terminals; (3) that a new three-tier computer structure should be introduced linking the central offices in Newcastle and North Fylde with area computers and, in turn, VDUs and micro-computers in local offices, and linking claimants' records held separately by the DHSS and Department of Employment (DHSS, 1982a, p. 48). The strategy will cost an estimated £700 million (on top of the £900 million that would in any case be spent on the current computer structure) over the 20 years 1982–2002, with estimated savings of £1,900 million over the same period.

Like the supplementary benefits review before it, the operational strategy study applies an administrative, and in this case technological, rationale to the problems that confront the social security system. As a result, the problems of staff and claimants alike are interpreted in managerial terms. Once again, crucial questions concerning the needs of claimants, the levels of benefit and the relationship between benefit officers and claimants are ignored in favour of technical and administrative issues. However, it is not that these fundamental questions have been simply overlooked, but rather that they cannot be addressed easily within a highly centralized bureau-incrementalist framework. There, the major issues are those concerning administration, and particularly administration from the perspective of the state bureaucracy. This is not to say that the administration of social security benefits is unimportant: the reverse is true. The way that benefits are delivered has an important bearing on access to them. Thus the simplification of administration can have beneficial spin-offs for claimants by making the system more comprehendable and more accessible. But the only way to *ensure* that such improvements in accessibility take place is to begin by examining the difficulties from the perspective of the claimant. And that requires an alternative form of administration and planning.

By concentrating on operational matters the DHSS is making, implicitly, a strategic decision. Furthermore there is a tendency to regard operational planning as non-contentious, technical and value-neutral. But operational decisions usually involve value choices, especially when these dominate administration at all levels, as in the social security system. So, priority is being given to the reduction in administrative manpower and the introduction of computers. This increases the degree of centralization of the social security system and at the same rime reduces further the prospect of radical developments such as the involvement of claimants in the administration of benefits. According to the strategy team, the implementation of the strategy 'will require a greater emphasis on the central direction and control of social security planning and projects to ensure that corporate objectives are achieved' (DHSS, 1982a, p. 48).

The operational strategy consists of a 20-year plan, and it is significant that the only recent public attempt at constructing such a long-term forward plan for social security is devoted to administration. The difference in the official attitude towards operational and strategic planning can be judged by trying to imagine the following statement by the Secretary of State for Social Services, in support of the operational strategy, being applied to strategic issues: 'Piecemeal changes can never be enough. We need a more radical approach if we are to modernise the way we run the system and give the public a quicker and more accurate service' (DHSS, 1982b, p. 6).

PLANNING THE HEALTH AND PERSONAL SOCIAL SERVICES

Strategic planning of the health and personal social services is conducted on a different basis to that of social security, because some power is devolved to locally based authorities and professionals. There is, therefore, scope for strategic and operational planning at both central and local levels. According to the DHSS, 'strategic "planning" activity relates to the role of broad oversight', and is supervised by a Departmental Planning Steering Committee, chaired at deputy secretary level and composed of senior administrative and professional staff (Social Services Committee, 1981, p. 1).

The main planning mechanism on the health and personal social services side of the Department is the programme budget. It was introduced in 1974 in order to relate ministerial policies and priorities more closely to expenditure and to facilitate tighter central control over the distribution of resources between programmes and client groups. The programme budget is an accounting mechanism that projects or programmes future expenditure, initially on the basis of past expenditure. Despite departmental denials (see DHSS, 1976b, p. 78), it is in effect a plan of expenditure (Banks, 1979, p. 164). Since its introduction and subsequent link-up with the PESC work in the DHSS, it has dominated strategic planning of the health and personal social services. All planning activities in this sector are conducted within the context of the financial projections determined through the programme budget. Its introduction accompanied the elaborations of the PESC system and reflected the same underlying preoccupation with the control of expenditure.

THE PROGRAMME BUDGET

The programme budget represents the main inroad into the administration of British social services by the systems analysis and programme budgeting techniques pioneered in the United States. We saw in chapter 4 that in 1970 the Heath government held back from the wide-scale introduction of the US Planning–Programming–Budgeting System (PPBS) into Whitehall departments, plumping instead for a selective review of the objectives of the major expenditure programmes and alternative policies by means of the Programme Analysis and Review (PAR) system. The DHSS had been discussing with the Treasury the possibility of introducing an output budget for health and personal social services, which would as a matter of routine relate expenditure to objectives. The Department decided to press ahead and set up a team of civil servants to conduct a feasibility study. The potential of the study was circumscribed by the instruction to produce proposals that could be implemented quickly using the existing sources of information (Banks, 1979, p. 155). This meant that priority was given to 'practicability rather than what would be ideal' (DHSS, 1972, p. 3), and relatively little effort was devoted to developing tools for monitoring and measuring output, particularly over the long term (DHSS, 1972a, p. 22). Because the reorganization of the NHS was still at an early stage in the planning process, the team was also instructed to concentrate in the first instance on the development of a programme budget for use at Departmental level.

The team reported in April 1971 and January 1972 (both reports were unpublished). The main recommendations of the initial report were that a programme budget for health and personal social services should be developed on the basis of client groups, and that its main aims should be to assist with the determination of priorities and with achieving the most cost-effective use of resources (DHSS, 1972a, p. 1).

The decisions to relate the programme budget to finance and departmental policies represented a crucial departure from the theory of PPBS and its development in the social services field in the United States (Rivlin, 1969), which concentrated on *outputs*. This means that, instead of providing a basis for assessments of the impact of services on patients and clients, the budget system is concerned simply with reconciling resources and level of provision. Hence the use of the term 'programme' rather than 'output'-budgeting. This is further confirmation of the inward-looking and bureau-incrementalist form of DHSS planning. But as Glennerster has pointed out, the adoption of output budgeting would have been a radical departure for Whitehall: the form of budgeting has been built around existing policy commitments and planning techniques. 'Since existing policies tend to be concerned with standards of provision in existing institutions or particular client groups, so do the budget structures' (Glennerster, 1975, p. 255).

The study team proposed that the programme budget should be

regarded as a forward plan, covering at least the current PESC period and probably five years beyond. It recommended the following steps:

(1)   an analysis of existing service provision to client groups over the previous five-year period;

(2)   forecasts for each main programme in the light of existing trends, demographic changes and present departmental policies;

(3)   reviews of policies for each client group, with special regard to the extent to which existing policies are being implemented and to any new priorities, and preparation of revised programmes for each client group;

(4)   amalgamation of revised programmes into a single plan, and consideration of total implications for resources: if the plan is incompatible with resource constraints, individual programmes would have to be modified.

It would have been remarkable too if the top DHSS officials and ministers had dissented from the format recommended by the study team (DHSS, 1972a; Banks, 1979). Not only did it facilitate even greater central control over strategic planning than previously, but it also represented a simple extension of the existing approach to policy-making and planning at the DHSS into its budgetary structure. Alongside this relatively simple framework of programme budgeting, PARs were supposed to provide in-depth studies of the costs and benefits of services and alternatives. While PARs never attained the degree of depth and sophistication to lend them great weight, their abolition in 1980 further weakened the analysis of policies as a basis for planning.

The study team recommended, and the ministers accepted, a programme structure based on (1) *specialities* in the hospital services and (2) *client groups*, divided by age and type of disability, in the personal social services (DHSS, 1972a, Annex A). Expenditure is allocated in the programme budget according to the following programmes (DHSS, 1976a, p. 82):

— primary care (for the whole population);
— general and acute hospital services;
— maternity services;
— services mainly for the elderly and physically handicapped;
— services for the mentally handicapped;

— services for the mentally ill;
— services mainly for children;
— other services (including social work).

The programme budget was used for the first time in October 1973, following the reorganization of the Department in 1972 and introduction of the new planning system four months earlier. The developments are linked; the programme budget provided the costings of policies essential to the new planning system, and the reorganization and planning system provided a framework, including client-group-based branches, within which the programme budget could be conducted (Banks, 1979, p. 165). The programme budget team was established permanently. It began an analysis of expenditure trends and conducted discussions with the policy branches on the costs of policies during the first planning cycle in 1974/5.

The consultative document issued in April 1976 represented the outcome of decisions on public expenditure and priorities conducted within the DHSS (see DHSS, 1976a, pp. 82–3). It was the first attempt at the public statement of priorities in the health and personal social services, and was issued in the now distant phase of flirtation with 'open government'. The departmental planning cycle in the following year took account of comments on the consultative document as well as further public expenditure constraints, and the results were published in a second document on priorities in the health and personal social services (DHSS, 1977a). Since then the programme budget has been given even greater power in the policy-making and planning process, in for example manpower planning in the health service.

Advantages and disadvantages of the programme budget

There is no doubt that the programme budget has facilitated more systematic planning in a department where at best piecemeal planning, and at worst no planning, characterized previous developments. It made priorities and difficult policy choices more explicit than before. Also, it has performed the valuable service of providing a link between changes in the structure of the population and service planning. Thus, when public expenditure restrictions are imposed, the programme budget facilitates the systematic rationing of resources between different programmes on the basis of population changes. Indeed, by demonstrating that resource growth is necessary to, effectively, stand still, it was instrumental in securing a slight growth in health and personal social services resources in 1976. *disadvantages*

Weighed against these positive features is the fact that the central planning system on this side of the DHSS is, in essence, a mechanism for programming and controlling expenditure. The main positive feature of PPBS — the evaluation of alternative policies in terms of their outcomes — was never imported from the United States. As a result, the Department has no planning mechanism for relating the performance of services to the operational definition of priorities. This absence of a method of allocating resources in line with priorities is a major deficiency in DHSS planning. It drew criticism from the House of Commons Expenditure Committee in 1977 and the recommendation that 'the expenditure planning and priority setting of DHSS should be synchronized so as to enable Parliament to examine the relationship between the two' (Expenditure Committee, 1977, p. vi). This recommendation has been endorsed subsequently by the Merrison Commission on the NHS (1979, p. 56) and the Black Committee (1980, p. 264) on inequalities in health.

Through its concentration on the cost of policies and subsequent integration with the PESC system, the programme budget is dominated by narrow economic, and specifically Treasury, assumptions about the availability of resources for social services. The need for services and the extent of any unmet need are relegated to a very low priority in relation to the cost of services. It is not that costs are unimportant; on the contrary, they are obviously an essential aspect of planning. But the planning process is biased overwhelmingly towards the analysis of financial inputs, and as a result other factors, such as the impact of policies, are overlooked or treated cursorily.

Partly as a result of this bias, the programme budget narrowly constrains the definition and assessment of need to service delivery categories. This creates an artificial separation when in fact there is a great deal of overlap between client groups — for example elderly people and those with disabilities — and many shared needs between them. At the same time, the moulding of the programme budget to the existing institutional structure in the DHSS confirmed the power of service professionals to protect their own specialisms and practice in the face of needs that cannot always be simply met by one specialism. In turn, this additional rigidity in service structure makes the transfer of resources between different categories of client or service even more difficult to achieve (Hurst, 1977, p. 232).

The programme budget is the perfect complement to bureau-incrementalism since it is the mechanism for costing policies based of past experience (DHSS, 1976a, p. 78). When economic growth was providing additional resources for the welfare state it was the mechanism for distributing increments. But it was constructed primarily to ration resources more systematically, and when the period of cuts took over, it became the device for redistributing resources *within* the overall DHSS budget. It is likely that the programme budget has weakened the position of those in the DHSS who seek a radical change in the structure of services, or who seek the positive expansion of services, because it emphasizes the resource implications of policies rather than their benefits and confirms the existing service structure. Since planning is cost-dominated, it does not generate any rationale for the alternative use of resources or increase in the proportion devoted to the social services. The abolition of PARs removed the only permanent means of constructing a case for expansion in the face of Treasury restrictions, and that may well be the reason for their demise.

PLANNING THE HEALTH SERVICES

The organizational structure of the NHS planning system, if not its scope and nature, contrasts with that of social security. On the social security side planning is conducted wholly at the centre, with the seven administrative regions being concerned solely with such management functions as staffing, statistical information and performance reviews. Health service planning takes a more elaborate form, reflecting the devolved managerial and consultative structure of the NHS. The considerable power wielded by the medical profession in determining the distribution of NHS resources necessitates a highly developed system of planning and control reaching all the way down to the level of service delivery. At the same time, this devolved structure has paved the way for a greater degree of consultation at local level than occurs in the social security system. The outcome is the most hierarchical and managerial planning system in the British social services, or in the United States for that matter (Glennerster, 1975, p. 153).

The NHS planning system has undergone two major overhauls in recent years, following the reorganizations of the health service in

1974 and 1981/2. Since 1974 the Secretary of State for Social Services has had ultimate responsibility for all health expenditure. The perceived need for greater control and planning resulted in pressure for a reorganization of the structure of the NHS in the early 1970s (West, 1980). The planning system introduced following the 1974 reorganization (DHSS, 1972b) reflected the same influences as those behind the general development of the PESC system at this time.

It is the PESC system that determines the allocation of resources to the health service over a three-year planning period. This is translated by the Department into guidance for the regions and, in turn, for the areas and districts. From 1974 regional health authorities (RHAs) were required to construct ten-year plans on the basis of the strategic guidelines received from the central Department. The local stage of planning began with the RHAs drawing up a list of priorities for their region. These were handed on to the area health authorities (AHAs) in order for them to prepare detailed strategic plans district by district. The outcome of discussions between the areas, districts and regions resulted in regional plans being drawn up and submitted to the Secretary of State. These strategic plans were to be reviewed every four or five years, with operational planning conducted by the three tiers to be revised annually (see for example DHSS, 1980c).

The organization of the NHS into three tiers was soon considered to be too cumbersome. Following the publication of a consultative document (DHSS, 1980d) and the passage of the Health Service Act (1980), separate area and district health authorities were replaced by district health authorities (DHAs). Since these were based on the old district authorities, the reorganization meant that AHAs were abolished. Most of the changes involved in this reorganization took place on or before April 1982. Each DHA is now responsible for the planning, development and management of health services within national and regional strategic guidelines (DHSS, 1980d).

A consultative document published in 1979 (DHSS, 1979a, p. 18) affirmed the government's commitment to the 'discipline of planning' in both the Department and the NHS but criticized existing arrangements as 'over-complicated and bureaucratic'. Thus in February 1981 health and local authorities were given notice of proposals to revise the NHS planning system (DHSS, 1981c). The new planning system is intended to reflect changes in the structure of the NHS.

The division of planning responsibilities between the different tiers is as follows. The DHSS continues to set and monitor national policies and priorities. It issues annually detailed guidance, including resource and manpower assumptions, to the RHAs. The role of the RHAs is to promote national priorities, allocate resources to DHAs, manage the capital programme and co-ordinate and reconcile DHAs' plans. It also has responsibility for services that are provided on a regional basis. The DHA is said to be the basic planning unit: 'Planning should start at district level, and as many decisions as possible should be left to local discretion' (DHSS, 1981c, p. 1). But, of course, resources and key strategic policies are determined centrally. As previously, the planning system has two main components: strategic and operational. Strategic plans are prepared by each district and region every five years instead of every four, to cover at least a ten-year period. Annual programmes of action are prepared for the next two years by each DHA.

The strategic planning process

Once every five years, the DHSS calls for new strategic plans and issues guidelines to RHAs, including assumptions about the availability of resources and a checklist of current national priorities. Each RHA then discusses an outline strategy with its DHAs in the light of these priorities. The outline strategy consists of a service-by-service statement or re-statement of broad policies and priorities, calling attention to any local or regional problems. It also includes details of individual DHAs' responsibilities for services managed on behalf of or in conjuction with other districts. The final component is agreed assumptions about revenue, capital, manpower and workloads.

This first stage, from the issue of DHSS guidelines to the issue of the outline strategy, takes up to four months, beginning in October. Over the next nine months each DHA prepares a district strategic plan within the regional outline. These plans consist of three elements: (1) a general commentary on the state of the district and progress since the last strategic plan; (2) detailed plans for each service, covering present provision and capital stock, surpluses, deficiencies and distance from targets set out in the planning framework, revenue, capital and manpower assumptions, workload assumptions, options, joint planning with the local authority and the strategy selected for the next ten or more years; (3) an overall plan for district services, including the determination of relative priorities such as timing and a reconciliation with revenue, capital and manpower assumptions.

The publication of these draft plans at the end of the first year of the process is followed by a period of local consultation. The DHAs are expected to submit their plans to the RHAs by January. The third stage, lasting from January to April, consists of the preparation of a regional strategic plan. The aim is to reconcile the DHAs' proposals and to secure compatibility among districts and between the districts and the regional strategy. The RHA is empowered to take final decisions if agreement cannot be reached with individual districts on any matter. The regional strategic plan comprises a general commentary on the state of the region and the adopted strategy; an overview of district plans; a concise summary plan for each service, with particular reference to those highlighted in the Department's guidelines and any major deficiencies or imbalances; a reconciliation of aggregate district proposals with the revenue, capital and manpower assumptions determined centrally for the regions, including a commentary on the progress being made towards achieving comparability between districts.

These regional strategic plans are submitted to the DHSS in April. The final stage is a series of meetings between the DHSS and the RHAs at which the plans are reviewed. This period of discussion is programmed to last six months, and therefore the whole process takes two years.

The strategic planning process is dominated by the DHSS (and through it the Treasury), which controls the resources available to the regions. The central Department determines strategic priorities. The 'basic planning units', the DHAs, are constrained by both the resource assumptions and the guidelines passed to them by the RHAs. The latter also have the power to override the DHAs in the planning process. The DHAs are the basic planning unit when it comes to annual operational planning and programming. But these plans must be consistent with the agreed strategy and the annual resource assumptions and planning guidelines circulated annually by the DHSS. The hierarchical structure of both strategic and operational planning processes ensures that local planning is closely scrutinized by the central Department and that, despite the local professional power games (Glennerster, et al., 1983, p. 90), plans are consistent with resource allocations.

Consultation is built into the planning system. It takes place during the preparation of strategic policies and plans for individual services and on the *forward* part of the operational programme. But since all of these consultations take place at district level, there is no opportunity to influence overall strategic priorities.

Resource Allocation Working Party

One further aspect of NHS planning deserves close attention. The Resource Allocation Working Party (RAWP) represents one of the very few central planning initiatives specifically designed to develop a framework within which to allocate resources according to need. Criticisms of wide inequalities in the availability of health care between different regions (for example, Tudor Hart, 1971; Townsend, 1974a) led to the appointment of the Working Party in 1975 (DHSS, 1976b, p. 5)

> to review the arrangements for distributing NHS capital and revenue to RHAs, AHAs and District respectively with a view to establishing a method of securing, as soon as practicable, a pattern of distribution responsive objectively, equitably and efficiently to relative need and to make recommendations.

The Working Party interpreted the underlying objective as being the need to ensure equal opportunity of access to health care for those at equal risk (DHSS, 1976b, p. 7). Their approach to resource allocation on the criterion of need was to use the age and sex structure of the population, together with standardized mortality rates (SMRs), to 'weight' regional populations for different groups of services. The groupings were: non-psychiatric in-patients; all day and out-patients; community health; ambulances; mental illness in-patients; mental handicap in-patients; and family practitioner committee administration (all of which were distinguishable within the programme budget structure − see p. 159).

Target revenue allocations for services were determined on the basis of the sum available nationally being apportioned between RHAs, AHAs and districts in proportion to relative needs, measured by population served, weighted to reflect age, sex, fertility, mortality and marital status. In the case of capital expenditure needs, populations were weighted according to family practitioner consultation rates. The recommendations represent a mechanism for translating an important strategic goal into practice. Support for the Working Party's approach, particularly the introduction of a morbidity factor in allocations, came from the Black Committee (1980, p. 247) on inequalities in health.

The RAWP methodology was adopted by the DHSS and instructions were issued to the RHAs in February 1977. At the same time, however, the growth of health care resources was being restricted, and this contributed to a reluctance to force the pace of change. Clearly too there were powerful interests, representing those areas and specialisms disadvantaged by the RAWP formula, lobbying ministers in favour of a slow rate of change and for modifications in the formula. For example, between 1977 and 1979 attention was called to provisions for teaching hospitals and 'certain specialist facilities which serve more than one region' (Black Committee, 1980, pp. 248, 409–11).

Reviewing progress over the first three years in operation, the Black Committee (1980, p. 249) concluded that, while the 14 RHAs had endeavoured to implement the RAWP methodology, four had not then applied the SMR principle; 'even among RHAs adopting the full methodology the progress made towards the restrictedly defined targets has been cautious.' Moreover, it had not been applied consistently at district level.

The RAWP formula was specifically designed to adjust the pattern of resource allocation that bureau-incrementalism produced and is therefore an important departure for social services planning. Some features of the RAWP approach, however, are characteristic of the traditional bureau-incrementalist perspective. For example, the Working Party accepted the existing pattern of services, the distribution of resources between in-patient and community services, and the prevailing national rates of utilization of different services. As the Black Committee (1980, p. 248) argued, 'What happens is not a good measure of what should happen, however convenient that may be.'

Then there is the fact that the more equitable distribution of resources between regions alone will not necessarily reduce inequalities in health (Black Committee, 1980, p. 263). What is also required is a change in the way those resources are utilized. In the first instance it is important to assess whether alternative uses of resources would have different implications for health status. One example is the case for a shift of resources towards community and preventive health care. The approach chosen by the Working Party suggests confidence in the pattern of services, if not in their precise distribution.

There are also problems with the RAWP methodology. For instance SMRs, especially non-age-specific ones, are not the best indicator of need in small areas. No attempt has been made subsequently to supplement the RAWP formula with other indicators of need. There is an urgent case for more refined indicators of the need for health care to be developed. Another problem is the exclusion of family practitioner services from the formula which should also be financed on the basis of need. Finally, the reallocation of resources under RAWP is on a very small scale — South Tyneside AHA obtained some £80,000 more in 1979—80 than it would have done under unmodified incremental planning — and so the pace of change is very slow indeed.

PLANNING THE PERSONAL SOCIAL SERVICES

Personal social services in England are not formally planned from the centre in the way the local health services are. This is not to say that links between central and local planning did not exist in the past. The national planning system was suspended by the Conservative government elected in 1979. (Curiously, this action did not apply to social services in Wales.) This is one indication of the total subordination of the strategic planning of priorities to the control of public expenditure, discussed in the previous chapter. Without a national planning system linking central and local government, the programme budget in conjunction with PESC is the only means of determining priorities for the allocation of resources to local authorities. Of course the authorities may, and often do, depart from centrally determined priorities. But this creates inconsistencies in the services available to people with similar needs in different parts of the country (see for example Davies et al., 1971; Shearer, 1981). Moreover, since the introduction of the block grant scheme in 1981, a more generous than average expenditure on services can incur financial penalties.

The relationship between the central Department, with its responsibility for providing general guidance on strategic priorities, and local authorities, which have a statutory responsibility to provide personal social services, is a longstanding source of conflict and discussion in social planning. It is a quite different relationship to that between the DHSS and DHAs, where some responsibility for decision-making has been devolved to local areas but where control remains firmly in the Department. One important difference is the fact that the personal social services are financed partly by revenue raised locally. Because of this constitutional division between central and local government, the problems of co-ordination and ensuring consistency between different authorities are much more acute than in the health service.

The precise nature of the division of responsibilities in strategic planning between the DHSS and local authorities, from the perspective of the DHSS, was expressed succinctly by an under-secretary at the Department: 'the Department's role is essentially a strategic role of, in fact, increasing or reducing resources in particular areas, . . . short, quick adjustments are . . . for local authorities working with the health authorities' (Social Services Committee, 1980, p. 35). As a consequence of this division of responsibilities, the history of planning between the DHSS and local authorities is more troubled. Also, the planning systems constructed have taken a different form to the highly centralized and hierarchical NHS planning system and the wholly centralized planning of social security. Local authorities, for example, have much greater freedom in determining strategic priorities and the levels of service provided in relation to demand than have DHAs or local social security offices.

It is the wide measure of divergence in progress towards national goals in the personal social services, which results from the existence of local autonomy and local democracy, that has been one of the main motivating forces behind successive attempts at creating a national planning system over the last 20 years. Seen from the centre, the problem has been how to reconcile national priorities with local decision-making. The very minimum that these systems have been designed to provide is information by which to monitor local progress in relation to central strategic objectives. The other major factor has been the ever-mounting desire to control public expenditure more and more tightly. Thus the first national planning system between the DHSS and local authorities followed quickly in the footsteps of the Plowden Committee's (1961) report and the establishment of the PESC system. The two factors — the desire to bring local services into line with national objectives and the desire to control expenditure — are not necessarily complementary, and since the mid-1970s have been in conflict (A. Walker, 1982b, p. 19).

In addition to routine restrictions on resources, periodically public expenditure cuts override the planning of priorities between the DHSS and local personal social services. From 1976 to 1978 and following the election of the Conservative government in 1979, public spending cuts took precedence over existing plans. As a result of cash-limit restrictions between 1976 and 1978, for example, local authorities underspent by 2, 1½ and ½ per cent each year (Webb and Wistow, 1982, p. 145). Some limited measure of protection was afforded by central government and some local authorities to the personal social services in the late 1970s; but, apart from the small transfer of resources from health to personal social services through joint finance (see p. 177). this minimal protection disappeared after 1979, partly as a result of the election pledge to sustain NHS resources.

In this recent period the central control of local expenditure has completely taken over from priority planning between the DHSS and local authorities. Thus, the abolition of the national planning system in 1979 followed the imposition of strict cash limits on local authority expenditure. Planning in relation to need has seemed an even less likely prospect since the transition to cash-based public expenditure planning and the parallel introduction of the block grant system (see p. 139). The full extent of the flight from planning may be gauged by the fact that, since 1979, the DHSS has not even required local authorities to make returns so that the level and standard of local provision might be monitored.

National planning systems in the personal social services

There have been three attempts by the DHSS to establish a national planning system in the personal social services (see Webb and Falk, 1974, pp. 72–85, Booth, 1979, pp. 134–45; Hambleton, 1982). The ten-year health and welfare plans, introduced in 1962, were abandoned in 1966 (Ministry of Health, 1963, 1964). This was mainly because of dissatisfaction on the part of the Labour government with the low extent to which national targets had been achieved by means of purely indicative planning. The ten-year planning system introduced in 1972 was abandoned after the first round, in 1974, primarily because of the dramatic change in the economic climate in the mid-1970s, which undermined the assumptions of growth on which the plans were based. The deficiencies of each of these DHSS initiatives in national planning can be illustrated by considering the last of them, the three-year plans introduced in 1977.

As a result of the failure of the two previous exercises, central planning was discredited to a large extent with local authorities. Also, long-term planning or programming at the centre was undermined by uncertainty about resources. But the DHSS still had to contend with the problems of co-ordination between central and local priorities and between health and personal social services, as well as with variations in provision between local authorities. Moreover, there was mounting pressure from the Treasury, over the course of the 1970s, for the Department of the Environment (DoE), as the department chiefly concerned with local authorities, and the DHSS to scrutinize more closely, and in some circumstances to control, the expenditure of local authorities. Consequently in June 1977 a new annual planning cycle was set in motion when the DHSS asked local authorities to submit Local Authority Planning Statements (LAPS) indicating their intentions with regard to the provision of personal social services (DHSS, 1977b).

The major departure from the two previous initiatives was the reduction in the planning period from ten years to three. Clearly the most significant factor here was the uncertainty about the future availability of resources. Also, no detailed guidelines were issued with the plans. Instead, local authorities were asked to follow the targets set out in the Department's consultative document issued the previous year (DHSS, 1976).

The consultative document on priorities in the health and personal social services marked the first attempt to open up the issue of priorities to public debate. Comments in response to the consultative document contributed to the slight increase of £6 million in the resources allocated to current expenditure on the personal social services in 1977/8, but capital expenditure was cut by £8 million. The document gave the main impetus to joint care planning (see below). Also, the painfully slow progress that had been achieved in some services in relation to modest targets was revealed by the document. For example, the number of home helps per 1,000 elderly was 6.5 in 1975/6 compared with the guideline of 12 per 1,000 that had previously been targeted for attainment in 1982. Financial stringency set back even further the achievement of guidelines. Thus, for example, the home help service was scheduled to grow by only 2 per cent a year (DHSS, 1976a, p. 38): at this rate, by 1979/80 there would have been only 7.1 home helps per 1000 elderly people (DHSS, 1977a, p. 24).

Analysis of the first round of LAPS returns showed that in 1977 local authorities as a whole were actually planning, in a number of services, to fall short of the levels of provision targeted for 1979/80. Taking the home help service again as an illustration, the 1977 returns showed that local authorities were aiming to reach 6.7 home helps per 1,000 elderly people by 1979/80 (DHSS, 1978a, p. 6); the LAPS returns from local authorities for 1978 showed a marginal improvement to 6.8 home helps per 1,000 elderly (DHSS, 1979b, p. 17). This indicates that in some community care services − including day care for the mentally ill and the mentally handicapped, home helps, meals and day nurseries − the priority planning exercise was not very successful in encouraging local authorities towards what were and remain extremely modest targets. Analysis of the first round of LAPS returns also revealed continuing wide variations in provision between different local authorities.

Social services departments were encouraged to take part in this third attempt at a national planning system by relating it closely to their existing annual administrative and financial routine. Thus, the process of completing LAPS returns was more straightforward than that for similar returns under previous exercises. This was due mainly to the fact that the DHSS had scaled down the amount of information requested to the level of that which local authorities were already preparing. But in addition, the changes in the structure of the personal social services (Seebohm Committee, 1968) and in local authority structure and management (Radcliffe-Maud Commission, 1969; Bains Committee, 1972) in the early 1970s had created a uniform pattern of administration into which the LAPS could be meshed more easily than before.

Local authority planning statements were submitted in 1977 and 1978. But within a few weeks of taking office the following year, the Conservative government had suspended three-year planning. Why was this swift action taken against the third, and so far the last, national planning system, especially when the DHSS was more convinced than ever of the need for such a system (see Booth, 1979, p. 143)? The answer lies, on the one hand, in the strong antipathy towards planning on the part of the incoming right-wing administration. In contrast to its counterpart of the early 1970s, the Conservative government elected in 1979 associated planning with state socialism. On the other hand, there were the central objectives of reducing the size and expenditure of the public sector.

The government by-passed the DHSS planning mechanism and intervened to control local authority's spending more directly. In Whitehall the Treasury and DoE had prevailed over the DHSS, whose three attempts at planning since the early 1960s had been designed partly to encourage laggardly local authorities to winch up their spending to the national target levels. There was strong opposition to this not only from the government, in the twin names of cutting expenditure and preserving local democracy, but also from Conservative local authorities, equally eager to restrain their expenditure and rate demands. By cancelling the planning system the government could control expenditure, while appearing to interfere less than its predecessors in local authority decision-making, and at the same time could provide a pretext for reducing civil service and local authority manpower.

Limitations of personal social services planning

The three attempts by the DHSS to establish a national planning system for the personal social services were characterized by the same deficiencies. They assumed that the determination of priorities was primarily a central matter, and so rode rough-shod over local democracy and reinforced the concentration of power locally in the hands of officials. They were narrowly directed at the personal social services, reflecting the preoccupation of the DHSS with its own internal problems of co-ordination. They relied on the steady growth of resources in line with service needs, a commitment that successive governments were unable to fulfil (for a full account see Booth, 1979).

In short, the national planning exercises were bureau-incrementalist in conception. Thus they were concerned with the development of existing services in relation to recognized needs, as if there were no alternative forms of services and no unrecognized needs. The guidelines published with each planning exercise reflected assumptions about the availability of resources rather than the extent of met and unmet need (Falk and Lee, 1978, p. 78). No rigorous attempt was made to assess need; instead, existing trends were extrapolated in line with resource assumptions. The plans and guidelines also reinforced the client group approach to service delivery, which overlooks elements of need common to all or several such groups. Social progress was conceived of as a matter of the *level* of services that are provided. This suggests a high degree of confidence in the existing infrastructure of services and in their success in achieving social goals.

In keeping with this perspective, no critical attention was paid to the objectives of personal social services and the extent to which they were being achieved. So, each exercise concentrated on the speedy return of planning statements. The DHSS did not encourage a local dialogue about priorities in advance of the preparation of the plans. None of the social services departments incorporated consumers in the preparation of plans. Also, although there were exceptions (see Falk and Lee, 1978, pp. 80–4), social service workers were involved only to a limited extent.

Finally, following on from the underestimation of need, the three planning exercises were based on narrow political assumptions concerning both the role of personal social services in society and the amount of money that should be made available to them. They assumed, for example, that these services would continue to operate on a casualty basis rather than taking a more progressive role in the prevention of social problems. Instead of encouraging local authorities to consider imaginatively the role that alternative objectives and forms of services might play in social development, and thereby providing a basis for a case to be put to the Treasury for increased resources, the plans reinforced the relatively low status of the personal social services as minimum provision entrenched in its existing forms (A. Walker, 1982d). Because services were cast in this limited role, they were not considered a high priority for public spending, and indeed suffered substantial cuts even when there were increasing demands for services stemming from officially recognized demographic pressures.

After the suspension of the national planning system in 1979, the problems that the DHSS set out to tackle through all three initiatives still remain.

With the removal of the, albeit gentle, encouragement towards national priorities that the filling out of LAPS returns entailed, planning is simply a matter of pointing to strategic priorities. The government has used local autonomy as an excuse not to provide coherent statements of policy, detailed monitoring and the provision of social indicators essential for strategic planning (DHSS, 1981b, p. 19):

> Statutory responsibility for the personal social services rests with elected local government. The Government indicates broad national policies, issues guidance where necessary and has a general concern for standards.

The need for personal social services planning

A national planning system would provide an opportunity for local authorities to contribute to the planning process in Whitehall (Hambleton, 1982, p. 424). While they can do so to some extent through the rate support grant procedure, there is a case, resting on the historically low priority given to the personal social services, for specific collaborative planning in this field. One element of this would be to fill the current information gap regarding local need and also the impact of social and economic changes on the personal social services. The annual surveys of cuts in services by the ADSS has made some contribution to filling this gap. But they are of limited value, partly because not all local authorities participate. A more detailed and comprehensive picture is required for planning, and this may help to build up momentum for a change in the treatment of the personal social services by the Treasury.

Second, a national planning system would provide a basis for a dialogue between central and local government about strategic priorities. This might encourage the DHSS to move away from a simple set of guidelines, towards a more informed discussion about the objectives of services and how they might be achieved in different areas. For example, even if the guideline of 12 home helps per 1,000 elderly people were achieved nationally, this form of provision is not necessarily the best method of meeting the needs of elderly people and their families in every case.

Third, a national planning system is necessary to facilitate joint planning between the health and personal social services. The DHSS knows what local health authorities are planning but is ignorant about the intentions of local social services. Without this knowledge joint planning between the NHS and personal social services cannot proceed very far.

Fourth, the establishment of social services planning machinery might encourage collaboration not only between health and personal social services but also between these services and other local services, such as housing and education.

The argument against revitalizing planning stems primarily from local authorities anxious to protect what little autonomy they have left from further Whitehall encroachment. As Hambleton (1982, p. 423) points out, this enables ministers to avoid the consequences of their own actions by passing the buck to the local level. In any case, the fear is not borne out by the continuance of LAPS in Wales. Equally key government departments, such as the DoE and Treasury, see no value in planning initiatives that employ more manpower when they can control more directly the expenditure of local authorities. It is indicative of the sorry state of social planning in Britain that the only two alternatives are considered to be local autonomy, with its inherent disadvantage of patches of underprovision, and central control, which rides rough-shod over local democracy and participation.

How can planning between the DHSS and personal social services be moved beyond this impasse? To replicate the approach of previous attempts to establish a national planning system would, at best, produce some information about levels of provision and perhaps encourage a dialogue between central and local government, as in Wales. What is required is that planning should be directed at the problem of choosing between strategic objectives and alternative forms of service provision, rather than at the extrapolation of existing trends. *It should be concerned with needs and standards of services, rather than just the level of services*. It should involve the clients and potential clients of services as well as chief officers. If planning is to be both needs-based and more democratic, fundamental changes are required in both the organization and control of social services and the form of planning employed.

Three requirements are paramount. First, personal social services planning must be more comprehensive than at present (Falk and Lee, 1978, p. 85). This means that it should be conducted in conjunction with the planning of other local authority and central services that impinge on its clients. Policies dealing with employment, social security and housing, including redevelopment, are obvious examples. But if the personal social services are to occupy a more positive role in development than simply responding to social problems and the social impact of economic changes, they must be planned together with other services and policies in a unified social strategy.

Second, social services departments themselves must be re-orientated towards meeting need and reducing social inequality and discrimination, rather than being concerned narrowly with the delivery of services. This requires careful analysis of social needs and of alternative means of meeting them.

Third, social services departments and local authorities generally must develop more democratic and participative forms of planning. This would encompass the clients of services as well as professionals, other social service workers and councillors. If clients' definitions of need are to occupy a central position in policy-making and planning they must hold power in the planning process. The opening up of the planning process should also involve social service workers at all levels and councillors, all of whom have found themselves increasingly excluded under corporate management and central planning.

JOINT CARE PLANNING

Since 1977 there have been formal arrangements for joint planning between the health and personal social services. This is the most explicit form of co-ordinated bureau-incrementalism within the British social services. The problem of co-ordination between social services is a longstanding one. The problem is particularly acute between the health and personal social services because of the overlap between the health and social service needs of the community. Often these services either are complementary or may be directly substituted for one another. Both come under the ministerial responsibility of the DHSS, yet because of their different statutory accountabilities and sources of finance they are organized along distinctly separate lines.

There has been a series of measures aimed at minimizing the effects of organizational and professional fragmentation on service delivery. Sargeant (1979, p. 173) distinguishes three forms of such co-ordination: 'case co-ordination' between practitioners over individual clients; 'operational co-ordination', involving the establishment of formal procedures to ensure the integration of complementary services; and 'strategic collaboration' over the planning of services and resources allocation. Informal discussions between doctors and social workers or health visitors and formal case-conferences are examples of the first two; we are concerned here with the latter.

The *Hospital Plan*, 1962, and its sister report *Health and Welfare* were early attempts to relate the provision of health and personal social services. The introduction of ten-year plans in 1972 represented a further step towards strategic collaboration because the annual planning exercise gave the DHSS and local authorities the opportunity to review services, including their relation with the health service. In anticipation of reorganization, a Working Party on Collaboration between the NHS and local authorities was set up in 1972. It stressed that the aim should be to secure 'genuinely collaborative methods of working throughout the process of planning' (DHSS, 1973, p. 10). In addition to providing a more effective service, the aim of collaboration was to 'open the way to the reallocation of the resources of both parties to conform to mutually agreed plans'.

The main impetus to joint care planning came with the publication of the consultative document on priorities in health and personal social services, which as I have already indicated was an important departure in a number of respects. The concept of joint planning was raised as a means of improving the effectiveness of services in a period of resources constraint. Subsequently the Secretary of State for Social Services issued a circular requesting health and local authorities to set up joint planning machinery (DHSS, 1977b). This reflected the thinking of the 1972 Working Party and was intended to be the first step towards realizing a full partnership in the planning of the interrelated services. The National Health Service Act (1977) laid a statutory duty on health and local authorities to co-operate in order to 'secure and advance the health and welfare' of the population. This duty, and the legal requirement to establish joint consultative committees, remain intact following the reorganization of the NHS.

In theory, joint planning covers more than just the health and personal social services. The recommendation of the Working Party on Collaboration that a statutory duty should be placed on health and local authorities to collaborate, which was enacted in 1977, included education, housing and environmental health as well as the personal social services. But joint planning has not developed in these other directions. The incentive to collaborate is not as strong as that between the health and personal social services because there is less overlap and less common interest in collaboration. Then there is the fact that collaboration with other services would involve another central government department.

Joint planning machinery

Collaboration is encouraged across a broad front. A primary function of DHAs, is to facilitate joint planning and collaboration with local authorities. In order to encourage this DHAs include members nominated by their relevant local authorities. Section 10 of the National Health Service (Reorganisation) Act (1973) placed a statutory duty on health and local authorities to collaborate in carrying out their functions. To this end it also enacted another recommendation of the Working Party on Collaboration, the duty to establish Joint Consultative Committees (JCCs) to advise on developing a joint approach to their services. Health and local authorities were reminded of their duty to set up JCCs in 1974 (DHSS, 1974b). In metropolitan areas there is one JCC for all local authority services and in non-metropolitan counties there are two JCCs, one for social services and education and the other for environmental health and housing. They provide a forum in which health and local authorities can discuss areas of common interest and potential collaboration. Formally, they are required to advise their respective authorities on strategic developments (for a fuller account see Sargeant, 1979, pp. 178–80).

Within this general collaborative framework there are two specific measures designed to ensure that joint planning, and not simply co-ordination of separately prepared plans, actually takes place between health and social services.

The first is Joint Care Planning Teams (JCPTs), established specifically to encourage joint planning between health and social services. They consist of groups of officers drawn from the DHA and local authority. Their main role is to consider the development of strategic plans, under the general guidance of the JCC. The JCPT is the main locus of joint care planning.

The second is joint finance (DHSS, 1977a). This is the mechanism for reallocating health service resources to fund local social services spending, where this will increase the total volume of care available to the community. So, each year a portion of the health budget is set aside for projects in the personal social services. In 1983/4 it was £96 million, 0.8 per cent of the health service budget and 4.5 per cent of the personal social services budget (Treasury, 1983, p. 55). The programme covers both revenue and capital expenditure. Joint finance is a small practical means of giving effect to the policy of switching care from institutions to community-based services. It is the main incentive to joint care planning (Sargeant, 1979, p. 181; Booth, 1981). In the years to 1982, 95 per cent of joint finance allocations were taken up (Social Services Committee, 1982, p. 82).

The limitations of joint planning

Joint care planning represents a considerable practical advance on previous *ad hoc* arrangements and political rhetoric about the need for both collaboration and community care (see A. Walker, 1982d, p. 13). Having said that, however, there are severe weaknesses both in the specific form of joint care planning and, more importantly, in the approach itself.

Viewed from the perspective of bureau-incrementalism and from within the confines of one central department, the DHSS, co-ordination and co-operation was a logical response to the interrelationship between client needs and services. When expenditure on the health and personal social services was cut back, it was equally logical to seek a redistribution within the overall budget between overlapping services (Social Services Committee, 1982, p. xxii). But as well as being, on the face of it, sensible responses to the fragmentation of services, co-ordination and collaboration were the *only* positive responses that could be made. It is not simply that resource constraints have forced a long-overdue cost imperative and collaborative tendency on the DHSS and other departments, but that the problems of co-ordination and liaison are seen as paramount. There are undoubtedly serious practical difficulties associated with the fragmentation of services, but these are certainly not the main problems confronting the clients and potential clients of services. The priority given to the issues of co-ordination and collaboration stems from the bureau-incrementalist service provider's perspective. Joint planning is, at best, joint bureaucracy planning.

It is assumed from this perspective that the only major improvements to social services that are necessary and possible are greater liaison and collaboration. However, co-ordinated planning alone cannot overcome, nor is it intended to, differences in the structure of services and between the professionals working in them; the inadequate coverage of many services; their domination by professional providers; and their lack of accountability to their clients and the wider community. These are not considered to be the main problems within the framework of bureau-incrementalism.

Turning briefly to the deficiencies of the particular machinery of joint care planning, the main problems are the lack of co-terminosity in health and social services boundaries, differences in constitutional and accountability structures, the wide measure of local discretion in the operation of JCCs and JCPTs, the small size of the programme, and the short duration of funding (for detailed accounts see Sargeant, 1979; Booth, 1981; Glennerster et al., 1983).

THE UNDERDEVELOPMENT OF SOCIAL SERVICES PLANNING

This outline of the organizational structure of DHSS planning indicates that, despite the extension of the central planning machinery and reduction in local planning since 1979, it is still bureau-incrementalist in character. In fact, recent changes in the planning machinery have reinforced this limitation.

In the first place, a large proportion of what is apparently considered as planning in the DHSS is not planning at all but monitoring and, to a lesser extent, research. Monitoring is a necessary and important component of strategic planning, but it concentrates on what has happened in the past rather than what should happen in the future (Hambleton, 1982, p. 423). This is not to suggest that policy monitoring in the DHSS is all that far advanced, but rather than the forward planning of services is even less developed. When the House of Commons Social Services Committee slated the DHSS (see the quotation on p. 149), it too was addressing itself to the effectiveness of monitoring rather than planning. At the same time, however, it also criticized the lack of strategic planning (Social Services Committee, 1980, p. xviii):

> rather than deciding upon an overall strategy and then adjusting the various elements of the strategy accordingly, policy is made by taking decisions about specific items (according to whatever criteria may be in use) and then having a retrospective look to see what their combined effect turned out to be.

It is not surprising, therefore, that in describing their strategic role DHSS officials put the word 'planning' in quotation marks (see p. 157 above).

Although a thorough analysis must wait for the publication of more results of the policy strategy unit's work, there is a firm indication that this new unit is even less concerned with detailed monitoring and appraisal of policy than its predecessor. Moreover, it has been removed purposely from a close involvement in planning (Social Services Committee, 1981, p. 73).

Second, planning is limited because it is focused primarily on existing services and their development. In so far as the Department conducts forward planning in relation to need, it takes the form of the *programming* of existing services. This means the forward projection of services in relation to available resources. To a large extent planning begins and ends there, although the procedures for such projection may change considerably from time to time.

There are two components to this programming that underline the bureau-incrementalist nature of DHSS planning. On the one hand, there is the projection of existing services to meet; on the other, needs that have already been recognized in the form of service provision. Unmet needs, and especially unrecognized needs, are not part of this programming, nor are alternative methods of achieving goals. This is less true of the social security side of the Department's planning than of the health and personal social services side, which is dominated by the programme budget. Because it is more closely controlled centrally and does not have powerful professional interest groups competing for different types of service, social security has witnessed more innovation in recent years than the health and personal social services, in the scope of provision if not in the administration of benefits.

The tendency for the DHSS to be insular, backward-looking and conservative is reinforced by the bureaucratic and incrementalist framework within which administration and planning is conducted. An important aspect of this framework is the pervasive ideology concerning the 'convergence' or gradual perfection of state services, discussed in chapter 2. Bureau-incrementalism and convergence go hand in hand. When civil servants firmly believe that the right sort of services exist to meet need, and all that is required is the adjustment of their level or mix, then the kind of fundamental reappraisal of needs and services implied by structural planning would simply not be considered relevant. Furthermore, when this approach is adopted the meaning and scope of planning is, at best, restricted, and perhaps the need for planning at all is called into question.

The institutionalization of incrementalism at the DHSS was clearly expressed by a principal/finance officer, again before the Social Services Committee (1980, p. 32), in answer to the question, How do you arrive at the public expenditure figure for the personal social services?

'Well, I think it is an incremental process essentially because from our knowledge of the services we know how much extra money is required year by year to meet the pressures of demography. . . . We also note the natural phenomenon that medical advances occur spontaneously throughout the service on a continuing basis. If you do not provide something extra as well as the demographic provision then you will slip behind in terms of medical technology so we know that as a matter of experience you have a margin.'

The confidence displayed here in the existing pattern of services is as inescapable as the paternalism hinted at.

Third, the priority given to economic policy, and therefore the susceptibility of social services planning to changes in economic fortune or policy, has contributed to a lack of commitment at the DHSS and in Whitehall generally to strategic planning. As a result, it is cast within relatively narrow bounds and remains *ad hoc*, despite the recent reorganization of the planning machinery. Outside of the programme budget, DHSS strategic planning tends to centre on specific issues rather than attempting to embrace a comprehensive range of departmental functions or client needs (Social Services Committee, 1982, p. xxi). Examples on the social security side are the reviews of disablement benefits and supplementary benefits published in 1974 and 1978, respectively (DHSS, 1974a, 1978a). On the health and personal social services side, there is the recent initiative on community care (DHSS, 1981d). There has been no official attempt to review the effectiveness of all social security provision or all health and personal social services, either separately or in conjunction with each other. There is, in fact, no permanent machinery in the DHSS for planning service provision in relation to need or for searching out new needs.

Social indicators

In the fourth place, the underdevelopment of DHSS planning is demonstrated by the low priority accorded to research and evaluation. The programme budget is officially recognized as an inadequate basis on which to evaluate policy options in detail (DHSS, 1976a, p. 78). Because planning is dominated by the financial requirements of the Treasury, so too are the indicators of service development (A. Walker, 1982b, p. 25). They are recognized by the DHSS as rough-and-ready and concerned only with measuring inputs rather than outputs (Social Services Committee, 1980, p. 32). This absence of social indicators by which to measure social progress is a *symptom* of the domination of economic over social priorities.

The nature and scope of information collected by the DHSS or any other government department is a direct function of its policies and planning role. If its involvement is minimal, then there is little point in collecting information. This is the case with the personal social services, where the barest statistics are collected centrally on the provision of services and an external body – the Chartered Institute of Public Finance and Accountancy (CIPFA) – is left to collate information from local authorities. Where the DHSS is more closely involved in administration and planning, some basic information is essential for it to carry out these functions. A vast amount of statistics are collected, as a matter of course, in the administration of social security and the health service. But the degree of centralization in planning does not alone determine the sort and quality of the statistics collected or the indicators constructed. These rest on a political decision about the scale of need to be met and, in turn, the type of planning to be conducted, whether indicative or imperative, bureau-incremental or structural. Research within the DHSS has been conducted as an adjunct to bureau-incrementalism, rather than critically to assess the *impact* of policy or to illuminate alternative approaches. While this is not surprising there are signs that, increasingly, research commissioned externally by the DHSS is being treated in the same way. Moreover there is a danger that the ESRC will interpret its role narrowly as being to provide answers to policy-makers' problems (see Thomas, 1983).

Social security planning is essentially financial in nature and, as the Department of Health, Education and Welfare (DHEW) in the

United States recognized in 1970, social indicators will not be obtained as a by-product of accounting or administrative routine (DHEW, 1970, p. xxxi). So, for example, the DHSS does not construct or consistently apply any indicators of need, either to existing social security claimants or to the population as a whole, as a basis for its planning. There is no test of the extent to which benefit rates are maintaining their purchasing power. There are no statistics collected by the Department, or previously by the SBC, showing the numbers of people with disabilities receiving supplementary benefit.

As we have seen, the NHS planning system is centralized, with strategic plans and resource distribution being determined by the DHSS. The inadequacy of health indicators reflects this central control and its concern with resources (Hurst, 1977, p. 232; Black Committee, 1980). As the Social Services Committee (1980, p. x) noted, echoing the DHEW report of a decade earlier,

> the kind of information provided in the White Paper and sub-sequent DHSS evidence — setting out the number of patients treated, the number of prescriptions dispensed and so on — is largely meaningless. Such statistics measure activity; they give no indication of impact.

Personal social services planning at the DHSS consists of passing on general indications or guidelines to the local authorities. The abolition of the LAPS system in 1979 demonstrated that central commitment to the strategic planning of the personal social services had weakened still further. As a result, the information available to the DHSS about the level and costs of personal social services provision is very limited and, in the words of the House of Commons Social Services Committee (1982, p. xxxix), 'rather broad-brush'. It concluded: 'It is plain that there are not at present sufficient sophisticated indicators for central Government to make serious assessments of local authority service provision.'

Although the Department has strategic responsibility for the personal social services, by its own admission it has 'no formalised or precisely quantified criteria of what represents minimum acceptable standards of personal social services provision' (Social Service Committee, 1982, p. 72). Nor does it carry out continual monitoring and evaluation studies of the *effectiveness* of services (see for example, Goldberg and Connelly, 1982).

Finally, the limited nature of DHSS planning is signalled by the absence of collaborative planning between the three different sectors of its responsibilities. While there is machinery established for joint planning between local health and personal social services, there is none whatsoever between social security and the health and personal social services. No assessment is made of the impact of changes in policy in one sector on provision in the other. There is no routine basis on which to assess the impact of reductions in personal social services expenditure on the health service.

It might be assumed, for example, that cuts in the personal social services would result in increasing numbers of elderly people being admitted to hospital. But the only available relevant information — per capita expenditure figures for different authorities — does not allow this hypothesis to be tested. Similarly, no assessment is possible in the short run of the link between cuts in personal social services and the take-up of benefits, such as the invalid care allowance.

These deficiencies in basic information about need and service provision would be significant enough on their own, but the fact that they occur within the same department is remarkable. Less surprising, perhaps, but also indicative of the underdevelopment of social services planning, is the absence of co-operation in planning between the DHSS and the Department of Education and Science, the Department of the Environment and the Department of Employment. Because it is department-based, Whitehall bureau-incrementalism encourages this insularity.

The potential for collaboration between the two sides of the DHSS was increased by the introduction of the Cross Sector Policy Review Group and the Policy Strategy Unit. The PSU has conducted studies of both benefits and services for people with disabilities and for poor families with children, and on the interaction of changes in benefits, taxes and charges. Although it is not possible at this stage to evaluate the impact of these bodies, their existence does at least recognize a key problem in social services planning. Yet even if they prove to be a major success, it must be said that the goal of collaboration between different social services in planning is actually very limited. The case for greater co-ordination tends to see that as an end in itself, and therefore overlooks other deficiencies in the planning and operation of services (Myrdal, 1960). Compartmentalization in Whitehall and the competitive quality inherent in the PESC process, however, militate against co-operation in planning and policy-making, and therefore it can be expected to make only limited progress. Meanwhile it tends to divert attention from other deficiencies in social services planning.

CONCLUSION

Planning carried out by the main social policy department of government is of a very rudimentary kind. The permanent planning machinery concentrates on two sorts of activity: monitoring and, to a much greater extent, programming. In fact, 'planning' in the DHSS, as in other government departments, is centred on the public expenditure process. There is very little forward planning of service development in relation to need. There is very little research and evaluation of policies. There is nothing to suggest that the DHSS is exceptional in these respects (see Glennerster, 1975, pp. 144–55). Planning is equally underdeveloped in the other social services.

8

Alternative Social and Economic Planning

INTRODUCTION

It is clear from Part II that social planning is grossly underdeveloped in Britain. In recent years it has regressed still further. The imperative to control social expenditure has overridden the need to plan social development in explicit conjunction with economic development (which itself has been narrowly interpreted).

We shall now turn from the largely theoretical concerns of Part I and the descriptive analysis of Part II, in which prescription was often implicit, to a more explicit discussion of alternatives to bureau-incrementalist policy and planning. How can we plan social development on the basis of a re-integrated, structural social and economic policy? And how can we plan society in the interests of all of its citizens in an open, democratic way? How can we move towards socialist welfare without the monolithic state apparatus associated with state socialism? These are the key questions to which this Part is addressed.

The underdevelopment of social planning has been recognized in Britain and other capitalist societies for a long time (Myrdal, 1960; Townsend, 1967; Abel-Smith, 1967; Miller, 1975). Various proposals have been made to improve the operation and status of social planning, and the purpose of this chapter is to review some of the main ones. Because structural social planning in a capitalist society is likely to be socialist in its objectives, the main political party of the Left, the Labour Party, is in a particularly important position with regard to the planning of alternatives to capitalist relations. Therefore I examine Labour's planning in Opposition. Since the election of the Conservative government in 1979, much of the energy of the broader labour movement has been directed towards the construction of an Alternative Economic

Strategy (AES), and it is important to assess its relevance for structural social planning. Finally, I outline the lessons that can be gained from the experience of planning in state socialist societies and Third World countries. First of all, though, Why do we need to establish structural social planning as the pre-eminent form of planning in Britain and other capitalist societies?

THE CASE FOR STRUCTURAL SOCIAL PLANNING

Three main factors underpin the case for structural social planning or, by implication in Britain, socialist social planning. A simple stock-taking of the key elements of planning outlined in Part II identifies these factors. Social planning is fragmented, bureau-incremental, centralized, elitist and undemocratic. As a result, it is unrepresentative of and unresponsive to the needs of citizens.

In the first place, then, *structural social planning is required in order to plan social development according to need*. It is a necessary vehicle for the achievement of socialist welfare. Structural social policy opens the door for a reintegration of social need and economic policy in order to create a more equal distribution of resources, status and power. Structural social planning is the necessary accompaniment of structural social policy. Both are intended to overcome economic hegemony in the policy process and thereby to enable social needs and priorities to be established as the basis for production and distribution.

Policies geared towards a radical change in the distribution of resources and power must be strategically planned, debated and subsequently revised if they are to be realized in a democratic way. This much is obvious from the previous account of the theory and practice of policy and planning. It cannot be assumed that planning by itself will result in redistribution according to social priorities. If policy-makers assume that planning in itself will create a more equal distribution of resources, without establishing a framework within which to secure that goal, then at best no significant change is likely to occur as a consequence of their activities (Townsend and Bosanquet, 1972; Miller, 1975). There is a bias not only in the capitalist system itself against redistribution and structural change, but also among professional planners, who are usually either economists in the orthodox neoclassical mould or subject to the constraints of the narrowest form of economic thought.

As Miller (1975) points out, 'Issues of equality and quality have to be imposed on the economic intellectual apparatus; they do not flow out of the current instruments of economic analysis.' This is crucial because it indicates that there is a powerful ideology dominating social planning, which effectively excludes from the political agenda major changes in distribution and redistribution. It is not that they are evaluated and rejected as impractical, but that they are never considered in the first place (see p. 21).

Structural social planning provides a framework within which to counteract the systematic historical and institutionalized bias against equality and to enable the reconstitution of national priorities. Thus, it is important to re-establish social goals alongside economic goals. At the moment, according to Townsend (1975, p. 55),

> precedence is given to the wrong values. If national progress were measured more against social objectives like the removal of poverty, the establishment of an effective system of civil rights and the integration of racial groups, instead of the rate of economic growth, different priorities for political action would be produced.

The establishment of explicit social goals and priorities will also encourage frequent assessment of performance in relation to objectives. This requires the introduction not only of a new scale of values but also of new planning machinery. These, then, are some of the elements involved in planning social development in relation to need.

Second, *structural social planning is required to overcome the present fragmentation of planning*. In particular, there are artificial divisions between social, economic and environmental or physical planning, and between planning in the 'public' and 'private' sectors. Planning is fragmented too, within the public sector. The administrative division of planning, particularly within the state, creates enormous practical difficulties for the clients of the welfare state. The obvious examples are the creation of the poverty, unemployment and invalidity traps through the interaction of the benefit and tax systems (Bradshaw, 1982, pp. 106–7; A. Walker, 1982c). All of these divisions are stultifying to the planning of social development according to need, which requires a comprehensive assessment of resources, needs and priorities.

There is a need for planning that encompasses all aspects of social and economic development in all sectors of society. It is not simply that separate developments need to be co-ordinated. Co-ordination may be achieved within the perspective of bureau-incrementalist planning. The different administrative sectors of planning may be linked, but this would not add up to a coherent overall social strategy. What is required, instead, is the *integration* of planning in different sectors, particularly between the public and private sectors. Now, this provides difficulty in establishing commonly acceptable criteria, and this problem cannot be ignored. But questions of number, scope and intensity of coverage can greatly reduce potential conflict.

The third important factor in the case for structural social planning is the need to democratize the planning process. Social priorities are implicit in the distribution of public expenditure, but they are rarely debated openly (A. Walker, 1982b). Once national priorities are made more explicit, as they would have to be within the framework of democratic structural social planning, their discussion will be encouraged, as will debate on the direction of social development. (This is not to suggest that more formal methods of facilitating participation in decision-making are not also required.)

If priorities were debated openly, it would help to undermine the economic domination of social planning, through the exposure of the narrow assumptions implicit in this order of precedence. It would, for example, question the public burden model of social welfare expenditure, and begin to reveal the social basis of the division between different systems of distribution in the public and private sectors. The democratic participation of citizens in local and national planning might also have the effect of restoring stability and cohesion in social life (Townsend, 1975; and see chapter 9). When they are excluded from participating in the formulation and application of policy, people are, rightly, more apt to feel that rules are being imposed on them (Myrdal, 1960, pp. 63–4).

It is important to democratize planning in order to diffuse power in the planning process. Citizens, and especially the clients of welfare services, must play an important part in the planning and development of services if they are to be more responsive to their needs. The crucial question here is, Who plans? At the present social planning is dominated by bureaucrats, professionals and 'bureau-professionals' (Parry, et al., 1979). Although there is a strong case for professional autonomy in social services (Hill, 1982), professional groups have been more concerned to secure improvements in their own freedom and status than to further the interests of their clients (Wilding, 1982). Unfortunately, what social planning apparatus there has been has tended to reinforce bureaucratic and professional power rather than form a bulwark against it. The growth of corporatism has, in turn, strengthened some aspects of professional power and further weakened the position of those in need.

COMPREHENSIVE SOCIAL PLANNING

It is a reflection of the underdevelopment of social planning in this country that there have been so few radical alternatives proposed to Treasury-dominated bureau-incrementalism. The most important proposal was made, more than 15 years ago, by Peter Townsend in his damning critique of social planning in Britain, 'The Need for a Social Plan' (1967, p. 56):

> Most social planning in Britain is narrowly departmental; it is conceived within administrative and not functional boundaries. Rarely is the risk taken to spell out its logic to the general public, on grounds either that this might reveal administrative ignorance and ineptitude or encourage criticism of central thinking and action.

As one way towards the reconstitution of social planning, Townsend suggested the creation of a Department of Social Planning. This would be 'not so much a co-ordinating instrument as a long-term planning instrument and a source of information about the social programmes of the Government and the local authorities' (Townsend, 1975, p. 62). Its functions would be to provide information on the distribution of resources, the level of services in different areas and so on; to review standards of deprivation; to prepare five-year and ten-year plans which would co-ordinate the activities of different departments; and to provide a forum for the discussion of national priorities.

This is the most important proposal yet to establish a more comprehensive form of social planning, although it was not developed in detail. It would be a considerable advance on the present absence of concerted social planning. Having said that, however, comprehensive social planning that co-ordinates the activities of the state and assesses national priorities is not structural social planning. This proposal is best viewed, therefore, as a first step along the road from bureau-incrementalism to structural planning. It is intended to initiate a debate about social priorities, out of which would come alternative forms of policy and planning.

While comprehensive social planning would represent a significant step towards planning for need, there are two main reasons why it must go further eventually if that goal is to be achieved.

In the first place, it cannot be assumed that the provision of information about inequalities in the distribution of resources and about the shortcomings of social policy would, on its own, create sufficient pressure for changes in policy. Information is a crucial aspect of planning: 'If needs are to be met they must first be perceived' (Townsend, 1967, p. 62). But it is optimistic to assume that it would have the desired impact on the social structure without major alterations in the institutional *response* to information. The scope and nature of the information generated by the state is a function of its decided policy role in relation to need, rather than information determining policy and planning. The institutions within which planning is conducted, and the sort of statistics they generate, are based on assumptions about the relative importance of different groups of people and economic and social activities. For example, roles within industrial production are valued in the national accounts, whereas those of 'housewife' or grandparent are not. Then there is the framework set by prevailing theories. Economic orthodoxy exerts a dominant influence over planning institutions (Myrdal, 1970, p. 53). Thus social statistics are a *reflection*, rather than a cause, of the absence of structural social planning in this country.

Second, a Department of Social Planning, even if it had solid political support, would by itself reinforce the central bureaucratic control of social planning. It cannot be assumed, in the light of the previous discussion of bureaucratic power in the planning process, that a simple departmental shift of focus would facilitate *structural* change. What is required is planning machinery that would counterbalance the centralist tendencies in comprehensive planning with a measure of local independence, as well as direct channels of local representation and participation.

The traditional department—minister framework is not sufficient to ensure structural social planning. There are good reasons to suggest that, unless an alternative institutional framework can be established, it will not be possible to superimpose radical planning machinery on the existing Treasury-dominated system. More importantly, it will not be possible to counteract economic hegemony and to establish democratic participation. Two examples can be quoted by way of illustrating the difficulties.

The Department of Economic Affairs

Following the election of the Labour government in 1964, the Department of Economic Affairs was established with the intention of co-ordinating economic policies (see p. 106). The DEA was specifically intended to act as a counterweight to the Treasury and thereby to wrest economic policy from orthodox financial control. However, despite a great deal of activity, including the production of the National Plan (DEA, 1965) within a year, the DEA never established itself as a significant force. The Treasury maintained control over short-term demand management and used this power to direct the response to the foreign exchange crisis of mid-1966, a response that destroyed the National Plan and also the DEA as a planning ministry (Opie, 1972, p. 177).

There were serious deficiencies in the National Plan and the DEA (chapter 5). Moreover, the new department was not given sufficient control over functions traditionally performed by the Treasury that were supposed to be transferred to it. The National Plan did not establish social priorities in any detail, and actually proposed relative reductions in the living standards of social security claimants (Townsend, 1967, p. 57). But the point is that, if this relatively modest attempt to establish an alternative power base in the central planning machinery failed, there can be little confidence in the long-term success of a similar, albeit far more radical, venture, unless a number of basic structural conditions for success are met.

The Central Policy Review Staff

The Central Policy Review Staff (CPRS), or government 'Think Tank', which was established in October 1970, owed much to the idea of a Department of Social Planning aimed at more comprehensive planning, but it was a much more limited initiative. It was created to improve policy analysis and decision-making at the centre and to give the Prime Minister some independence of the Treasury (Heclo and Wildavsky,

1974, pp. 266–8). But it was never intended to produce comprehensive social plans. It resulted, in part, from the reaction among Labour ministers to the Treasury domination of economic policy during and following the devaluation crisis of 1967, and also from discussions conducted within the Conservative Opposition. The four main aims of the CPRS, set out in 1970, were (1) to assist ministers in working out the policy implications of their strategy; (2) to establish relative priorities; (3) to identify new directions or choices in policy and (4) to ensure that the implications of alternative courses of action are fully analysed and considered (Teasury, 1970).

Here was the basis, then, for a shift in the Whitehall machinery towards long-term strategic planning. But the CPRS was not able to perform this role; in Heclo and Wildavsky's (1974, p. 308) terms, it never succeeded in 'rocking the boat'. A number of interesting and relatively independent reports were published (see for example, CPRS, 1975), but the programme was fitful and eclectic. Its role was ill-defined, it was detached from the Treasury machinery of economic and social planning, and it had too little time for deliberation. Like the DEA before it, the CPRS was imposed on an existing Treasury-dominated civil service machinery. Without direct ministerial responsibility, and without a power base in the central administration, its role was confined to reminding politicians about issues they would rather not consider. 'They want attractive issues for next time and not necessarily those that might go on at a later date' (Heclo and Wildavsky, 1974, p. 338). In other words, the CPRS was powerless to affect bureau-incrementalism along the lines suggested by the 1970 White Paper. It was abolished in 1983, following the re-election of the Conservative government.

SOCIAL INDICATORS AND SOCIAL ACCOUNTING

The success of economists in influencing government policy, and the domination of economic indicators in policy-making, led social scientists in the 1960s to believe that the construction of analogous social indicators might be just as effective in directing social policy (Carley, 1981, p. 17). The 'social indicators movement' (Duncan, 1969) was strongest in the United States, although the UK's *Social Trends* was one of the first to appear, in 1970. By the end of the decade 30 countries had issued social reports (Carley, 1981, p. 19).

The term 'social indicator' was defined by the US Department of Health, Education, and Welfare (DHEW, 1970, p. 971) as a

statistic of direct normative interest which facilitates concise, comprehensive and balanced judgement about the condition of major aspects of a society. It is, in all cases, a direct measure of welfare and is subject to the interpretation that if it changes in the 'right' direction, while other things remain equal, things have gotten better, or people are better off. Thus, statistics on the numbers of doctors or policemen could not be social indicators, whereas figures on health or crime rates could be.

Although this definition has been criticized subsequently (see Carley, 1981, pp. 23–5), it is sufficient to underline the concern of social indicators, as opposed to social statistics, with normative measurement and outputs rather than with inputs. Related to social indicators are 'social accounting' – statistical accounts of the social welfare of a country, or part of it, which therefore complement economic accounts – and 'social reporting' – descriptions of the social state of the nation based on qualitative and quantitative measures.

In the United States, where planning is even more discredited than in Britain, there was a great deal of pressure in the 1960s in favour of the production of social indicators and an annual social report. The call was for social accounting in direct parallel to economic accounting (Mondale, 1967, p. 29):

The valuable lessons learned over the past two decades regarding economic indicators suggests that, if we had more and better data on social conditions, and if these could be molded into a coherent system of social indicators comparable to their economic counterparts, we would be able to do a far better job of decision-making regarding social progress.

In 1967 Senator Mondale introduced the Full Opportunity and Social Accounting Act, requiring, among other things, the submission of an annual social report. The Act was re-introduced in 1969, but again was not passed.

Although an interesting development, the call for social indicators suffered several deficiencies, which suggests that, had it been successful, it would not have challenged the traditional definitions of economic accounting that continue to dominate national policy-making and planning in the United States as much as in this country.

First, the coalition of interests that led the pressure were predominantly social scientists, and, not surprisingly, they were concerned primarily with the generation of statistics and information. A comparison was made, rightly, with the development of economic statistics and the power of professional economists, but it was mistakenly believed that the production of more and better information was sufficient to create, directly or indirectly, alternative plans, or even backdoor socialism (Kopkind, 1967). This was a plea for better social indicators and social research methods rather than for better planning machinery. Moreover, although a powerful critique of economic indicators as tools for social policy was constructed, this did not include criticism of those same indicators as a poor basis for economic policy (Bell, 1969, p. 73). So the intention was to establish social indicators and social accounting alongside economic accounting, and not to supercede economic policy with social policy in the planning process. For example, according to one of the leading actors in the pressure for social indicators, they are 'a logical extension of PPBS and other forms of operations and systems analysis' (Olson, 1969, p. 93).

Second, there was a tension in determining the relevant scope of social accounts and reports between the evaluation of *government* programmes and the broader measurement of *societal* changes (Bell, 1969, p. 82). This tension was not resolved. Moreover, when it is coupled with the third deficiency, namely the centralized, bureaucratic nature of this initiative, its limitations are even more clearly exposed. The construction of social statistics is a specialized, not to say professionalized, task. Senator Mondale's proposal to establish an expert Council of Social Advisers to supervise the production of the annual social report underlines the fact that this was to be a highly specialized and centralized development. Indeed, one of the chief criticisms of the proposed Council was that there were too few competent macro-sociologists to staff it! (Bell, 1969, p. 83). It was recognized too that the Council would not have much of a constituency. Social indicators and social reporting were seen as a substitute for democratic participation in planning. Participation was to be provided by social survey and research.

In view of the longstanding failure of officially sponsored research and officially sponsored professions to provide a critical commentary on state activity and policy (see p. 24), there can be little confidence that either the required social statistics or the necessary subsequent action would have emerged from this framework.

Without institutional changes in planning and the planning machinery, therefore, and these comprise the fourth deficiency, there is little chance that social statistics and social research will result in the required policy response. The pressure for social indicators was not concerned with the institutional framework within which planning is conducted. Social indicators, although important, are only one aspect of planning.

Although limited in the ways outlined, the idea of a social report was an important contribution to the planning debate. As Olson (1969, p. 97) has pointed out, 'If future social reports could do nothing more than increase the orderliness of thought, and the quality of debate, about our urgent social problems, they would still be worth doing.' Unfortunately, the proposal was not extended into a more comprehensive social planning machinery and was not even pursued in its limited form. Like the idea for a Department of Social Planning, this important initiative would be flawed as an end in itself. In particular, there is assumption about the simple causal relationship between information and change, and its failure to develop an institutional framework through which to supercede, and not simply match, narrow economic considerations with social ones (for a full account of social indicators see Carley, 1981).

Social audit

In Britain there was a similar reaction to the American one against the deficiencies of narrow economic accounting; in the early 1970s this created pressure for the preparation of social audits. Although more limited than its US counterpart, the British initiative stems more directly from the consumer movement; both have similar historical origins. However, being based on an 'ardent support for consumerism' (Social Audit, 1973, p. 3), the British experiment is potentially more democratic and participative than the more elitist social indicators pressure group in the United States. 'It will be one of our objectives to illustrate the feasibility of progress towards the day when reasonable safeguards for economic democracy will be embodied in law, and social audits universal' (Social Audit, 1973, p. 3). The two are similar, also, to the extent that they are both based on an analogy with economic accounting. But, whereas social indicators are concerned usually with overall national well-being, social audit is more narrowly confined to examining the consequences of corporate activity (Medawar, 1978, 1980).

In recent years, the academic critique of the absence of social statistics by which to assess social progress has been enjoined by parliamentary pressure, especially through the House of Commons Social Services Committee. It has criticized the main spending department, the DHSS, for having no strategic planning and no comprehensive information system by which to assess the effects of changes in expenditure levels and patterns on the quality and scope of services provided (Social Services Committee, 1980, p. xviii; see also DHSS, 1980a).

There is definitely a need for social indicators and social statistics that are constructed independently of administrative processes. It is unlikely, though, that these alternative statistics will be derived officially until the social planning machinery has been transformed (A. Walker, 1982b). This, in a nutshell, is the primary weakness of the approach that calls for social statistics without at the same time arguing for more fundamental changes in policy-making and planning. It puts the cart before the horse.

PLANNING AND THE LABOUR PARTY

Because structural social policy and planning under capitalism are likely to be socialist in objectives and methods, it is to the Labour Party and the labour movement that we should turn for alternatives to current practice. Yet, as we saw in chapters 3 and 6, the Labour Party flirted with, and quickly abandoned, concerted economic planning in 1966, and a decade later began the transition to the cash-based planning of public expenditure that eventually buried social planning. Since 1979 the Labour Party has been in turmoil, largely because of what was seen by the Left as the desertion by the Wilson and Callaghan governments of socialist policies agreed at party conferences, and their determination to ensure that those experiences are not repeated. This is another expression of differences over a fundamental question that is as old as the Party itself: 'namely, whether the Labour Party is to be concerned with attempts at a more efficient and more humane administration of a capitalist society; or whether it is to adapt to the task of creating a socialist one' (Miliband, 1972, p. 344).

I am not concerned here with assessing either the history of policy-making in the Labour Party or the record of previous Labour governments (see Abel-Smith, 1967; Townsend and Bosanquet, 1975; Bosanquet and Townsend, 1980). Attention is directed instead at the results of the re-thinking process since 1979. How far do Labour's policies contain elements of structural social planning? If the policies were implemented, would they begin the planned transition to socialism?

The answer to both questions is No. The Labour Party's (1983) programme of action 'to save British industry and rebuild the welfare state' did not represent a radical departure from previous plans. At the heart of the programme was Keynesian-style reflation aimed at economic growth (Labour Party, 1983, p. 8):

> Our programme is . . . heavily dependent upon the achievement of our basic objectives: namely, a large and sustained increase in the nation's output and income and a matching decline in the numbers out of work. It is this that will make the resources available for higher public spending programmes.

Neither the social objectives nor the assumption of growth were spelt out. This perpetuated the myth that there is competition between economic and social objectives, and hence the 'public burden' assumption that social objectives depend on economic policies (see p. 28). The plans were overwhelmingly bureau-incremental — concerned with small-scale reforms in welfare state benefits and services, such as the restoration of Conservative cuts and the ending of some of the more glaring anomalies, including the failure to pay the long-term rate of supplementary benefit to the unemployed after one year.

Another example of the bureau-incrementalism of Labour's plans is the mistaken belief that the existing benefit and tax systems could be made to operate 'fairly' as between the sexes. But the establishment of real equality would require a more radical restructuring, including a move away from the allocation of benefits and reliefs based on the family unit, a recognition of conflict within the family, and an end to the present domestic division of labour (Rights of Women, 1982).

Finally, the proposals were concerned with central planning and a return to the corporatism which underscored the 1965 National Plan. A Department of Economic and Industrial Planning would have been created and a 'national economic assessment' worked out between the trade unions and government. The two proposals for participative planning — workplace planning agreements and land use planning — were not matched by public participation in social services planning or management.

Policy-making in the Labour Party remains elitist and centralized. It is based on Westminster and is, at best, corporatist rather than democratic. Fabian centralism is still the dominant strand in thinking about social policy within the Party (Kerr, 1981), and is reinforced by the corporatist approach of the trade unions. This encourages the belief that it is only a matter of Labour politicians getting into power for the ship of state to be steered in the required direction. The lack of detailed planning and preparation in Opposition that this self-confidence and absence of democratic accountability fosters creates two problems. On the one hand, there is no concerted social strategy prepared in Opposition. This makes difficult the displacement of economistic Treasury values once in office. On the other hand, when Labour gets into power it is unprepared for a war of attrition with the bureau-incrementalism of the civil service (see for example, Barnett, 1982, p. 59). So, it is not simply that the civil service will subvert the radical intentions of Labour ministers, as they usually claim: the dice are loaded by attitudes and decisions taken by the Party in Opposition. (For a fuller account of Labour's planning see A. Walker, 1983.)

THE ALTERNATIVE ECONOMIC STRATEGY

The case for structural social planning is based not only on the inadequacies in the practice of social services planning, but also on the inadequacies of economic planning. It was pointed out in chapters 3 and 7 that economic planning has been as narrowly constructed as social planning in recent years by financial accounting. When this is translated into the economic planning machinery, as we saw in the last section, its overriding concern is with financial control, and planning is effectively replaced by economic forecasting. Together with the mystification of economic planning has been the reduction in the influence of Parliament over economic affairs (Coombes and Walkland, 1980; Committee of Public Accounts, 1981).

These inadequacies, coupled with the failure of previous attempts at economic planning by Labour governments (see p. 105), the adoption of restrictive monetarist policies from 1975/6 and the eventual breakdown of corporate relations between the Labour government and trade unions in 1979 with the 'winter of discontent', led to discussions within the broader labour movement about alternative forms of policy and planning. This activity was galvanized by the Conservative propaganda claim that 'there is no alternative' to their policies (Sharples, 1981, p. 71). Thus the policies that emerged from the labour movement were known collectively as the 'alternative economic strategy' (AES).

In fact, the AES is a broad consensus on economic policy, the basic elements of which are (London CSE Group, 1980, p. 6):

(1)   a policy for expansion aimed at restoring full employment and raising living standards, based on a planned reflation of the economy primarily through increases in public spending;

(2)   planned controls on foreign trade and international capital movements to protect the balance of payments and prevent the flight of capital;

(3)   an industrial strategy based on extended public ownership (including financial institutions), and planning at the level of the firm through planning agreements tied to an extensive network of industrial democracy;

(4)   a national economic plan co-ordinating macroeconomic policies with industrial planning;

(5)   control of inflation based on price control.

Beyond this broad outline, however, there is no clear agreement on the precise structure of the| AES (Rowthorn, 1981, p. 4). For example, some variants include a wealth tax (Communist Party, 1978; Glyn and Harrison, 1980, p. 149); others do not (TUC, 1982).

The AES is underpinned by a policy for planned economic expansion or 'structural reflation', intended in the first place to bring unused resources into production and to achieve full employment, and, second, to use resources more efficiently. Furthermore, it addresses the question of what is produced and for what purpose. But these questions of quality are left until the second stage (London CSE Group, 1980, p. 36).

The AES is not simply a policy of reflation. Expansion is coupled with import controls, industrial planning and price controls to avoid balance of payments crises, 'supply bottlenecks' and inflation. Thus, planning is a central feature of the AES, in economic expansion, industrial democracy and trade. The AES also addressed the integration of

British capitalism in the world economy and the crucial role of multi-national companies in determining its economic fortune (although its response has been criticized as nationalistic – Cripps, 1981, p. 93).

At the heart of the AES is an industrial strategy aimed at the regeneration of industry (London CSE Group, 1980, p. 61). It is concerned primarily with economic and particularly industrial planning in order to ensure, first, that economic expansion takes place; second, that production responds to an expansion of demand; third, that the long-term structural decline of British industry is arrested; and fourth, that the long-term development of industry in the face of declining oil production and new technology is controlled. These aims would be achieved by means of planning agreements, public ownership, national economic planning and control of the financial system (London CSE Group, 1980, pp. 65–6).

Planning agreements would be negotiated between the largest companies, the government and the trade unions. They would be backed by sanctions, such as making the provision of public finance and tax relief conditional on their completion. Public ownership would be extended to 'key firms' in each sector of manufacturing industry, whose role would be to act as an example 'to guide the level of investment of other firms in the sector' (London CSE Group, 1980, p. 66). Industrial planning would be co-ordinated by a National Planning Commission. The financial system would be controlled by public ownership and the 'channelling of institutional funds'.

An inadequate basis for structural social planning

On paper, the AES is clearly a more radical and comprehensive economic strategy than has been applied hitherto in this country outside of wartime. But it does not provide a basis for structural social planning. Because of the variety of alternative economic strategies this statement is necessarily a generalization. But their common core does not, in fact, propose a radical structural change in economic relations. This is obvious in the weaker Keynesian versions, which concentrate on demand management and regulation (see for example, TUC, 1982). Even the more radical variants, however, do not address the fundamental question of the continued private ownership and control of the means of production, and therefore of the potential conflict between planning and profit: 'advocates of the planning-agreement system are badly mistaken in believing that capital would act against its own interests to fit in with a plan devised to protect those of workers' (Glyn and Harrison, 1980, p. 158).

While capital, and especially multinational capital, controls the means of production, it is impossible for the AES to secure both full employment in the short term and longer-term economic success. The Liberal Beveridge (1944, p. 23) was prepared to go this far in the interests of full employment:

> Whether private ownership of means of production to be operated by others is a good economic device or not, it must be judged as a device. It is not an essential citizen liberty in Britain, because it is not and never has been enjoyed by more than a very small proportion of the British people. . . . On the view taken in this Report, full employment is in fact attainable while leaving the conduct of industry in the main to private enterprise . . . . But if, contrary to this view, it should be shown by experience or by agreement that abolition of private property in the means of production was necessary for full employment, this abolition would have to be undertaken.

Second, the AES is concerned primarily with industrial policy and planning and does not encompass an explicit social strategy (A. Walker, 1982e). The fact that economic goals are thereby assumed to have primacy over social goals is yet another demonstration of the breadth of the influence of economic hegemony. It is assumed by proponents of the AES that economic policy and social policy, and in turn economic relations and social relations, are independent. It is, to recap the argument in chapter 3, economic policy that generates resources and social policy that distributes them.

Incidentally, this argument can be applied with equal force to those who have called for a social counterpart to the AES (see for example, Aaronovitch, 1981b, p. 111; Meacher, 1982), since to do so is to accept the orthodox division between economic and social policy. Given this acceptance, it is difficult then to mount a sustained argument against the preferential treatment of the former over the latter, and to counter the assumption that the private sector is productive and the public sector is unproductive (London CSE Group, 1980, p. 70).

In fact, the AES embodies the same 'public burden' model of welfare as orthodox economics (Hall, 1983, p. 92). Public spending on social services occupies a subsidiary position to its role in boosting demand and industrial regeneration. So emphasis is placed on capital spending rather than on current spending. Social spending is seen primarily as an economic tool and public services are viewed, negatively, as 'a problem of financing' (Hall, 1983, p. 96).

An example helps to illustrate the inadequacy of the AES as a basis for structural social planning. Because of its narrow concentration on the economic relations of production, the AES is apt to ignore the social relations embodied in or arising out of economic relations. This reinforces the orthodox definition of production and employment. So the often unpaid role of women in production, through the provision of care for children and male workers, is ignored (Coote, 1981). This male orientation is mirrored in development planning (see p. 214) and derives from the same orthodox economic categories of productive and unproductive labour. The contribution of other groups excluded from access to industrial production – the elderly and people with disabilities – is also undervalued. Moreover, concern for these groups cannot simply be tacked on to the AES in the form of social policy, because an approach based on social need implies a fundamentally different pattern of priorities and relations. It might, for example, tackle the division of labour and resources between men and women or waged and unwaged, and reorganize work roles, as well as altering the relationship between labour and capital.

Third, the AES relies heavily on centralized and bureaucratic planning. Like the political economy approach to social policy discussed in chapter 2, it over-emphasizes the role of the central state. The extension of workers' control and the negotiation of planning agreements are important mechanisms for promoting organized working-class power and democratic control in private industry. But there is no comparable mechanism for initiating democratic control over public institutions in both the industrial and social welfare fields. The TUC–Labour Party Liaison Committee (1982, p. 15) proposals, which were embodied in the 1983 Labour Party plans, envisage the continuance of financial control by the Treasury. The National Economic Assessment would take over the Treasury's economic forecasting role, but would leave the Treasury in control of public spending. Most of the central features of the AES – import controls, price controls and nationalization – may in fact strengthen state bureaucracy and inhibit democratization.

It is, then, another proposal for planning from above, 'and schemes for popular involvement remain just an embellishment on what remains primarily a programme for greater state control of the economy' (Rowthorn, 1981, p. 7). This effectively excludes people from contributing to decisions about the economic and social prorities embodied in the strategy. So the AES is likely to encounter the same kind of antipathy that the current institutions of economic and social planning attract.

Finally, related to this concentration on the state bureaucracy is a confusion about the form and purpose of planning. It is not clear, for example, whether the AES is proposing macro-planning or targeting, indicative planning or direct control. The AES is centred on planning agreements (London CSE Group, 1980; p. 71; Devine, 1981, p. 114) but it is difficult to see how these can work without the power of central direction. The analogy with the corporate planning techniques of private companies (Glyn and Harrison, 1980, p. 166) underlines the point that central control and direction is a necessary feature of this approach. Also, the experience of the worker's plans in the Lucas and Vickers companies suggests that democratic planning alone cannot develop on the basis of enthusiasm and innovative ideas (Beynon and Wainwright, 1979). At the macro-level the introduction of a special Cabinet Committee, Department of Planning (Aaronovitch, 1981, p. 69) or a National Planning Commission (Devine, 1981, p. 117) has been suggested. There is no indication of how broader social development might be planned.

The AES is concerned primarily with industrial planning. It derives more from the experience of industrial relations and workers' plans than from the more elitist social indicators or consumerist social audit approaches. Although it is in many respects a radical departure from economic orthodoxy, it does not provide a basis for structural social planning because it is narrowly directed towards industrial regeneration — an important goal, but one that falls far short of the structural change necessary to set in motion a socialist transition.

PLANNING IN STATE SOCIALIST SOCIETIES

Structural social planning is a normative concept in Western capitalist societies, but do state socialist societies furnish any examples of such planning in practice? Planning is more developed and entrenched in these countries than anywhere else. Indeed, the 'aversion' to planning in Western societies (Myrdal, 1960, p. 53) is related to the close association between planning and state socialism. Just as capitalist societies have similarities in their approach to planning, so too do state socialist societies.

The common features of planning in all of these countries are the use of state ownership of the means of production, national economic planning and political dictatorship as the chief means of mobilizing national resources to achieve economic objectives. 'These normally include rapid economic growth and in particular rapid industrialization, an egalitarian income distribution, and the development of the armed forces' (Ellman, 1979, p. 15). There are both positive and negative lessons to be learned from the experience of Soviet-type countries for planning the transition from capitalism to socialism.

Economic planning in state socialist countries is concerned not simply with production but also with ownership and distribution. Alternative economic strategies in Britain have concentrated on planning production and to a lesser extent on ownership, but have given hardly any thought to distribution (see for example, TUC, 1982; London CSE Group, 1980). Under state socialism production occupies a central role, the whole national economy is based on the production of material by labour. Therefore 'it is a basic principle of socialist planning that the only source of the national income is labour in the productive sphere' (Ellman, 1979, p. 16). The similarity between this and the position of the right-wing economists Bacon and Eltis (1976) is inescapable. Although the two are based on widely different reasoning, they suffer from the same deficiencies in making an artificial separation between productive and unproductive forms of employment based on a narrow concept of material production, and in giving precedence to growth in the former.

Planning in Comecon countries, particularly in the USSR, is imperative. In Stalin's words, 'our plans are not forecasts but instructions' (quoted in Ellman, 1979, p. 17). This form of planning was contrasted earlier with the indicative planning that is more characteristic of capitalist countries.

Clearly, imperative planning in itself is not undesirable; it depends on how the plans are constructed and managed. Unfortunately, in state socialist societies planning consists primarily of instructions from above. There is a part for 'feedback' from the periphery in the planning process, but this is largely an administrative process and there is little active participation by citizens in the formation of plans.

Planning is highly centralized and oppressively bureaucratic. For example, in the USSR the State Planning Commission (Gosplan) works out production plans and sends them on to the relevant departments for execution. There is a wide range of central organizations including those for planning the distribution of commodities (the State Committee on Material-Technical Supplies, Gossnal) and for determining prices (the State Committee on Prices). Draft plans are constructed on the basis of a complicated and long-winded process of planning and counter-planning which takes place within both the administrative hierarchy and the party (for an excellent description of this process see Ellman, 1979, pp. 16—29).

Social and economic policies are supposed to be integrated in state socialist countries, but again they are highly centralized and geared primarily to the needs of production, for example through the control of wages and consumption. The principle of distribution according to need has not been consistently pursued in these countries. Moreover, the definition of need adopted for minority groups is often very low (Lane, 1982, pp. 55, 59), and socialist social policies have not been more vertically redistributive than have capitalist ones (George and Manning, 1981, p. 172). Inequalities based on nationality and sex also persist (Lane, 1982, pp. 54—103).

On the positive side, once plans are constructed in the Soviet-type system of imperative planning, they are concrete and not simply targets, with a clear allocation of responsibilities for carrying them out. Moreover, the planning process is an endless one; it is an integral part of the economic system, being based on a series of one-year and the basic five-year plans. The major 'problem' of socialist planning is usually taken to be the slower pace of work and lower level of effort than in capitalist societies (not reflected in the health and safety record of Soviet production — see Ellman, 1979, p. 157). But this may be a positive advantage for a socialist employment policy in facilitating the promotion of full employment.

Chinese variations on the Comecon and especially the USSR model are more democratic, at least in the Western sense, in rejecting the highly technical and over-bureaucratic organization of planning and attempting to get more feedback from citizens. 'Leaders do not reach decisions simply by studying incoming statistics, reports and computer printouts. They go out into the field to collect information by personal observation' (Ellman, 1979, p. 30). The planning machinery too is less elaborate; plans are less detailed than their Soviet counterparts and are not even published. China also operates a more decentralized planning system than the USSR, though this does not necessarily mean that it is actually democratic (a point I return to in chapter 9).

While decision-making is devolved to some extent in Soviet planning, to local farmers and factory managers for example, the Chinese have devolved decision-making to local authorities, via the political process. Finally, in China there are a large number of small enterprises wholly outside of the national planning system.

In sum, planning in the Comecon countries is highly centralized, rigidly bureaucratic and closely associated with industrial production. It is not structural; that is, it is not seeking to transform social and economic relations, but is primarily an economic tool used to support the status quo. Despite the undoubted importance of planning in state socialist societies, in all of them both planning and the market co-exist.

The underdevelopment of social planning under state socialism

Why is it that planning has remained so restricted, and in particular that social planning has remained so underdeveloped, in these countries? The answers to this question have important implications for the planning of socialist alternative economic strategies in advanced capitalist societies.

In the first place, planning in state socialist societies is an adjunct to the ideologies of Marxism—Leninism, or in the case of China Marxism—Leninism—Mao Tse-tung; and these may be described as the 'ideologies of state-directed industrialisation in backward countries' (Ellman, 1979, p. 274). Like liberalism in Victorian Britain, which provided a motivating force for industrial advance through capitalism, Marxism—Leninism emphasized rapid industrialization and military expansion. Economic liberalism succeeded in its immediate industrial aims at the cost of gross deprivation, huge inequalities, absence of democracy and imperialism. Marxism—Leninism achieved rapid industrialization, but at the expense of democracy, political freedom, national independence in satellite countries, centralized bureaucracy and a hierarchical socio-political system. Planning systems in state socialist countries have reflected these key structural features, and particularly the autocratic tradition in the USSR that was reinforced by Marxism—Leninism.

Second, it has been assumed in state socialist countries that, once revolution had changed basic economic and social relations, particularly ownership of the means of production, then socialist society was well on the way to being achieved (Ferge, 1979, p. 307). Structural social change was expected to follow from a revolution in economic relations. Hence planning concentrated on maintaining post-revolutionary society rather than transforming it. The assumption that a new socialist way of life would simply follow from a change in the relations of production was based, as Ferge (1979, p. 307) points out, on a simplified conception of the relationship between material conditions and social consciousness, 'positing it as an automatic connection, neglecting the role of traditional attitudes, folk customs, ideals and also the impact of the models presented by Western consumerism'.

Third, the deprivations of early post-revolutionary society have been associated falsely with austerity in the longer term. While it may have been a vital necessity under conditions of scarcity and in the face of the possible re-assertion of class-based inequalities, asceticism has proved difficult to sustain in a period of improving conditions. This created obvious difficulties for those generations who had fully accepted the earlier ideological orientation and who could only equate prosperity with a bourgeois way of life. A push in the opposite direction was bound to come from the younger generations, who had not experienced the earlier period of austerity or been subjected to the ideological force that accompanied it. The new challenge confronting the Comecon countries is, therefore, the transition to socialist well-being (Ferge, 1979, p. 309).

The implications of this experience for the planning of alternative strategies in capitalist countries are obvious. Foremost is the fact that the transition to socialism does not necessarily follow from revolution or the election of a socialist government; its achievements must be carefully planned and assiduously worked for. But there are, in addition, at least two good reasons why the package of planned socialism is likely to be a difficult one to sell politically in the West.

Socialism is still associated with austerity, and despite the wholly different conditions pertaining in capitalist societies, the transition to socialism remains firmly linked to relatively underdeveloped countries.

Western governments have, of course, exploited the link between social-ism and austerity and contrasted it with capitalist prosperity.

Moreover, because of the dominance of the Soviet model, socialist planning is associated with a highly centralized and bureaucratic state machine, or with a state dictatorship. People brought up in the liberal—democratic tradition and within the consumerist prosperity of capitalism would, quite naturally, find it difficult to accept autocratically imposed austerity. This is especially true in those countries, including Britain and the United States, where liberal—democratic and capitalist values, such as self-help, are deeply entrenched.

The contrast, however, is entirely false. The prosperity of advanced capitalist countries and their democratic tradition suggests a wholly different model of planned socialism to that pursued in state socialist countries. The fact that the prime goal of planning in state socialist countries is industrialization indicates that it is inappropriate as a basis for planning in capitalist countries. Furthermore, the model of planning under state socialism, as we have seen, is not appropriate because it is not socialist in either its form or its content.

Social planning in Hungary

A penetrating assessment of the current status of social planning in one state socialist society, Hungary, has been provided by Ferges's (1979) book, *A Society in the Making*. She notes a range of different orien-tations towards social policy and planning and especially towards the relationship between economic and social policy. They include the position that gives clear priority to economic over social considerations and that most closely approximates the approach in Western capitalist societies, the position in which the two are given roughly equal import-ance, and a third 'main position' where, in the long run at least, economic rationality or optimization is subordinated to the social aim of human-ization (Ferge, 1979, p. 69).

Although all three approaches agree with the ideal of a socialist society and with the observation that Hungary is at an early stage of post-revolutionary development, they differ on their proposed paths for development. It is the third and main model that is best described as structural social policy. Its goal is to assure (Hegedüs and Márkus, 1969; quoted in Ferge, 1979, p. 68) the evolution of social conditions in a way that enables each member of society to develop his personality to the greatest extent possible under given economic conditions, and to fulfil himself in everyday life, including the sphere of work and the activities outside work . . . . In our opinion the correct amalgamation of goals of optimisation and humanisation is the basic question for long-range planning. And when we said earlier that it is possible to develop the civilizational model of socialism, we think that this would not be achieved solely, perhaps not even primarily, by the increase of economic efficiency, but only if it is offered more to people in terms of the humanisation of social relations.

To a large extent, however, this still remains a normative prescription for planning in Hungarian society. According to Ferge (1979, p. 307), 'the characteristics of a socialist way of life, its chief roles and the instruments promoting it have not yet found adequate expression in the social plans.' Despite very considerable progress against social problems, structural social planning has yet to be fully developed in Hungary. This can be illustrated easily with reference to the Hungarian Commission for Perspective Planning on Manpower and Standard of Living, which published its hypotheses concerning the direction of social development over a fifteen-year period, in 1969. The public debate that followed encouraged comments from only a hundred or so people, and they were mostly professionals. Some of these comments are illuminating (quoted in Ferge, 1979, p. 306):

It is somewhat disheartening that the forecasts of a socialist country up to 1985 . . . do not say much more than that the structure of consumption will follow a pattern very similar to that of more developed countries . . . . If we want more than just to create a kind of bourgeois welfare, then we have to take into account more seriously the specific nature of a socialist country.

If socialism implies the requirement and the goal of the creation of a new way of life, it cannot be uncritical towards the cultural patterns, values and stereotypes inherited from the past . . . . While on the one hand, we cannot force upon people any imaginary utopias of a socialist way of life because this has to emerge from their everyday activity and they themselves have to create it, we cannot on the other hand refuse to influence this evolution in the name of the basic values of socialism.

The final version of this long-term plan was amended to include, in addition to material progress, the following proposals: to assure a secure and stable life for everybody; to strengthen the open character of society by maintaining mobility at a high level; to enhance the socialist character of income distribution, implying the reduction of the distance between extremes; and to build up a more consistent system of preferences in consumption. In the mid-1970s the need to narrow regional inequalities in living standards was also added.

SOCIAL PLANNING AND SOCIAL DEVELOPMENT

While social planning in developed societies is relegated to a relatively minor role, in some countries in the Third World it has recently become a prominent element in development planning. Although the degree of change should not be overstated, the rise of social planning in some parts of the Third World, such as Tanzania and Zambia, reflects important changes in the concept of development, and in the approach to planning in those societies. In particular, the traditional focus of development solely on economic growth has been broadened in some cases to include a range of social and economic goals (Conyers, 1982, p. 3). There has also been a critical reappraisal of the achievements of development and development planning up to the 1970s, and an attempt to overcome some of the deficiencies of a strategy based on the pursuit of narrow economic goals in such planning.

The restricted interpretation of social planning in advanced capitalist and state socialist societies is, in part, a function of the dominant role of the state in the provision of social services. In the Third World the role of the state in social welfare is much more limited, and therefore social services planning is potentially less institutional and mechanistic, and the definition of social welfare broader.

But in addition, as has already been noted, social planning – and, it may be argued, planning itself – is associated primarily with developing societies. Such countries are 'engaged in a comprehensive and continuous effort to bring about calculated changes in the nature of their society and economy' (Conyers, 1982, p. 9). This definition includes those societies that would be considered conventionally as developed, but which are transforming the nature of their economic and social relations (Hungary is one example – see p.211).

When a society considers itself to be developed, it is obviously unlikely to assign structural social planning, or for that matter radical social change, to a position of political priority. Instead, planning is confined chiefly to the role of co-ordination (see p. 92). It is not structural; it is for the most part piecemeal and directed at smoothing out relatively minor blemishes in the operation of what are considered to be fully developed institutions and services. In the Third World, development planning is much more important than in the advanced societies, although it is often undertaken to gain favour for aid and investment. In recent years social planning has emerged in some countries, such as Tanzania, as a distinct pursuit and discipline with the realization that, not only are social factors important in determining the outcome of economic development plans, but they are also important as ends in themselves (Conyers, 1982, p. 10).

This is not to say that there are not substantial deficiencies in the form of social planning adopted in the Third World. Often planning is highly centralized and bureaucratic. Frequently planning and welfare are the inappropriate creatures of Western influence and values, managed through international agencies, multinational corporations and the state under external influence. Development planning is overwhelmingly male-orientated, with women being segregated and relegated to the 'underdeveloped' subsistence sector (Rogers, 1980, p. 11). These deficiences, and especially discrimination against women, are present under even the most progressive planning regimes in the Third World. Caution is required, therefore, in drawing out the positive aspects of planning in some developing societies.

The presumption of development

A proposal for structural social planning in advanced capitalist societies is inevitably at variance with the assumption of development that underpins welfare states. But although these societies may be advanced in terms of their per capita income, they are still characterized by deep-seated inequalities and large-scale need. Furthermore, their social services may be developed in terms of their administrative complexity, but not necessarily in terms of the production of welfare. In other words, the case for structural social planning in Britain is based on its *social* underdevelopment and on the need, therefore, for a radical transformation in the distribution of power and resources in order to create a more just society.

A positive intervention in social affairs is required, in the form of structural social policy and planning, to deliberately transform the basic cycle of reproduction. Social planning in this sense is concerned with social development, but also with economic development, and is more akin to the practice in some Third World countries than in advanced capitalist ones. Social services planning is only a small part of this broad conception, rather than the sum total of social planning.

There are important lessons for social planning to be gained from the experience of development planning and development studies in parts of the Third World. In contrast to the conservatism and at times arrogance about the success of their institutions of 'developed' societies, there is often a more radical appreciation of the need for social change in underdeveloped ones. Certainly in one or two countries there is a recognition of the need for purposeful efforts to change the nature of society.

Underlying this radicalism in countries such as Tanzania there is, first, the fact that some inequalities are considered to be social problems (a major exception being sex inequality – see Rogers, 1980). Thus one of the main aims of development policy is the reduction of inequality and the creation of a fairer distribution of resources. So social planners are more likely than their counterparts in advanced capitalist societies to consider the impact of policies on the distribution of resources, and to formulate policies that are specifically designed to reduce inequalities. Although, in general, inequalities in income are wider in developing than in developed societies, and the gap is not as large as might be expected, there is considerable variation between different countries (Atkinson, 1976).

Second, there are signs of a recognition of the interrelationship between economic and social policy and also of the possibility of a conflict between the two. This is resulting from the ending of the long-standing domination of economists in development planning, and the rising awareness among development economists of the importance of questions of distribution (Conyers, 1982, p. 21). According to Seers (1969, p. 3),

The questions to ask about a country's development are therefore: What has been happening to poverty? What has been happening to unemployment? What has been happening to inequality? If all of these have declined from high levels, then beyond doubt this has been a period of development for the country concerned. If one or two of these central problems have been growing worse, especially if all three have, it would be strange to call the result 'development', even if per capita income doubled.

The underdevelopment of social planning in Britain and other advanced capitalist societies, as both a practice and a discipline, is obvious by the incongruity of this statement to the pursuit of planning in these countries. The suggestions that there is a conflict between economic goals, such as growth, and social objectives, such as equality and full employment, and that the latter should take precedence over the former, are particularly alien to the advanced societies.

Finally, in a few Third World countries there is more direct participation in social planning by ordinary citizens (Conyers, 1982, p. 15), and in these countries, therefore, social planning can be less elitist, less centralized and less bureaucratic than anywhere else.

CONCLUSION

This review of the main alternatives to centralized bureau-incrementalism in Britain, including some of those proposed by both academic experts and the political Left, provides further evidence of the underdevelopment of our thinking about social planning. The alternative that is usually caricatured as the only one — state socialism — has been shown to be rigidly centralized and oppressively bureaucratic, and therefore unacceptable as a basis for democratic structural planning, although the long experience of state socialist societies with explicit planning processes affords important negative lessons for the discussion of alternative forms of planning in Western democracies. A more positive alternative model of planning is provided by one or two Third World countries, which appear to have far more developed conceptions of social planning and social objectives than so-called developed societies. Some of these lessons are taken up in the final chapter.

Before turning to a discussion of my own proposals for structural

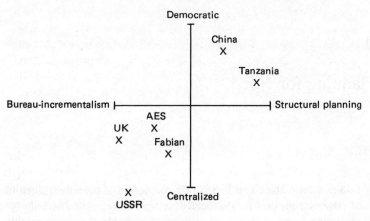

Figure 4 Dimensions of social planning

social planning, we might recall the planning continuum outlined in chapter 4. The alternative models reviewed in this chapter can be placed on the continuum as in figure 4. The object of the next chapter is to make proposals for moving social planning under capitalism from the bottom left-hand segment of the figure to the top right-hand one, and thereby to provide a basis for a planned transition to socialism.

9

Planning for Need

I do not share Marx's mid-Victorian conviction of the inevitability
of progress; nor do I regard social development as an automatically
ascending spiral with Socialism as its climax. On the contrary, I
think that, in the absence of sustained and strenuous efforts,
the way is as likely to lead downhill as up, and that Socialism,
if achieved, will be the creation not of any mystical historical
necessities, but of the energy of human minds and wills.

Tawney (1966, p. 178)

INTRODUCTION

The preceding chapters have discussed the deficiencies of traditional
conceptions of social policy and social planning and suggested that their
dominant forms in different societies are centralist, undemocratic,
bureau-incremental and subordinate to narrow economic goals. Social
policy and social planning in capitalist societies do not conflict with,
but embody and reflect, capitalist values. The social and economic
priorities implicit in social policy and planning are related to production
and the reproduction of these values. The centrality of the market to
distribution, production for profit, the goal of economic growth,
inequalities in original income and so on have not been challenged
to any significant extent by social policies under either Conservative
or Labour governments in Britain. Even when policies result from
direct working-class pressure, the institutionalized form of the response
is framed within the context of dominant values and assumptions.

Until some of the basic structures of society are altered – the
dominant values in production and distribution for example –
socialist goals, such as equality of conditions between social classes
and groups, are not likely to be pursued seriously. It is not simply

the observed persistence of wide inequalities in income and wealth despite the postwar welfare state (see for example Townsend, 1979; Le Grand 1982), but also the absence of any effective challenge to these inequalities that supports this contention. 'Alternative' social and economic strategies have been framed within the broad context of capitalist social relations, giving precedence to economic priorities, such as growth, and not seeking to alter the principles on which resources are distributed.

In this final chapter I want to forget momentarily how things are and think about how they might be. My purpose is to outline a basis for one type of structural social planning. It is socialist, in that it seeks to transform social relations, production and distribution according to socialist principles. It was argued in chapter 3 that socialist goals are essential for the achievement of 'welfare' in the form of distribution according to need. A package of measures or manifesto is not proposed, but some elements of socialist social planning are set out. I examine the nature of structural social planning which aims to achieve socialist goals, and the form it might take.

The concern of this chapter is not with revolutionary change, but with the planned transition from capitalism to socialism. It is assumed, therefore, that it is possible to establish the foundations for policies leading towards distribution according to need within a capitalist society. This requires, among other things, the adoption of a wholly different meaning to 'planning' from that put into practice in either capitalist or state socialist societies.

Regardless of whether or not a system of socialist social planning can be introduced into Britain and other advanced capitalist societies, there will be an important role for social planning in attempting to harmonize the mixed economy. Many people, chiefly Conservatives and Social Democrats, will wish to set the limit to social change there. But this chapter starts from the assumption that *planning for need* is incompatible with a predominantly capitalist society. This does not necessitate the abolition of the market, but rather the assertion of socialist values over capitalist values. The method proposed for achieving that aim, structural social planning, is seen as the only viable alternative to the delusion of some Conservatives and Social Democrats, who try to seek welfare and social justice within capitalist relations, and to the anti-humanitarian tendency of Marxism to subordinate people to economic change and progress.

SOCIALIST SOCIAL PLANNING

Neither of the two main organizational models of planning in operation provides an adequate basis for planning the transition to socialism in advanced capitalist societies. The problem with indicative planning is its ineffectiveness. Its targets are not binding on participants in the economy, and the guidelines flow in one direction from the centre to the periphery. It is not surprising, therefore, that, in both the economic (Holland, 1978, p. 1) and the social (Townsend, 1975, pp. 56–76) spheres, this form of planning has been discredited. Imperative planning, on the other hand, is even less democratic and is highly centralized.

A model of revolutionary change, based on Eastern European experience, is also inadequate. Not only is this model of change an outdated 'fantasy' of some leftist groups (Aaronovitch, 1981a, p. 113), but it is in direct conflict with a social theory or programme based on the pursuit of welfare. Socialism achieved through bloody violence is no more compatible with need-based welfare than is capitalism at the cost of the injuries of class. Moreover, the simplistic revolutionary position misconstrues the multi-faceted nature of the capitalist state and institutions, which are already the location of a whole range of struggles and not just those between capital and labour. In other words, there is no bastion to be stormed, and the military analogy is inappropriate.

This model of change also detracts from the need to plan a long-term strategy for social progress, both before and after the accession of socialism. The revolutionary Left rarely has anything to say about the practical steps needed to realize a post-revolutionary, socialist way of life. Contrary to the implications of some modern Marxist thinking, a change in the relations of production is not the end-product of socialist transformation, but only the start.

Instead of violent and decisive change arising out of a workers' revolution, *it is necessary to conceive of structural change in advanced capitalist societies occurring over a long period and involving a wider range of groups than just key groups of industrial workers.* Planning is an integral part of this process of change, but not as a series of blueprints drawn up at the centre and passed to the periphery for action.

From participation to democratic control

The meaning and practice of planning as an expert pursuit carried out exclusively by administrators or professionally qualified planners, which is common to advanced capitalist, state socialist and most Third World countries, must be transformed. At the moment planning is something that is done *for* people by others acting in professional roles; it is patronizing, elitist and remote from the experience of ordinary people. At best there may be opportunities for feedback or consultation. For example, there are the institutionalized forms of economic plan revision in state socialist societies, or the *ad hoc* public inquiries conducted in conjunction with environmental planning. Such consultation is virtually unknown in the social planning process in Britain. Consumers' groups, such as single-parent family groups or claimants' unions, are not included in the planning process. Where consumers are represented in the organizational structure of social institutions, as on Community Health Councils, they are not part of the planning machinery (Phillips, 1980). The one postwar example of public involvement in the central planning of social security in Britain was primarily a public relations exercise (C. Walker, 1983).

Most commonly, planning is conducted by administrators consulting and bargaining with each other in complete secrecy, with only the results of this process being published. As we saw in Chapter 6, public expenditure planning in Britain, which is in effect the main form of social planning, is a good example of this prevailing form of bureau-incrementalist planning.

Central administrative and expert planning will have a role in structural planning for socialist welfare, but the limitations of this approach must be recognized. Even in the hands of Fabian socialists, it often remains elitist, centralized and at times patronizing. Moreover, because the locus of planning is not at the point where people *experience* welfare institutions and services, the outcome is likely to be simplistic and relatively unresponsive to their changing needs. 'Utopias elaborated in minute detail are necessarily naive: it is only in their everyday experience that people gradually find adequate solutions to the problems emerging under continuously changing conditions' (Ferge, 1979, p. 19).

This is not to rescind the point made in the previous chapter about the role of Utopian thinking. An important aspect of socialist planning, particularly in opposition, is the projection of possible 'Utopian' relations and institutions. But in a genuinely democratic socialist society these could not be planned in detail by experts and successfully imposed on people. What is more, the interests of those administering services do not always coincide precisely with the interests of those receiving them, and centralized, expert planning inevitably gives more weight to the former.

Rather than being confined to the centres of power, socialist planning should be diffuse and democratic, a dialogue before it is an expert activity. Thus, instead of being located primarily in central and local government bureaucracies, social planners would be locally based outside the main administrative machinery, as community workers or community development officers, subject to local control and veto. Clients, claimants and other citizens would be at the centre of the planning process.

This is not to suggest that needs are peculiar to one locality – the definition of 'local' is itself problematic – but that planning must be a dialogue between citizens and government and socialist planning should facilitate and not prevent this sort of dialogue.

Any proposal that differs radically from existing practice is bound to be viewed with suspicion, especially by the academic and professional groups involved. There can be no serious dissension from the fact that social and economic planning in advanced capitalist societies is a specialist pursuit, which, with one or two minor exceptions in a few local authorities, is far removed from the everyday experience of ordinary citizens. Second, this form of planning has not had any notable success in reducing inequalities or promoting need-based welfare; it has been used as an adjunct to and not an engine for policy-making. Third, as previously argued, the dominant elitist and centralized form that planning takes in capitalist societies – bureau-incremental-ism – is a major factor in the lack of responsiveness of state social services to need.

We might begin to construct an alternative planning system that would lead to a transformation in these institutions and in the quality of life of citizens. To achieve such a change, our main emphasis would not be with the creation of a Department of Planning or Department for the Family or any other department of central government, but with citizens, whether as individuals or in groups.

Since the planning machinery would be transformative in operation, and therefore would not be compatible with a bourgeois government and state, its full introduction rests on the election of a socialist party to power with a commitment to change. But the planning process must begin at once. It will contribute to, and often will be indivisible from, the formation of socialist policies to be implemented following an election. The labour movement should be a key channel for planning and policy-making in Opposition, involving a dialogue between individuals and groups — trade unions, women's groups, tenants' groups, claimants' unions and so on. All would, effectively, be involved in the planning and policy-making process.

Following the election of a socialist government, this planning process would be institutionalized with the appointment of social planners, who would combine with local politicians to begin, or in many cases continue, the social planning dialogue with local citizens. The aim would be to create the conditions for socialist evolution. The election of a socialist government committed to planned change would, therefore, translate existing oppositional planning and relations into a formalized planning process. *To some extent, therefore, socialist planning is underway already, in the form of struggles, in a wide range of relations, that counterpose alternative institutions, methods of work and relationships.*

In the building of an open or covert 'oppositional practice' (London Edinburgh Weekend Return Group (LEWRG), 1979), socialists working within the state machine are beginning to discuss and mentally construct alternative economic and social relations. The women's movement, groups of pensioners, people with disabilities, single parents, people in environmental pressure groups and others are all the time defining alternative relationships, values and expectations to those that dominate the market. The intention is *not* to unite these struggles into one cataclysmic revolution which would, overnight, transform existing capitalist institutions into socialist ones: that strategy has already been dismissed as naive. The planned structural change proposed here would build on and not attempt to sweep away existing institutions and relations. These will already contain the seeds of change in the form of the oppositional relationships presently being practised and the values they are based on. So there will be a 'continuity between the oppositional forms within the old society and the way the new society comes to be organised' (LEWRG, 1979, p. 132). Reserving the issue of planning in Opposition for later discussion: once a socialist government is elected, on what basis should social planning be conducted?

PRINCIPLES OF SOCIALIST SOCIAL PLANNING

Which principles distinguish socialist structural planning from other forms of social planning? First and foremost, it is socialist in its objectives. But this does not tell us very much, because the constituent elements of this goal and the relative priorities between them will differ between socialists. To my mind the principal socialist goal is the replacement of privilege and inequalities in the distribution of resources and life-chances with social and economic equality. This is coupled with, and dependent on, the dispersal of power. The goal is the development of a socialist way of life based on equality according to need, democratic freedom and fellowship; a classless society, which does not countenance adverse discrimination based on age, sex, race or any other social category.

If the goals of planning are socialist, then the means must be no less so. Planning is a means and not an end. This is where the conception of social planning put forward here diverges sharply from the practice under state socialism. Replacement of the tyranny of capitalism by a tyranny of state power, even if it were operated through a participative planning system, would not correspond to democratic socialism. In the transformative conception of social planning proposed here socialism is pursued not as a 'gospel of economic planning' (Terrill, 1973, p. 257), which, quite simply, treats people as the means to an end, but rather as a mechanism for developing social relations between free and equal citizens. Thus, rather than a means of exerting control over social and especially productive relations, socialist social planning should be a means of dispersing power and facilitating social as well as economic equality. In the sense it is used here, therefore, planning is an attempt to encourage people to liberate themselves politically in order that they may also secure their own social and economic freedom.

Social priorities in planning

If the essence of socialist social planning is the democratic pursuit of equality and the promotion of a socialist way of life based on fellowship, what priorities and organizational form does this imply for planning?

First of all, the achievement of economic and social equality requires a reordering of economic and social priorities. Under both capitalism and state socialism, people are subordinated, to different degrees, to economic values and the goal of economic progress. It was argued in the previous chapter that those on both the Right and the Left of the political spectrum, from the Institute of Economic Affairs to the Conference of Socialist Economists, have concentrated on economic policy on the assumption that economic growth is an essential prerequisite for social development. Those who have been effectively marginalized by capitalist society would with good reason be sceptical about the promise of an improvement in their living standards relative to others following economic growth. They have yet to see the results of a long series of such promises. The economic hegemony that underpins this scale of priorities however is very influential on all sections of society. Yet, as was argued in detail in chapter 3, it is often incompatible with the achievement of social priorities.

Economic policies are also social policies, to the extent that they imply certain social relations or discriminate in favour of or against different groups. These implicit policies, for example the creation of unemployment under monetarism, may conflict with explicit social policies, such as protecting families from poverty. Throughout the world priority is given in national planning to economic goals. Economic hegemony is reinforced in both capitalist and state socialist societies by quite different ideologies, and in the Third World by international capitalist institutions such as the IMF and the World Bank. The task of changing this 'natural' order is a major one. *The planning system can play a central role in this through the combination of economic and social policies.* Socialists must recognize the interrelationship between economic and social policies in order to ensure consistency in policy, and the transformation from distribution based on class and status to distribution based on need.

Instead of economic planning being concerned primarily with macroeconomic policy, with social planning depending on the resources made available through the economic system, socialist social planning and the organization of production and distribution would start with social need and social priorities based on need. These would in turn determine the form and content of economic policy and planning. The social organization of work and the nature of production would therefore be determined primarily by social priorities, not by economic or financial motives. This would require a reorientation of economic policy as well as social policy.

In more concrete terms, under market capitalism production rests on the relationship between demand and profit. The decision of whether or not to produce and in what form is made without reference to citizens, except indirectly as consumers. But the relative social priority afforded to a particular good is determined at the point of consumption and not at the point of production. This is not only wasteful, but means that social priorities are overridden by narrow financial motives. The interests of citizens, as consumers, workers and so on, are not represented in a market-based economic system, and democratic socialist planning requires the reverse.

So the decision of whether or not to produce a good would not rest simply on potential demand, but also on the priority that is allocated socially to that good and to the production of it. Moreover, this decision would not be based primarily on the potential return on investment, but on the social usefulness of a particular good or service and on the social costs|or benefits of production. The latter would include the effects on employment, the type of employment and the impact on health of both workers and local communities.

Interest in these matters is not confined solely to workers, as some proposals for workers' co-operatives and planning agreements seem to suggest. The wider community and local citizens would be represented through the social planning system. This would link workplace planning – covering such things as production targets, investment and work facilities – with broader interests, including social needs, the use of scarce resources and the social costs of production. Decisions on priorities would rest between local areas and national government. Conflicts can be expected, but these are likely to be far fewer than at present because planning in both central and local government will be orientated towards similar, socialist goals.

The goal of equality

The realization of equality through planning requires not only the reversal of the prevailing scale of social and economic values, but also a change in the social meaning of 'need'. The character of demand would be different under socialist planning to that under capitalism — because it would be articulated through the planning system as well as the market, and also because it would be determined by socialist social priorities and not capitalist commodity fetishism. Production and distribution would be based on need as measured by the resources required by individuals and families to enable them to participate, in the first instance, in customary roles and relationships and, secondarily, in a socialist way of life comprising equality, mutual respect and fellowship.

Equality in this context means equality of conditions, which must be guaranteed by socialist social planning. It does not imply that people are or ever should be the same, but that their social and economic status and power, within a relatively broad band based on variations in need, should be. As Tawney (1964, p. 57) wrote in a famous passage:

> So to criticise inequality and to desire equality is not, as is sometimes suggested, to cherish the romantic illusion that men are equal in character and intelligence. It is to hold that, while their natural endowments differ profoundly, it is the mark of a civilised society to aim at eliminating such inequalities as have their source not in individual differences, but in its own organisation, and that individual differences, which are a source of social energy, are more likely to ripen and find expression if social inequalities are, as far as practicable, diminished.

This sort of structural change requires democratic control over systems of distribution in both of the so-called public and the private sectors — control, that is, over the direct distribution of resources through wages, dividends, non-wage benefits and so on, as well as over the redistribution of resources through the tax and social security systems. Thus wages would vary, above a minimum participation standard (Townsend, 1979), according to family size and other needs such as disability. At the same time, a social wage would be paid to those not currently in employment. This would be coupled with a progressive tax system, including wealth and corporation taxes.

The importance of reproduction

A thorough transformation is required in systems of distribution in order to create social equality. But this is only part of the story, because distribution is only one aspect of the process of *social reproduction*. If key capitalist social relations are to be replaced with socialist ones, then the whole process must be transformed (Ferge, 1979, p. 21). To concentrate on the distribution of resources alone is to overlook the fact that this is only one facet of social organization. As Marx pointed out (in McLellan, 1977, p. 570), even some 'socialists' have failed to recognize that radical changes in distribution rest on changes in the relations of production:

> Vulgar socialism (and from it in turn a section of the democracy) has taken over from the bourgeois economists the consideration and treatment of distribution as independent of the mode of production and hence the presentation of socialism as turning principally on distribution.

What is meant by reproduction? The cycle of reproduction comprises the reproduction of people, values, the structure of relationships and power as well as the production and reproduction of goods and services (Ferge, 1979, p. 23). All of these processes are taking place at once within all societies. Therefore the social structure itself and the social relations on which it is built are being constantly reproduced.

As indicated in chapter 1, it is the cycle of reproduction that offers a resolution to the metaphorical contradiction between structural inequality and the need for radical change. The image of powerlessness in the face of an impregnable structure of values, relationships and power is at least partly transformed when it is realized that, in Marris's (1982, p. 118) words, 'we make the citadel, we constantly recreate it, inside ourselves and in our dealings with each other, and so surely, we can begin to unmake it.'

Thus it is to the reproduction of existing social structures and values that planning must be directed. Moreover, because we are all part of the cycle of reproduction, planning alternatives become rather less remote and instead are seen as something that we can be involved in directly. The dynamic notion of 'reproduction', therefore, puts ordinary people in a much more influential position in relation to social change than the more static one of 'social structure'.

The social division of work is at the centre of the cycle of reproduction of the basic structural relations and the social classes formed
by the way work is organized; it is 'the most important and most
dynamic layer of the reproduction of social life' (Ferge, 1979, p. 27).

Ferge (1979, p. 33) distinguishes three basic productive relations:
ownership, power and knowledge. Ownership of the means of production
is important in determining the nature of the cycle of reproduction.
The owners of capital directly and indirectly determine the structure of
present and future needs and are the key figures in decisions about the
distribution of resources from production. But in addition, ownership
is an important basis of power. It creates power through the access it
provides to political and economic means to further the capitalists'
own interests. This much is evident in capitalist societies from the
permanence of structural inequality despite the existence of welfare
states. The capitalist class, through ownership or control of the means
of production, is able to defend its position and interests very easily.

This does not mean though that a change in ownership will on its
own result in socialist social relations. *A change in the social organization
of work does not necessarily follow from a change in ownership.* In
Hungary, for instance, 'the organisation of the social division of work
. . . has followed the former, capitalist, pattern even under new socialist
conditions' (Ferge, 1979, p. 31).

The social division of work is mirrored and in turn supported by a
social division not only of power, but also of knowledge (Ferge, 1979,
p. 33). Thus the transition to socialist society depends on a transformation in the process of social reproduction, which rests first on
changes in the relations of ownership, power and knowledge. Ownership
and control would be altered following the election of a socialist
government through an increase in public ownership, the establishment
of more workers' co-operatives and a system of public influence and
control. Power too would be dispersed by these measures and also
through the planning system. The social organization of work is
accompanied by the hierarchical organization of education. This
creates the paradoxical distribution of education services whereby
those who need the least tend to get the most (A. Walker, 1982f).
Gradually a more equal distribution of knowledge would follow from
radical changes in social conditions and in the meaning and institutions
of education and training.

Second, arising out of these basic structural relations, there are relations formed in the sphere of distribution and redistribution that can be tackled through the tax and social security systems. Finally, there are relations formed in the sphere of consumption that would also be expected to be transformed following the other changes already outlined.

Transformation in the social division of work is, then, crucial to the development of a socialist society. This does not imply that all work will be made the same, of course — it could not be. The intention is to eliminate those inequalities that are based on hierarchical differentiation, not all forms of differentiation. This means, in effect, that the aim is vertical and not horizontal change (Ferge, 1979, p. 40).

THE ORGANIZATION OF SOCIALIST PLANNING

It would be of little practical value, except heuristically, to attempt to provide a detailed proposal for the administrative structure of socialist social planning. To do so would suggest that there is only one, or one best form, when practice is likely to reveal a number of different arrangements whereby the transition to socialism could be achieved. There is also the risk of falling into the same trap as traditional social administration, in concentrating on the organizational structure of institutions to the exclusion of the principles and assumptions that underlie them. None the less, some proposals are made for the organization of socialist social planning. The acceptance of these specific proposals rests on a judgement about how effective they are likely to be in practice, and hopefully from practical experiments in opposition.

The acceptance of the principle of socialist planning is a matter of political philosophy, not of academic assessment. Because socialist planning sets out to change basic structural relations it is bound to entail mistakes and may appear to be less polished than bureau-incrementalist planning. This must be expected in view of the complexities of social reality, and the fact that knowledge about the potential for intervention is often non-existent or is interpreted in a biased form (Ferge, 1979, p. 46). There are bound to be defects in the early phase of the transformation, but the goal of distribution according to need, which is another way of describing socialist welfare, is one worth striving for.

In contrast to the practice of planning in state socialist societies, social planning must be socialist in organization and operation. This requires above all that it should be democratic, a forum for citizen planning and a channel for citizens' influence on the state. The goal, then, is a socialist planning method and not simply a participatory one. Within capitalist society social planning will conflict with the capitalist free market. This is not, however, a conflict between the market and planning — the two co-exist in all forms of society — but rather a political struggle between those working to preserve the status quo and those wishing to transform it (Ellman, 1979, p. 271).

Thus, in seeking to change from capitalism to socialism, the social planning system must embody both democratic planning and a socialist logic or imperative. In other words, although there may be variations between different groups and geographical areas in their programme of progress towards socialism and in the precise form that it takes, the end result of the planning process must be to achieve socialism. Planning would not be open-ended in the long term.

The case for democratic planning and control

Why is democratic control of economic and social institutions essential?

First, uncontrolled and socially unplanned capitalist enterprise will continue to accumulate profit without reference to the needs of workers or other citizens. The result is that labour and material resources are not necessarily employed in a way that ensures maximum *social efficiency* (see chapter 7). The social costs of capitalism, such as unemployment and poverty, must be planned out of existence.

Second, the manufacture of need by capitalist enterprise is socially wasteful, and planning is necessary to end this and to ensure the achievement of production according to need.

Third, democratic planning is essential to avoid the growth of corporate power, which may be exerted through the central or local state. Thus, the democratic planning system would be the embodiment of the dispersal of power essential for the achievement of democratic socialist relations. While decisions about production and distribution — what is produced, where and how, and how resources are distributed — are concentrated in few hands, there is little chance of achieving a significant shift towards democratic socialism.

In fact, the case for a limited form of participatory planning is recognized across a wide range of countries, particularly those that are classified as underdeveloped. For example, according to Myrdal (1968, p. 851), 'Even the ruling elites of those South Asian countries that have moved toward a more authoritarian regime are aware that there is little hope of effective planning for development without popular support.' The concentration of economic and political power under capitalism stands four-square in front of the development of socialism. So a radical change in the distribution of power is an essential component of socialist social planning.

Participation and community development

Such a transformation requires not only the election of a socialist government, but also a change in the democratic process at central and local levels. The simple parliamentary model of representation, with its inherent elitism and centralism, is an inadequate basis for democratic socialism. Changes are required in order to disperse power more widely and also to increase the accountability of public institutions. These would include increased powers for local government, providing greater local autonomy and more control over resources than at present, and more devolved powers from local government to smaller geographical areas and groups of citizens. Increased, but genuinely 'public', ownership is also required to ensure democratic control over investment and production.

Ideally, a socialist society would include a system of 'perfectly decentralized' decision-making, wherein all decisions would be made by individuals, local authorities and firms entirely independently of the wishes of the central government (Ellman, 1979, p. 33). But while this might be a feasible goal for a socialist society in which the majority of citizens is committed to socialist development, for one that is in transition from capitalism to socialism, it is not. The ideal type of 'perfect centralism' has already been dismissed as being undemocratic and involving too many restrictions on freedom.

The alternative to these models is, according to Ellman (1979, p. 33), 'perfect indirect centralism', by which is meant 'an economy in which all decisions are made by individuals, local authorities or firms, but whose decisions are exactly those that would have been made if the central authorities had made them'. By determining the criteria and scope of planning, through its control of economic planning or, as in the case of China, through the political system and control of labour, the state may achieve its desired ends although operating on the basis of apparently decentralized planning. If the transformation from capitalism to socialism is to be successful, it will require a planning system that is nearer to indirect centralization than the other ideal types, but with one important proviso.

Although socialist hegemony will be exerted throughout society, as capitalist ideology operates currently, the state will not be in a position to impose its will in all cases as under capitalism and state socialism. Thus socialism will be achieved through argument and persuasion at local level, with central state power being used as a last resort in exceptional circumstances. The model of decision-making being proposed here for the pre-socialist stage of the development of British society might be properly regarded as *imperfect direct decentralization*.

The Chinese planning system is often regarded as a model of decentralized planning. Its planning 'from the top down and from the bottom up' involves citizen participation in a national planning framework. There are 29 administrative units — provinces, autonomous regions and municipalities — each of which is subdivided into a series of successively smaller units: areas, districts, neighbourhoods, communes, right down to production teams in rural areas and streets in urban areas.

Although there is 'a remarkably high degree of genuine "grass roots" participation' (Conyers, 1982, p. 110) in the Chinese planning system, it is not a useful one for our purposes because of its narrow limitation to production and the restrictions on individual liberty that it entails. While there have been some relaxations in state control since the death of Mao Tse-tung and the overthrow of the Gang of Four, it is doubtful whether this sort of participatory planning is compatible with a Western-style democracy. This does not however mean that there are no important lessons to be learnt from the Chinese planning system — for example, the need for decentralized decision-making in small local areas, and for effective communication between the different levels of the planning machinery.

Participation in planning and decision-making has a long history in Britain. One example is the planning hearings on the use of land; another is the citizens' representation on Community Health Councils.

But these exercises have been strictly limited. Power has remained concentrated. Moreover, the incorporation that they produced has emasculated criticism and has resulted in very little significant change in the distribution of resources. There is no form of public participation in planning and decision-making processes that have a significant impact on welfare, such as the PESC system, or in decisions on employment or redundancy. In contrast to the illusory freedom of liberal democracy, wherein leaders are selected from a narrow class and political views are dominated by that capitalist class, whose interests the state represents, and in contrast to the absence of political freedom in state socialist societies, socialist social planning should provide a basis for the dispersal of power to citizens. The active participation of individuals in decision-making on all of those social and economic issues that have an important bearing on their lives through the planning system will enable people to govern themselves in a more real sense.

In Third World countries participatory planning initiatives are becoming more common (Conyers, 1982, p. 116), although participation remains selective (Rogers, 1980). One means of encouraging such participation is the process of community development through involvement in local programmes and the establishment of local organizations. These are usually confined to one or two areas, however. India is one of the few countries that has attempted to establish community development on a nationwide basis, and therefore to provide a basis for national participation in planning. The Indian community development programme, launched in the 1950s, combines decentralized administration, local government and trained community development workers (Conyers, 1982, p. 120). Unfortunately, it has not allowed any genuine involvement in planning by the majority of the population. Attempts to mobilize the villages themselves into overcoming gross economic and social deprivations have, not surprisingly, been a failure. In contrast, the Chinese national community development approach (though it is not known as such) has been used successfully to consolidate changes following the revolution and has had a beneficial effect on the standard of living of the population.

The concept of community development has been discredited in Britain and the United States through the ineffective Community Development Programme and American War on Poverty (Higgins, 1978; Moynihan, 1968). The concept has been used in a wide range of forms and, like the similar concept of community care, is full of ideological connotations. These are related particularly to the notion of 'community' and the association of the concept with self-help. There is also the mistaken assumption, underlying some previous community development programmes, that communities or local areas in advanced capitalist societies are separate from the national economic and social structure. Despite these difficulties, it does have some relevance here in denoting the activities and efforts of citizens, which together with those of government attempt to improve the economic and social condition of 'the community'. It underlines the fact that change will come about through the efforts of citizens in conjunction with the state, and stresses the need for local areas to have greater control over their own economic and social development.

In contrast to participation initiatives in capitalist and Third World countries, which assume that planners and politicians plan and people participate, a radically different concept of planning and community development is proposed below, which attempts to open up the planning process and enable people to plan for themselves. Thus, an integral part of planning the transformation to a socialist way of life would be a network of locally based social development workers or community development officers. Their role would be to overcome the tendencies of the parliamentary system of representative democracy and capitalist organization to discourage active participation in decision-making and to exclude citizens from planning those developments that have a direct bearing on their living standards and their way of life.

The dual nature of this role stems, first, from the fact that citizens who have been prevented for so long from participating in planning need positive encouragement and practical assistance to do so. Second, people who have lived under capitalism all of their lives, although many of them will have voted for a socialist government, will require convincing that a socialist way of life is feasible and can work. So community development workers have an important role to play within the social planning system, in encouraging participation in planning and decision-making and in the transformation to socialism. What they would be expected to do is outlined in greater detail in the next section, where I turn to the discussion of a possible form for socialist planning.

ONE FORM OF SOCIALIST PLANNING

Social planners would be employed in every locality as part of a national planning network. Their brief would cover economic and social policy and so would be concerned with industrial development as much as with social services. Local planners must be subject to local control, so they would report to a newly created committee in each local authority, a planning committee, with responsibility for planning local social and economic development.

This committee would be the key planning authority and would, in effect, become the main committee of local government, superseding even the finance committee. It would be charged with establishing local priorities. All planning − social economic, environmental − whether currently conducted nationally or locally, would come under the aegis of this local planning authority, although local plans would be subject to national priorities. Social planning (and all forms of planning, including social services planning, would be subsumed under this heading) would not be based on departments or existing client groups. In fact existing departments, such as the personal social services, might be reconstructed or amalgamated with other departments or authorities, for example the NHS. The distinction between mainly central and mainly local responsibilities would disappear.

Members of the local planning committee would be designated 'social planners'; they would be full-time politicians elected by local citizens, and would have planning/community development staff working for them. The objective of these workers would not be fact-finding, although local opinion surveys and social audits might be used as part of their armoury, but primarily initiating and taking part in the planning dialogue. This would entail detailed discussions with local citizens and groups. In this dialogue socialist principles would be confronted with the everyday experiences of citizens, with the aim of equating principles and needs.

Another important aspect of the local planners' role would be to encourage the formation of local planning groups, based on discrete geographical areas such as housing estates, or groups of workers in, say, factories, or people sharing a common status, for example single-parenthood. The intention is not to create an elaborate planning structure, along Chinese lines, based on communes, streets or teams;

a structure such as this cannot simply be translated to advanced capitalist societies where natural communities do not exist everywhere. Rather, planning must begin with those institutions and groups formed under capitalism. Local planning would encompass economic and social institutions. Workers' groups within all forms of employment would work in conjunction with local planning committees to assess priorities in re-ordering the social organization of work. Despite the extension of public ownership in key areas, such as banking, finance and important productive enterprises, the market would remain a significant feature of society because there is a danger of over-bureaucratizing the economic system (Aaronovitch, 1981a, p. 51), but its activities would be orientated towards socially defined needs.

The socialist imperative

The purpose of the planning system is to create a society organized along socialist lines. Thus, rather than a completely open-ended commitment to the planning process, there would be an in-built imperative towards socialism. This means that the role of social planners would be not simply to reflect locally expressed needs, but to confront experience under capitalism with a socialist critique, and to encourage a dialogue about socialist policies. Put another way, the social planners are intended to be not researchers or reporters, but catalysts and facilitators. This means, of course, that local planners would often have to counter expressed needs and expectations with alternative explanations, needs and priorities. This would particularly be the case in the first stage of socialist reconstruction, lasting at least 15 or 20 years, when needs created under capitalist organization would continue to be articulated during the transition to socialism. But while there could be no question about adherence to socialist principles in planning, the precise nature of policies and plans and the manner of their implementation would be a matter for discussion and local variation.

This locally based planning machinery would not be independent of national planning but would be an integral part of it. Local authorities would have increased powers in planning economic and social development and would command a much greater proportion of revenue than at present, raised through local taxation. There would also be central and regional planning authorities. The purpose of the latter would be to provide a forum for local representatives to discuss plans and priorities.

The central planning department, like its local counterpart, would supersede all other central government departments planning functions, including those of the Treasury. It would be charged with the task of allocating national funds according to national priorities, and with the difficult job of attempting to match these with local need. The Department of Planning would have four major responsibilities: (1) preparing information on national socialist priorities for local planners; (2) ensuring that socialist principles are translated into local planning machinery; (3) preparing national planning guidelines; and (4) collating local plans.

Local plans would be assessed by central government and would be subject to amendment only in terms of their adjustment to national goals and priorities, and of the time period set for the achievement of local plans in order to fit them in with national social and economic development. Local planning authorities would have the power to override centrally determined priorities, provided they had the backing of regional authorities and were using locally raised revenue. The planning and direction role of the central government would, therefore, be reduced considerably, and would be concerned chiefly with national macroeconomic decisions such as investment and taxation and with external economic policy, though with reference to local areas.

Decentralized planning

The net result of these proposals would be, first, to unify social and economic planning and, second, to democratize the planning process by moving the locus of planning from town hall or Whitehall to citizens. But in addition, local authorities would have the responsibility for carrying out plans. The combination of these two functions, planning and plan implementation, is, as Conyers (1982, p. 108) points out, crucial for the success of decentralized planning:

> If plans are merely prepared at the local level and then forwarded to the national level, where they are incorporated into a national plan and implemented through ministerial or departmental head-quarters, those involved in planning at the local level are unlikely to feel a great deal of genuine involvement in, or commitment to, the plans.

Examples of decentralized planning in Third World countries, such as Tanzania, Zambia, Papua New Guinea and the Solomon Islands, support the conclusion that commitment to the planning process is related to power over the implementation of plans and over the distribution of resources (Conyers, 1982).

Third World experience is also helpful in indicating some of the possible limitations or pitfalls of decentralized planning. In the first place, there is the danger that local plans may be subsumed by national plans and local priorities by national priorities. Thus, if local control over national social planning is to be genuinely democratic, local authorities must have the power to override national priorities. Second, even when planning is decentralized, ordinary citizens at community level may still not be directly involved in the planning process (Rogers, 1980). There is a danger that planning will remain an expert activity. This is why stress has been put on the role of local planners as facilitators rather than as dictators in the planning dialogue, on the integration of community groups in the planning process and on the local political control of planning. In addition, there might be further democratic safeguards, such as allowing a group of citizens powers in some circumstances to overrule local planners, in order to prevent social planning from developing into another profession that operates more to control than to liberate people. This problem stems from the obvious difficulty of introducing a democratic and socialist planning machinery in the face of a legacy from current practices of non-democratic, non-participative and non-socialist planning.

It is the task of social planners and community development workers to extend small-scale oppositional planning to all local areas, and in doing so they may attempt to take on too much responsibility. There is, moreover, a contradictory element in this role, which on the one hand expects planning and action to derive from local citizens and groups, and on the other embodies facilitating powers (Conyers, 1982, p. 118). The role is made even more difficult by the need to ensure that socialist principles are adhered to in the planning process. These difficulties should not be underestimated; their resolution rests on the workers' balancing their different responsibilities and on central and local politicians' ensuring that it is the citizens and not the planning and community development staff who, step by step, occupy the centre stage in planning.

PLANNING IN OPPOSITION

Most of this chapter has been concerned with the goals of socialist planning and with the conditions through which a democratic socialist society may be encouraged to evolve. Much of this will already have been dismissed in some quarters as Utopian. But planning for change is a crucial element of both socialism and social policy. And the need for structural social policy and planning arises directly from the fact that the aim of welfare to meet need is frustrated by capitalism. Large-scale change is required, therefore, and this is only likely to follow from the election of a government that is determined to establish the institutional framework within which socialism may evolve freely. It is reasonable to ask, however, what we can do meanwhile to contribute to the sort of changes discussed and the promotion of socialist goals. What can we do to create better conditions for socialist evolution, so that the transition may come about all the more quickly and smoothly?

Structural changes in the direction of socialism will not be planned by the capitalist state since they would be fundamentally opposed to its central values. Therefore planning must take place, in the first instance, in opposition to those values. But because the goals it seeks to promote are radically different to those that dominate society, it may also entail conflict and struggle. Oppositional relationships and struggles were referred to earlier, and it is important to spell out here precisely what this means.

Socialist evolution is not a matter of constructing a blueprint plan for socialism, presenting it to the people and expecting to get the go-ahead. Because the dominant institutions in society are geared to reproducing capitalist rather than socialist relations, socialist planning implies an attack on the dominant forces and policies in existing institutions. But in addition, there are a large number of, usually interpersonal, conflicts going on all of the time under capitalism. There is, for example, the social security claimant arguing with the supplementary benefit officer about the demeaning nature of life on benefit; the trade union official negotiating with an employer for an improvement in working conditions; the tenant trying to persuade the landlord to carry out basic repairs; and the women trying to renegotiate the domestic division of labour. In other words, in their everyday lives ordinary people are constructing, mentally or in practice, ways of interacting, relationships, divisions of labour, methods of work and so on that offer alternatives to dominant relationships and values, and therefore a critique of them. These are essentially small-scale attempts to intervene in the reproduction of the distribution of power and to counterpose an alternative form. In doing so those involved are not conscious of the strategic implications of their activities: they are simply trying to secure what for them are better, or more just, relationships.

Frequently these common personal struggles are also representative of a smaller number of characteristic features of market-based relations: authoritarian and demeaning public services, injustice, production for profit and private ownership. There is some potential then for combining some of the conflicts and struggles that capitalism atomizes. They might be built piece by piece into a movement that is at the same time in opposition to the reproduction of existing relations and is sowing the seeds of socialist evolution (for a detailed account of oppositional struggles see LEWRG, 1979). Oppositional relationships and struggles then are dual in nature, because they comprise arguments both against existing unacceptable capitalist relations and for the construction of alternative socialist plans. The idea is *not* to disrupt the existing order as a means of creating change, but to establish and legitimate alternative, socialist relationships and ways of acting: 'the hardest and most crucial task is to establish a sense of the relationships we want to create so clear, so persuasive, and so mundane that people's behaviour will begin to converge upon these expectations in all the transactions of everyday life' (Marris, 1982, p. 118).

The Labour Party and socialist planning

The obvious focus for this oppositional planning is the Labour Party and labour movement. The former is rightly perceived as the only political party of the Left at the moment that has the remotest chance of being elected to power. This does not mean, however, that it can be assumed that the Labour Party *will* adopt a transformative socialist programme; in fact, one important aspect of oppositional planning for socialism is to persuade the official parliamentary Opposition to do precisely that.

At the present time the Labour Party is caught in the trap of having to defend its own record and the institutions it created, however poor these may have proved (see for example, Labour Party, 1980, 1981a, 1981b, 1981c).

The natural reaction on the political Left to right-wing Conservative policies aimed, for instance, at cutting back welfare state services is a defensive one. The dilemma is obvious and by now familiar to many inside and outside of the Labour Party. At the same time as defending services or institutions from attack, we may also be defending undesirable forms of management and administration simply because, in comparison with the right-wing alternative, they are the lesser of two evils (LEWRG, 1979, p. 104). Additionally, there is the danger 'of appearing to endorse, as we struggle for the retention of certain state services, the state itself. We may become caught up in a defence of the "state form" as well as of state provision' (LEWRG, 1979, p. 104).

The Labour Party appears to be stuck in this position at the present time. Its planning is statist as well as capitalist (see A. Walker, 1983). But, as I have already indicated, this dilemma stems in part from the way in which power is conceived of as static and immutable and the implications that this holds for the kinds of action that are thereby defined as possible or impossible (Marris, 1982, p. 118).

Reformist pressure groups

In addition to the labour movement, there is a wide range of pressure groups that may potentially operate in opposition to certain aspects of the state. Quite reasonably however, these groups — representing single parents, poor families, people with disabilities, elderly people and many others — have adopted relatively short-term, reformist goals, and have tended therefore to imitate the state rather than to adopt an oppositional form. The rationale for this reformism has been clearly stated by Bull (1970, p. 23) in response to criticism of welfare rights activity:

> It would be difficult to persuade families who are a pound or two better off each week, as a result of visiting our (welfare rights) stalls, that we should have concentrated on (pressure for) family allowances.

These pressure groups have sought, and to a large extent have been granted, incorporation. This is not to say they are uncritical, far from it; but the criticism and planning is primarily incremental and reformist.

Nor is it to suggest that there is no need for such groups to keep a watching brief on the state, and to represent within the state machinery the interests of the large numbers of marginalized people. Indeed, many of those working in such groups see their activities as contributing to the longer-term struggle against capitalism. But these groups have been too uncritical of capitalist relations, notwithstanding the spectre of the Charity Commissioners removing their financially essential charitable status for engaging in 'political' activities. There are exceptions — some pressure groups in the 'poverty lobby', claimants' unions and some groups of people with disabilities have sought to create oppositional relationships and values. But many of those involved are among the very groups that find it most difficult to combine in a concerted struggle; owing to grossly inadequate incomes and battles with individualizing bureaucracies, they often have difficulty in managing their own lives from day to day.

The individualistic nature of capitalism is reproduced in welfare institutions, social security, the personal social services and so on, which in turn atomize claimants and clients. (One of the ways in which the bureaucracies manage this is through the atomization of workers: supplementary benefit officers and social workers.) Furthermore, the traditional pressure groups as a rule have not been receptive to the formation of claimant and client self-help groups.

Yet despite these barriers, and to some extent because of them, some groups of socially marginalized people have begun to establish themselves in opposition to the state. An example of what can be achieved when individuals who have been marginalized by capitalism combine in a common struggle and gain strength through unity is the successful pressure exerted by the Grey Panthers on the US federal government to raise the retirement age to 70. Another major example of a potential basis for oppositional struggle is the increasing strength and self-confidence of the women's movement in arguing against the patriarchal form of social relations. Often the embryonic struggles are located in the realm of the welfare state, since it is there that many people have their most direct experience of the state, and there that the contradictions between welfare services seeking to meet need and capitalism are most apparent.

LAYING THE FOUNDATION FOR AN ALTERNATIVE SOCIAL
AND ECONOMIC STRATEGY

On what basis could these actual and potential oppositional relationships and struggles, which are at the same time forms of oppositional
planning, be encouraged to develop? What can we do in the short term
to lay the practical foundations for structural social policy and socialist
evolution?

Popular planning

First, as has already been stressed in this chapter, structural planning
for socialism must be derived from and reflect people's own experiences.
Allegiance to socialist goals cannot be forced on people in a democracy:
it must be built on their understanding of social affairs (LEWRG, 1979,
pp. 143–4):

> People's views and feelings cannot simply be dismissed as 'false
> consciousness'. There are often coherent and plausible reasons
> why people turn to private medicine or want to buy their council
> house. Unless we listen to these and take account of them in
> formulating a socialist approach to health care, or housing, as the
> case may be, it is quite unlikely that we will ever be able to build
> a mass movement.

This means, often to our discomfort, that we have to accept divisions
and prejudices between people as a starting point in arguing for socialism. It is important to recognize the inconsistencies and contradictions
that capitalism encourages, and not to be in any way surprised when
they are manifested, if we are to be in a position to counter them. Thus
we must search for common goals between different individuals and
groups — against unemployment, poor services, expenditure on armaments, discrimination and so on — in order to reveal that the issues that
divide us are often insignificant in comparison with those that should
unite us.

One such example is the social division of unemployment and
employment policy between young and older workers. For obvious
reasons, the state and media have concentrated in the present recession

on unemployment among young people. The numbers of young people out of work are larger than those of older workers, but a similar proportion of both groups is involved and, most significantly, a greater proportion of the latter are liable to be unemployed for very long periods (A. Walker, 1982a). Employment policy is overwhelmingly concerned with young people and has reinforced the social pressure on older workers to withdraw from the labour market in order to help younger workers to get jobs. The Job Release Scheme, introduced by the Labour government in 1977 and enlarged by the Conservatives in 1981 and 1983, is designed specifically to replace older with younger workers. The alternative economic strategies of the Left too have argued for earlier retirement to help reduce unemployment, when the majority of older workers do not want to leave work prematurely. Available evidence suggests that the younger unemployed do not consistently benefit from the withdrawal of older workers from the labour market; instead, jobs are frequently lost altogether.

But my main point is that, owing to the social division between young and older workers, many of the latter believe that it is their *duty* to make way for younger people. This is one example of the historical marginalization of older workers and their use as a reserve army of labour (A. Walker, 1982a). In this way, unemployment is attributed in part to older workers remaining in employment. Young and older workers are divided, when in fact they both share a common interest in increasing employment and in ensuring that these jobs do not result in ill health, disability or fatigue and thereby cause them to leave employment prematurely.

Cutting across these divisions based on age, there is an underlying division based on social class; unskilled and semi-skilled older and younger workers are most likely to be unemployed. Thus both groups have an interest in the transformation of the social division of work, together with the social division of unemployment that accompanies it.

Such superficial divisions between people, which serve to obscure their potential for a common struggle for social justice, may be found in every sphere of social life – social security, economic relations, housing, consumerism, the sexual division of labour, caring for relatives and so on. In order to help remove the individualizing veil that engulfs social relations, it is necessary to demonstrate the common social causes of particular experiences and to encourage people to discuss and argue about them together. The struggles that may slowly and falteringly emerge must take place in every aspect of social affairs. It is misleading to hold back from discussing personal relations in the belief that the main struggle is within the labour movement, because the cycle of reproduction is all-embracing. It is to every sphere of this cycle that the struggle for socialism must be directed. 'There is no politics-free zone' (LEWRG, 1979, p. 145).

Socialist vision and practice

There is a need for a Utopian vision to counterbalance the conservative ideology that there is no viable alternative to present policies and institutions. The sheer weight of opinion supporting this historical fatalism − government, civil service, media, business, academics − means that socialists have a massive problem to overcome. Utopianism is also important to demonstrate that short-term gains are not the end of the road: that there is, in short, no final answer to social problems such as poverty, inequality and discrimination under predominantly capitalist relations.

Then there is the damage done to socialism by the deficiencies of state socialism and to some extent by those of the public welfare state in this country. A Utopian vision is necessary to argue that both of these models are far from the goals of socialist social planning. Ironically, the Conservative governments elected in 1979 and 1983 have proved helpful in showing the potential for change in existing institutions.

The Utopian construction of a socialist way of life emphasizes the fact that the peaceful transition of society will take a very long time indeed, at least 30 years. Oppositional relationships and struggles cannot be expected to produce immediate large-scale changes; they are not intended to do so. *They are supposed to prepare the ground and encourage the conditions in which structural change can take place.* For much of the time, therefore, socialists involved in these struggles cannot expect them to lead to concrete changes in public policy. More often, they will be the focus of discussion, education, the forging of common bonds and planning. Parliamentary and state-based interest groups have avoided this less tangibly productive activity.

Socialists have an important responsibility as bearers of the vision of an alternative future; they have a difficult and often isolating task. For many this has meant a long period of covert activity, of not declaring themselves and of fighting on a series of relatively minor issues. This is the politics of the unfinished (Mathieson, 1978), a series of skirmishes in which the individual or group does not reveal his or their politics fully, in order to avoid being labelled and pigeon-holed. This has proved a useful, but strictly limited, strategy in that it has helped to make some changes within organizations (Cohen, 1979), but it has reinforced the tendency to relate criticism to issues and not to the reproduction of structures. It is time for these socialists to 'come out' and put their case more forcefully. (The analogy is with the world of gay liberation, but it has been successfully used by people with disabilities: Sutherland, 1981). Thus they may take 'a seat at the table' but do not have to appear to accept the structural relations on which it is based.

In addition to arguing openly for a socialist way of life, it will be necessary to *demonstrate* how socialist relations can work. This will be difficult, to say the least, within the confines of a market economy. As individuals, however, we may recognize that socialism entails the equal sharing of power, and in our everyday relations – for example our professional relations as teachers, social workers and doctors and our personal relations as wives, husbands, partners, lovers or parents – we can begin to share power and knowledge. Collectively, too, there is some scope for the practical demonstration of socialist relations. Some local authorities, such as Sheffield, have begun in recent years to develop relatively small-scale initiatives in socialist planning and service provision. Although it is too early to judge the outcome of these initiatives, they do suggest that there is some scope for establishing alternative, socialist policies at the local level (Alcock and Lee, 1981).

One of the main requirements for socialist evolution is the gradual reduction of social inequality, and as argued earlier, the main key to this change is a transformation in the social division of work – not simply paid employment. Each of us, as workers, trade unionists, members of families and so on, can therefore contribute to the building of socialist relations by reorganizing work over which we have some control and arguing for control where it does not exist. Together we can counteract capitalist values in small ways and prepare the ground for an alternative way of life. Collective activities, for example, militate against individualism and consumerism and may help to weaken acquisitiveness (Ferge, 1979, p. 323). We can also contribute to the humanization of need, which is essential for a socialist way of life, by reducing conspicuous or status-enforcing consumption. Trade unions are in a particularly powerful position to reorganize work and to establish a role for workers in planning production. But, so far at least, they have not been particularly interested in furthering these sort of developments, concentrating instead on narrow economism. Again, local authorities are well placed to encourage socialist evolution, for example through the promotion of collective activities such as child care, and the re-organization of services to reflect more directly the needs of citizens.

Socialist indicators and accounting

Objective evidence is an essential feature of socialist as much as any other form of planning. It also has an important part to play in putting the case for socialism. The deficiencies of capitalism are not always as evident as some of those on the political Left believe them to be (LEWRG, 1979, p. 139), and they require detailed exposure. The state controls information, both through the collection of statistics (state-istics) and through the sponsorship of research. There are numerous examples of the implications of this political control of information (see for example Townsend, 1975, pp. 306—18, and Irvine, Miles and Evans, 1979).

One such example is the production of the very barest official statistics on the numbers of individuals and families in poverty in Great Britain. On taking office in 1979 the Conservative government cancelled the annual publication of these figures in favour of bi-annual production. Thus, the estimates 'published' (they were not strictly published but were 'made available' in the House of Commons library) in mid-1982 were for 1979, and those for 1981 were released in late 1983. More-over, the statistics had been 'massaged' by taking an average for the whole year and not an end-of-year count as was previously the case, which resulted in a reduction in the true figures. In general, official statistics, collected as a by-product of bureau-incrementalism, are an inadequate basis for structural social planning.

Detailed research and inquiry is also necessary to establish the basis for planning the socialist alternative to capitalism, and this sort of expert activity therefore has a legitimate part to play in the oppositional struggle. This is not to say that the collection and interpretation of statistics should remain the sole province of academic experts, nor that this activity should continue to masquerade as non-political. The structural planning system will need indicators of group mobility and way of life in order to assess social development. In order to plan for need, some account of need is required. But indicators are required of *real* social needs and not those that arise primarily out of capitalist relations (Archibugi, 1979, p. 57).

Planning for welfare requires the construction of new indicators of the quality of life. Social indicators may be used to project alternative forms of social relations, to be compared with existing ones and to identify social priorities in development. A new system of accounting is also required in order to judge the social usefulness of production or expenditure as opposed to their economic or financial value. At the same time, a system of social accounting can be used constructively to highlight the deficiencies of the assumptions built into conventional accounting, and the extent to which capitalism must be transformed in order to realize socialist goals. It is unlikely that conventional financially based accounting will prove an adequate basis for socialist accounting, which requires an assessment based on the social rather than the financial return on investment and expenditure. Together, socialist indicators and socialist accounting could create a framework for the allocation of resources according to social rather than private criteria.

Work has already progressed on such 'socialist indicators' in Italy (Archibugi, 1978). This could be built on to derive indicators that show not simply the degree of social well-being but also the extent to which socialist goals such as equality have been achieved. Again, these indicators, such as the distribution of resources between social classes and groups, might be applied at the local level in advance of the election of a socialist government. The distribution and redistribution of resources in socialist local authorities could be assessed by means of these indicators.

Finally, a new system of social accounting would provide another basis for arguing against economic hegemony and for the assertion of social priorities above narrow financial ones. This would, in turn, further the long-term aim of subordinating economic goals to social ones.

CONCLUSION

Socialist evolution rests on a change in social relations, the relations that are embodied in capitalist institutions. We cannot reasonably expect to take over those institutions, and in any case, 'There is no way that society can be transformed through institutions that have been developed precisely to take away our power' (LEWRG, 1979, p. 132). But capitalist values, relations and institutions have to be reproduced constantly. Therefore they do provide scope for oppositional relations and planning, and it is these that, in turn, offer the best hope for building a socialist alternative strategy. The key, as the quotation from Tawney at the beginning of this chapter suggests, is the commitment and energy of all of us involved in the reproduction of existing structures.

References

Aaronovitch, S. (1981a) *The Road From Thatcherism*, London, Lawrence and Wishart.

Aaronovitch, S. (1981b) 'Discussion: alternative economic strategies', in Currie and Smith (1981), pp. 109–12.

Aaronovitch, S., Smith, R., Gardiner, J. and Moore, R. (1981) *The Political Economy of British Capitalism*, London, McGraw-Hill.

Abel-Smith, B. (1967) *Labour's Social Plans*, London, Fabian Society.

Alcock, P. and Lee, P. (1981) 'The Socialist Republic of South Yorkshire?' *Critical Social Policy*, 1 (2), 72–93.

Algie, J. (1979) 'Priorities in personal social services', in M. Brown and S. Baldwin (eds), *The Year Book of Social Policy in Britain 1978*, London, Routledge & Kegan Paul. pp. 159–80.

Alt, J. (1979) *The Politics of Economic Decline*, Cambridge University Press.

Amos, F.J.C. et al. (1982) *Perspectives for Planning*, Birmingham, Institute of Local Government Studies.

Archibugi, F. (1978) 'Capitalist planning in question', in Holland (1978), pp. 49–68.

Armstrong Committee (1980) *Budgetary Reform in the UK*, Oxford University Press.

Atkinson, A.B. (1976) *The Economics of Inequality*, Cambridge University Press.

Atkinson, A.B. and Stiglitz, J.E. (1980) *Lectures on Public Economics*, Maidenhead, McGraw-Hill.

Bachrach, P. and Baratz, M.S. (1970) *Power and Poverty*, London, Oxford University Press.

Bacon, R. and Eltis, W. (1976) *Britain's Economic Problems*, London, Macmillan.

Bains Committee (1972) *The New Local Authorities: Management and Structure*, London, HMSO.

Baker, J. (1979) 'Social conscience and social policy', *Journal of Social Policy*, 8 (2), 177–206.

Balogh, T. (1965) *Planning for Progress: A Strategy for Labour*, London, Fabian Society.

Banks, G.T. (1979) 'Programme budgeting in the DHSS', in Booth (1979), pp. 150–72.

Banting, K.G. (1979) *Poverty, Politics and Poverty*, London, Macmillan.

Baran, P. (1973) *The Political Economy of Growth*, Harmondsworth, Pelican.

Barclay Committee (1982) *Social Workers and Their Roles*, London, Bedford Square Press.

Barnett, J. (1982) *Inside the Treasury*, London, André Deutsch.

Barras, R., and Geary, K. (1979) 'A review of the Cleveland county plan cycle 1977/78', *Local Government Studies*, 5 (1), 39–54.

Beckerman, W. (ed.) (1972) *The Labour Government's Economic Record 1964–70*, London, Duckworth.

Bell, D. (1965) *The End of Ideology*, New York, Free Press.

Bell, D. (1969) 'The idea of a social report', *The Public Interest*, 15, 72–84.

Benn, T. (1980) 'Manifestos and mandarins', in RIPA, *Policy and Practice*, London, RIPA, pp. 57–78.

Bennington, J. (1976) *Local Government Becomes Big Business*, London, CDP Information and Intelligence Unit.

Berger, P.L. and Luckman, T. (1971) *The Social Construction of Reality*, Harmondsworth, Penguin.

Beveridge, W.H. (1909) *Unemployment: a Problem of Industry*, London, Longmans.

Beveridge, W.H. (1942) *Social Insurance and Allied Services*, Cmnd 6404, London, HMSO.

Beveridge, W.H. (1944) *Full Employment in a Free Society*, London, Allen & Unwin.

Beynon, H. and Wainwright, H. (1979) *The Worker's Report on Vickers*, London, Pluto Press.

Black Committee (1980) *Inequalities in Health*, London, DHSS.

Blackaby, F.T. (ed.) (1979) *British Economic Policy 1960–74*, Cambridge University Press.

Blake, D. and Ormerod, P. (1980) *The Economics of Prosperity*, London, Grant McIntyre.

Booth, T.A. (ed.) (1979) *Planning for Welfare*, Oxford, Basil Blackwell/ Martin Robertson.

Booth, T.A. (1981) 'Collaboration between the health and social services. Part 1: A case study of joint care planning', *Policy and Politics*, 9 (1), 23–49.

Booth, T.A. (1982) 'Economics and the poverty of social planning', *Public Administration*, 60 (Summer), 197–214.

Bosanquet, N. and Townsend, P. (1980) *Labour and Equality*, London, Heinemann.

Boulding, K. (1967) 'The boundaries of social policy', *Social Work*, January, 3–11.

Bradshaw, J. (1982) 'Public expenditure on social security', in A. Walker (1982b), pp. 91–112.

Braybrooke, D. and Lindblom, C.E. (1963) *A Strategy of Decision*, New York, Free Press.

Briggs, A. (1961) 'The welfare state in historical perspective', *European Journal of Sociology*, 2 (2), 221–58.

Brittan, L. (1982) 'The Government's economic strategy', in Kay (1982), pp. 7–18.

Brittan, S. (1973) *Is There an Economic Consensus?* London, Macmillan.

Brown, M. (1976) *Introduction to Social Administration in Britain* (3rd edn), London, Hutchinson.

Bruce, M. (1961) *The Coming of the Welfare State*, London, Batsford.

Buchanan, J.M. and Tullock, G. (1965) *The Calculus of Consent*, Ann Arbor, University of Michigan Press.

Budd, A. (1978) *The Politics of Economic Planning*, London, Fontana.

Bull, D. (1970) *Action for Welfare Rights*, London, Fabian Society.

Bull, D. (1979) 'Open government and the review of supplementary benefits', in S. Baldwin and M. Brown (eds), *The Year Book of Social Policy 1978*, London, Routledge & Kegan Paul, pp. 22–56.

Bull, D. and Wilding, P. (eds) (1983) *Thatcherism and the Poor*, London, CPAG.

Burgess, T. and Travers, T. (1982) *Ten Billion Pounds*, London, Grant McIntyre.

Carley, M. (1981) *Social Measurement and Social Indicators*, London, Allen & Unwin.

Carrier, J. and Kendall, I. (1977) 'Social administration as social science', in Heisler (1977), pp. 25–32.

Castles, F.G., Murray, D.J., Potter, D.C. and Pollitt, C.J. (eds) (1978) *Decisions, Organisations and Society* (2nd edn), Harmondsworth, Penguin.

Caves, R.E. and Krause, L.B. (eds) (1980) *Britain's Economic Performance*, Washington DC, Brookings Institution.

CDP (1977) *The Costs of Industrial Change*, London, CDP Inter-Project Editorial Team.

Clarke, Sir R. (1978) *Public Expenditure Management and Control*, London, Macmillan.

Cockburn, C. (1977) *The Local State*, London, Pluto Press.

Cohens, S. (1979) 'It's alright for you to talk', in R. Bailey and M. Brake (eds), *Radical Social Work*, London, Edward Arnold.

Committee on Abuse of Social Security Benefits (1973) *Report*, Cmnd 5228, London, HMSO.

Committee on Policy Optimisation (1978) *Report*, Cmnd 7148, London, HMSO.

Committee of Public Accounts (1981) *The Role of the Comptroller and Auditor General*, vol. 1, Session 1980–81, HC 115–1, London, HMSO.

Communist Party (1978) *The British Road to Socialism*, London, Communist Party.

Conyers, D. (1982) *An Introduction to Social Planning in the Third World*, London, John Wiley.

Coombes, D. and Walkland, S.A. (eds) (1980) *Parliament and Economic Affairs*, London, Heinemann.

Cooper, M.H. (ed.) (1973) *Social Policy: A Survey of Recent Developments*, Oxford, Basil Blackwell and Martin Robertson.

Coote, A. (1981) 'The AES: a new starting point', *New Socialist*, November/December, 4–7.

Corrigan, P. and Leonard, P. (1978) *Social Work Practice Under Capitalism*, London, Macmillan.

CPRS (1975) *A Joint Framework for Social Policies*, London, HMSO.

CPSA (1979) *Behind Closed Doors*, London, CPSA.

Cripps, F. (1981) 'The British crisis: can the left win?' *New Left Review*, 128, pp. 93–6.

Cross, R. (1982) *Economic Theory and Policy in the UK*, Oxford, Martin Robertson.

Crossman, R.H.S. (1977) *Diaries of a Cabinet Minister*, London, Weidenfeld & Nicolson.

Crouch, C. (ed.) (1979) *State and Economy in Contemporary Capitalism*, London, Croom-Helm.

Culyer, A.J. (1974) *The Economics of Social Policy*, Oxford, Basil Blackwell and Martin Robertson.

Culyer, A.J. (1981) *The Political Economy of Social Policy*, Oxford, Martin Robertson.

Currie, D. (1981) 'What's left of monetarism?' in Currie and Smith (1981), pp. 129–50.

Currie, D. and Smith, R. (eds) (1981) *Socialist Economic Review 1981*, London, Merlin Press.

Dahl, R.A. (1956) *A Preface to Democratic Theory*, Chicago, University Press.

Dahl, R.A. (1961) *Who Governs*? Yale University Press.

Davies, B. (1968) *Social Needs and Resources in Local Services*, London, Michael Joseph.

Davies, B., et al. (1971) *Variations in Services for the Aged*, London, Bell.

Davies, B. et al. (1972) *Variations in Children's Services Among British Urban Authorities*, London, Bell.

DEA (1965) *The National Plan*, Cmnd 2764, London, HMSO.

Devine, P. (1981) 'Principles of democratic planning', in Currie and Smith (1981), pp. 113–27.

DHEW (1970) *Towards a Social Report*, Ann Arbor, University of Michigan Press.

DHSS (1972a) *Planning Programming Budgeting System for the Health and Personal Social Services*, London, DHSS.

DHSS (1972b) *Management Arrangements for the Reorganised NHS*, London, HMSO.

DHSS (1973) *A Report from the Working Party on Collaboration Between the NHS and Local Government on its Activities to the end of 1972*, London, HMSO.

DHSS (1974a) *Social Security Provision for Chronically Sick and Disabled People*, HC276, London, HMSO.

DHSS (1974b) *Better Pensions*, Cmnd 5713, London, HMSO.

DHSS (1974c) *Collaboration Between Health and Local Authorities*, Circular HRC (74) 19, London, DHSS.

DHSS (1976a) *Priorities for Health and Personal Social Services in England*, London, HMSO.

DHSS (1976b) *Sharing Resources for Health in England*, London, HMSO.

DHSS (1977a) *The Way Forward*, London, HMSO.

DHSS (1977b) *Joint Care Planning: Health and Local Authorities*, Circular HC (77) 27, London, DHSS.

DHSS (1978a) *Social Assistance*, London, DHSS.

DHSS (1978b) *A Happier Old Age*, London, HMSO.

DHSS (1978c) *Local Authority Personal Social Services: Summary of Planning Returns 1976–77 to 1979–80*, London, DHSS.

DHSS (1979a) *Patients First*, London, HMSO.

DHSS (1979b) *Local Authority Personal Social Services: Summary of Planning Returns 1977–78 to 1980–81*, London, DHSS.

DHSS (1980a) *Reply by the Government to the Third Report from the Social Services Committee, Session 1979–80*, Cmnd 8086, London, HMSO.

DHSS (1980b) *A Strategy for Social Security Operations*, London, DHSS.

DHSS (1980c) *DHSS Planning Guidelines for 1980/81*, Circular HC(80) 9, London, DHSS.

DHSS (1980d) *Structure and Management*, Circular HC(80)8, London, DHSS.

DHSS (1981a) *Growing Older*, Cmnd 8173, London, HMSO.

DHSS (1981b) *Care in Action*, London, HMSO.

DHSS (1981c) *Review of the NHS Planning System – A Consultative Document*, Circular HN(81)4, London, DHSS.

DHSS (1981d) *Care in the Community*, London, DHSS.

DHSS (1982a) *Social Security Operational Strategy*, London, HMSO.

DHSS (1982b) *Social Security Operational Strategy: A Brief Guide*, London, DHSS.

Dillard, D. (1950) *The Economics of J.M. Keynes*, London, Crosby Lockwood.

Dobb, M. (1969) *Welfare Economics and the Economics of Socialism*, Cambridge University Press.

DoE (1974) *Rate Fund Expenditure and Rate Calls in 1975/76*; Circular 171/74, London, DoE.

DoE (1977) *Local Government Finance*, Cmnd 6813, London, HMSO.

DoE (1980) *Local Government Finance*, HC 56, London, HMSO.

Donnison, D.V. (1962) *The Development of Social Administration*, London, Bell.

Donnison, D. (1982) *The Politics of Poverty*, Oxford, Martin Robertson.

Donnison, D. (1975) *An Approach to Social Policy*, Dublin, Stationery Office.

Donnison, D. et al. (1975) *Social Policy and Administration Revisited* (rev. edn), London, Allen & Unwin.

Donzelot, J. (1979) *The Policing of Families*, London, Hutchinson.

Downs, A. (1957) *An Economic Theory of Democracy*, New York, Harper and Row.

Downs, A. (1967) *Inside Bureaucracy*, Boston, Little Brown.

Dror, Y. (1964) 'Muddling through — "science" or "inertia"?' *Public Administration Review*, xxiv, 153—7.

Easton, D. (1965) *A Framework for Political Analysis*, Englewood Cliffs, NJ, Prentice-Hall.

Eddison, T. (1973) *Local Government: Management and Corporate Planning*, London, Leonard Hill.

Ellman, M. (1979) *Socialist Planning*, Cambridge University Press.

Else, P.K. and Marshall, G.P. (1979) *The Management of Public Expenditure*, London, PSI.

Etzioni, A. (1967) 'Mixed scanning: a "third" approach to decision-making', *Public Administration Review*, 27, 382—96.

Expenditure Committee (1974) *Public Expenditure, Inflation and the Balance of Payments*, Ninth Report, Session 1973—74, HC 328, London, HMSO.

Expenditure Committee (1975) *The Financing of Public Expenditure*, First Report, Session 1975—76, HC69, London, HMSO.

Expenditure Committee (1976) *Planning and Control of Public Expenditure*, Thirteenth Report, Session 1975—76, HC 718, London, HMSO.

Expenditure Committee (1977) *Ninth Report*, Session 1976—77, London, HMSO.

Falk, N. and Lee, J. (1978) *Planning the Social Services*, London, Saxon House.

Ferge, Z. (1979) *A Society in the Making*, Harmondsworth, Penguin.

Foster, J. (1982) 'The community and industry', in A. Walker (1982d), pp. 76—94.

Foster, P. (1983) *Access to Welfare*, London, Macmillan.

Fox Piven, F. and Cloward, R.A. (1972) *Regulating the Poor*, London, Tavistock.

Frey, B.S. (1983) *Democratic Economic Policy*, Oxford, Martin Robertson.

Friedman, M. (1962) *Capitalism and Freedom*, Chicago, University Press.

Fulton Committee (1968) *The Civil Service*, vol. 1, Cmnd 3638, London, HMSO.

Galbraith, J.K. (1975) *Economics and the Public Purpose*, Harmondsworth, Penguin.

Galper, J. (1978) 'What are radical social services?' *Social Policy*, January/February, 37–41.

Gans, H. (1972) *People and Plans*, Harmondsworth, Penguin.

George, V. and Manning, N. (1980) *Socialism, Social Welfare and the Soviet Union*, London, Routledge & Kegan Paul.

George, V. and Wilding, P. (1976) *Ideology and Social Welfare*, London, Routledge & Kegan Paul.

Ginsburg, N. (1979) *Class, Capital and Social Policy*, London, Macmillan.

Glennerster, H. (1975) *Social Service Budgets and Social Policy*, London, George Allen & Unwin.

Glennerster, H. (1976) 'In praise of public expenditure', *New Statesman*, 27 February, 252–4.

Glennerster, H. (1979) 'The determinants of public expenditure' in Booth (1979), pp. 3–22.

Glennerster, H. (1981a) 'From containment to conflict? social planning in the seventies', *Journal of Social Policy*, 10 (1), 31–52.

Glennerster, H. (1981b) 'Social service spending in a hostile environment', in C. Hood and M. Wright (eds), *Big Government in Hard Times*, Oxford, Martin Robertson, pp. 179–96.

Glennerster, H. with Korman, N. and Marslen-Wilson, F. (1983) *Planning for Priority Groups*, Oxford, Martin Robertson.

Glyn, A. and Harrison, J. (1980) *The British Economic Disaster*, London, Pluto Press.

Goldberg, E.M., and Connelly, N. (1982) *The Effectiveness of Social Care for the Elderly*, London, Heinemann.

Golding, P. (1983) 'Rethinking commonsense about social policy', in Bull and Wilding (1983) pp. 7–12.

Golding, P. and Middleton, S. (1978) 'Why is the press so obsessed with welfare scroungers?' *New Society*, 26 October, 195–7.

Golding, P. and Middleton, S. (1982) *Images of Welfare*, Oxford, Basil Blackwell and Martin Robertson.

Goldman, Sir S. (1973) *The Developing System of Public Expenditure Management and Control*, Civil Service College Studies, no. 2, London, HMSO.

Goldthorpe, J.H. (1962) 'The development of social policy in England, 1800–1914', *Transactions of the Fifth World Congress of Sociology*, 4, 41–56.

Gordon, A. (1982) *Economics and Social Policy*, Oxford, Basil Blackwell and Martin Robertson.

Gough, I. (1978) 'Theories of the welfare state: a critique', *International Journal of Health Services*, 8 (1), 27–40.

Gough, I. (1979) *The Political Economy of the Welfare State*, London, Macmillan.

Gould, F. and Roweth, B. (1980) 'Public spending and social policy: the UK 1950–77', *Journal of Social Policy*, 9 (3), 337–57.

Gouldner, A.W. (1970) *The Coming Crisis of Western Sociology*, London, Heinemann.

Grant, R.M. and Shaw, G.K. (eds) (1975) *Current Issues in Economic Policy*, Oxford, Philip Allan.

Graycar, A. (ed.) (1983) *The Retreat of the Welfare State*, Sydney, Allen & Unwin.

Green, D. (1981) 'The Budget and the plan', in P.G. Cerney and M.A. Schain (eds), *French Politics and Public Policy*, London, Methuen, pp. 101–24.

Greenwood, R. (1979) 'The local authority budgetary process', in Booth (1979), pp. 78–96.

Greenwood, R., Hinings, C.R., and Ranson, S. (1975) 'Contingency theory and the organisation of local authorities. Part 1: Differentiation and integration', *Public Administration*, 53, 1–23.

Greenwood, R. and Stewart, J.D. (1974) *Corporate Planning in Local Government*, London, Charles Knight.

Hall, A. (1975) 'Policy making: more judgement than luck', *Community Care*, 6 August.

Hall, D. (1983) *The Cuts Machine*, London, Pluto Press.

Hall, P. (1976) *Reforming the Welfare*, London, Heinemann.

Hall, P., Land, H., Parker, R. and Webb, A. (1975) *Change, Choice and Conflict in Social Policy*, London, Heinemann.

Hall, P. (1981) *Great Planning Disasters*, Harmondsworth, Penguin.

Halsey, A.H. (1981) 'A sociologist's viewpoint', in OECD (1981) pp. 13–28.

Hambleton, R. (1982) 'Planning social services', *New Society*, 10 June, 423–4.

Harvey, D. (1976) *Social Justice and the City*, London, Edward Arnold.

Haverman, R. and Margolis, J. (eds) (1977) *Public Expenditure and Policy Analysis* (2nd edn), Chicago, Rand McNally.

Hayek, F.A. (1967) *Studies in Philosophy, Politics and Economics*, Chicago, University Press.

Healey, D. (1976) *Letter of Intent to the IMF*, London, HM Treasury.

Heclo, H. and Wildavsky, A. (1974) *The Private Government of Public Money*, London, Macmillan.

Heisler, H. (ed.) (1977) *Foundations of Social Administration*, London, Macmillan.

Hepworth, N.P. (1976) *The Finance of Local Government*, London, Allen & Unwin.

Hicks, J. (1974) *The Crisis in Keynesian Economics*, Oxford, Basil Blackwell.

Higgins, J. (1978) *The Poverty Business: Britain and America*, Oxford, Basil Blackwell.

Higgins, J. (1980) 'Social control theories of social policy', *Journal of Social Policy*, 9 (1) 1–24.

Higgins, J. (1981) *States of Welfare*, Oxford, Basil Blackwell and Martin Robertson.

Hill, M. (1979) 'Social work teams and the allocation of resources', in Booth (1979), pp. 115–32.

Hill, M. (1981) *Understanding Social Policy*, Oxford, Basil Blackwell and Martin Robertson.

Hill, M. (1982) 'Professions in community care', in A. Walker (1982), pp. 56–75.

Hirsch, F. (1977) *The Social Limits to Growth*, London, Routledge & Kegan Paul.

Holland, S. (1978) *Beyond Capitalist Planning*, Oxford, Basil Blackwell.

Hood, C. and Wright, M. (1981) *Big Government in Hard Times*, Oxford, Martin Robertson.

Horne, D. (1970) *God is an Englishman*, Harmondsworth, Penguin.

House of Commons (1979) *Hansard*, vol. 968, 12 June, London, HMSO.

Hunt, E.K. and Sherman, H.J. (1981) *Economics* (4th edn), New York, Harper & Row.

Hurst, J.W. (1977) "Rationalising social expenditure – health and social services', in M.V. Posner (ed.), *Public Expenditure*, Cambridge University Press, pp. 221–36.

Hyderbrand, R. (1964) 'Administration of social change', *Public Administration Review*, 19, 160–72.

Irvine, J., Miles, I. and Evans, J. (eds) (1979) *Demystifying Social Statistics*, London, Pluto Press.

Jenkins, R. (1972) *What Matters Now*, London, Fontana.

Johnson, H.G. (1971) 'The Keynesian revolution and the monetarist counter-revolution' *American Economic Review, Papers and Proceedings*, 61, 1–14.

Jones, C. and Novak, T. (1980) 'The state and social policy', in P. Corrigan (ed.), *Capitalism, State Formation and Marxist Theory*, London, Quartet Books, pp. 143–70.

Jordan, B. (1973) *Paupers*, London, Routledge & Kegan Paul.

Judge, K. (1978) *Rationing Social Services*, London, Heinemann.

Judge, K. (1979) 'The financial relationship between central and local government in the personal social services', in Booth (1979), pp. 24–50.

Judge, K. (1982) 'The growth and decline of social expenditure' in A. Walker (1982b), pp. 27–48.

Jutsum, C. and Walker, G. (1979) *Public Expenditure 1977/78: Outturn Compared with Plan*, Treasury Working Paper no. 11, London, HM Treasury.

Kahn, A.J. (1969) *Theory and Practice of Social Planning*, New York, Russell Sage.

Kapp, K.W. (1978) *The Social Costs of Business Enterprise*, Nottingham, Spokeman Books.

Kay, J. (ed.) (1982) *The 1982 Budget*, Oxford, Basil Blackwell.

Kerr, H. (1981) 'Labour's social policy 1974–79', *Critical Social Policy*, 1 (1), 5–17.

Kilroy, B. (1982) 'Public expenditure on housing', in A. Walker (1982b), pp. 113–36.

Kincaid, J. (1973) *Poverty and Equality in Britain*, Harmondsworth, Pelican.

Kopkind, A. (1967) 'The future planners', *New Republic*, 25 February, 19–23.

Labour Party (1969) *Labour's Economic Strategy*, London, Labour Party.

Labour Party (1980) *Private Schools*, London, Labour Party.

Labour Party (1981a) *Taxation*, London, Labour Party.

Labour Party (1981b) *Social Security*, London, Labour Party.

Labour Party (1981c) *A Future for Public Housing*, London, Labour Party.

Labour Party (1983) *The New Hope for Britain*, London, Labour Party.

Land, H. (1978) 'Who cares for the family?' *Journal of Social Policy*, 7 (3), 275–84.

Land, H. (1980) 'The family wage', *Feminist Review*, no. 6, 55–79.

Lane, D. (1982) *The End of Social Inequality?* London, Allen & Unwin.

Lansley, S. (1980) 'Is this the end of local democracy?', *New Society*, 11 December, 510–1.

Lansley, S. and Weir, S. (1983) 'Towards a popular view of poverty', *New Society*, 25 August, 283–4.

Lecomber, R. (1979) 'Economic growth and social welfare' in W. Beckerman (ed.), *Slow Growth in Britain*, Oxford, Clarendon Press, pp. 23–40.

Le Grand, J. (1978) 'Who benefits from public expenditure?' *New Society*, 45 (833), 614–6.

Le Grand, J. (1982) *The Strategy of Equality*, London, Allen & Unwin.

Le Grand, J. and Robinson, R. (1976) *The Economics of Social Problems*, London, Macmillan.

Lewis, P. et al. (1975) *Inflation and Low Incomes*, London, Fabian Society.

Lindblom, C.E. (1959) 'The science of "muddling through" ', *Public Administration*, 19, 79–99.

Lindblom, C.E. (1968) *The Policy-Making Process*, Englewood Cliffs, NJ, Prentice-Hall.

Lipsey, R.G. (1979) *An Introduction to Positive Economics* (5th edn), London, Weidenfeld & Nicolson.

Lister, R. (1978) *Social Assistance: The Real Challenge*, London, CPAG.

Lister, R. and Wilson, O. (1976) *The Unequal Breadwinner*, London, NCCL.

Lockwood, D. (1956) 'Some remarks on "the social system" ', *British Journal of Sociology*, 7 (2), 134–46.

London CSE Group (1980) *The Alternative Economic Strategy*, London, CSE Books.

London Edinburgh Weekend Return Group (LEWRG) (1979) *In and Against the State*, London, Pluto Press.

Loney, M., Boswell, D. and Clarke, J. (eds) (1983) *Social Policy and Social Welfare*, Milton Keynes, Open University Press.

Lukes, S. (1974) *Power: A Radical View*, London, Macmillan.

MacDougall, Sir D. (1977) 'Economic growth and social welfare', *Scottish Journal of Political Economy*, 24 (3), 193—206.

Marris, P. (1982) *Community Planning and Conceptions of Change*, London, Routledge & Kegan Paul.

Marsh, D.C. (ed.) (1979) *Introducing Social Policy*, London Routledge & Kegan Paul.

Marshall, G.P. (1980) *Social Goals and Economic Perspectives*, Harmondsworth, Penguin.

Marshall, T.H. (1975) *Social Policy* (4th edn), London, Hutchinson.

Mathieson, T. (1978) *The Politics of Abolition*, Oxford, Martin Robertson.

Maud Committee on the Management of Local Government (1967) *Report*, vol. 1, London, HMSO.

Mayer, R.H. (1972) *Social Planning and Social Change*, Englewood Cliffs, NJ, Prentice-Hall.

Meacher, M. (1982) 'Socialism with a human face', *New Socialist*, March/April, 18—21.

Medawar, C. (1978) *The Social Audit Consumer Handbook*, London, Macmillan.

Medawar, C. (1980) *Consumers of Power*, London, Social Audit.

Mencher, S. (1969) *From Poor Law to Poverty Program*, Pittsburgh, University Press.

Merrison Commission (1979) *Report of the Royal Commission on the NHS*, Cmnd 7615, London, HMSO.

Midgley, J. (1978) 'Developmental roles for social work in the Third World: the prospect of social planning', *Journal of Social Policy*, 7 (2), 173—188.

Miliband, R. (1969) *The State in Capitalist Society*, London, Weidenfeld & Nicolson.

Miliband, R. (1972) *Parliamentary Socialism* (2nd end), London, Merlin Press.

Miller, S.M. (1975) 'Planning: can it make a difference in capitalist America?', *Social Policy*, September/October, 12—22.

Miller, S.M. and Rein, M. (1975) 'Can income redistribution work?' *Social Policy*, May/June, 3—18.

Ministry of Health (1962) *A Hospital Plan for England and Wales*, Cmnd 1604, London, HMSO.

Ministry of Health (1963) *Health and Welfare: the Development of Community Care*, Cmnd 1973, London, HMSO.

Mishan, E.J. (1967) *The Costs of Economic Growth*, Harmondsworth, Penguin.

Mishra, R. (1975) 'Marx and welfare', *Sociological Review*, 23, (2), 288—9.

Mishra, R. (1981) *Society and Social Policy* (2nd edn), London, Macmillan.

Mitchell, J. (1966) *Groundwork to Economic Planning*, London, Secker & Warburg.

Mondale, W.F. (1967) 'New tools for social progress', *The Progressive*, 31, 28–31.

Moroney, R.M. (1976) *The Family and the State*, London, Longmans.

Moynihan, D. (1968) *Maximum Feasible Misunderstanding*, New York, Free Press.

Mydral, G. (1960) *Beyond the Welfare State*, London, Duckworth.

Mydral, G. (1968) *Asian Drama: an Enquiry into the Poverty of Nations*, Harmondsworth, Penguin.

Myrdal, G. (1970) *Objectivity in Social Research*, London, Duckworth.

NEDC (1963) *Growth of the UK Economy to 1966*, London, HMSO.

North Tyneside CDP (1978) *North Shields: Living with Industrial Change*, Newcastle, North Tyneside CDP.

Novick, D. (1965) *Program Budgeting*, Cambridge, Mass., Harvard University Press.

O'Connor, J. (1973) *The Fiscal Crisis of the State*, New York, St James Press.

OECD (1981) *The Welfare Stare in Crisis*, Paris, OECD.

Olson, M. (1969) 'The plan and purpose of a social report', *The Public Interest*, 15, 85–97.

Opie, R. (1972) 'Economic planning and growth', in Beckerman (1972), pp. 157–77.

Pahl, R. (1975) *Whose City?* Harmondsworth, Penguin.

Paris, C. (ed.) (1982) *Critical Readings in Planning Theory*, Oxford, Pergamon Press.

Parker, J. (1975) *Social Policy and Citzenship*, London, Macmillan.

Parry, N. and Parry, J. (1979) 'Social work, professionalism and the state', in Parry, et al. (1979), pp. 21–47.

Parry, N., Rustin, M., and Satyamurti, C. (eds) (1979) *Social Work, Welfare and the State*, London, Edward Arnold.

Paterson Committee (1973) *The New Scottish Local Authorities: Organisation and Management Structures*, Edinburgh, Scottish Development Department.

Peacock, A. (1975) 'Foreward: studying economic policy', in Grant and Shaw (1975), pp. 1–9.

Pechman, J.A. (1980) 'Taxation', in Caves and Krause (1980), pp. 199–260.

Pemberton, A. (1983) 'Marxism and social policy: a critique of the "contradictions of welfare" ', *Journal of Social Policy*, 12 (3), 289–308.

Perrow, C. (1973) 'The neo-Weberian model: decision-making, conflict, and technology', in Salaman and Thompson (1973), pp. 281–92.

Peston, M. (1981) 'New paths for socio-economic policy', in OECD (1981), pp. 94–109.

Phillips, D. (1980) 'The creation of consultative councils in the NHS', *Public Administration*, Spring, 47–66.

Pinker, R. (1971) *Social Theory and Social Policy*, London, Heinemann.
Pinker, R. (1974) 'Social policy and social justice', *Journal of Social Policy*, 3 (1), 1–19.
Pinker, R. (1979) *The Idea of Welfare*, London, Heinemann.
Plowden Committee (1961) *Control of Public Expenditure*, Cmnd 1432, London, HMSO.
Pond, C. (1982) 'Taxation and public expenditure', in A. Walker (1982b) pp. 49–69.
Popper, K. (1961) *The Poverty of Historicism*, London, Routledge & Kegan Paul.
Prest, A.R., and Coppock, D.J. (1980) *The UK Economy* (8th edn), London, Weidenfeld & Nicolson.
Price, R.W.R. (1979) 'Public expenditure', in Blackaby (1979), pp. 77–134.
Radcliffe Committee (1959) *Report of the Committee on the Working of the Monetary System*, Cmnd 827, London, HMSO.
Redcliffe-Maud Commission (1969) *Report of the Royal Commission on Local Government in England*, Cmnd 4040, London, HMSO.
Reddin, M. (1980) 'Utopia and social planning', unpublished paper.
Rein, M. (1968) 'Welfare planning', in *International Encyclopaedia of the Social Sciences*, pp. 142–53.
Rein, M. (1983) *From Policy to Practice*, London, Macmillan.
Riffault, H. and Rabier, J. (1977) *The Perception of Poverty in Europe*, Brussels, Commission of the European Communities.
Rights of Women (1982) *ROW Response to the Labour Party Discussion Documents on Taxation and Social Security*. London, ROW.
Rivlin, A.M. (1969) 'The planning, programming and budgeting system in the DHEW: some lessons from experience', in *The Analysis and Evaluation of Public Expenditures: the PPB system*, vol. 3, Washington, US Government Printing Office.
Robinson, D. (1972) 'Labour market policies' in Beckerman (1972), pp. 300–34.
Robinson, J. (1962) *Economic Philosophy*, London, Watts.
Robinson, J. (1966) *Economics: an Awkward Corner*, London, Allen & Unwin.
Robinson, J. (1971) *Economic Heresies*, London, Macmillan.
Rodgers, B. with Doron, A. and Jones, M. (1979) *The Study of Social Policy, A Comparative Approach*, London, Allen & Unwin.
Rogers, B. (1980) *The Domestication of Women*, London, Tavistock.
Roll, Sir E. (1968) *The World After Keynes*, London, Macmillan.
Room, G. (1979) *The Sociology of Welfare*, Oxford, Martin Robertson.
Rose, H. (1978) 'Towards a political economy of welfare', paper presented to the Research Committee on Poverty, Welfare and Social Policy, Ninth World Congress of Sociology.
Rose, H. (1981) 'Rereading Titmuss: the sexual division of welfare', *Journal of Social Policy*, 10 (4), 477–501.
Rose, R. and Peters, G. (1979) *Can Government Go Bankrupt?* London, Macmillan.

Rowthorn, B. (1981) 'The politics of the AES', *Marxism Today*, 25 (1), 4—10.

Royal Commission on Civil Liability and Compensation for Personal Injury (1978) *Report*, vol. 1, London, HMSO.

Rubin, I.I. (1979) *A History of Economic Thought*, London, Ink Links.

Salaman, G. and Thompson, K. (eds) (1973) *People and Organisations*, London, Longman.

Sandford, C. (1977) *Social Economics*, London, Heinemann.

Sandford, C. (1982) *The Economic Structure*, London, Longman.

Sargeant, T. (1979) 'Joint care planning in the health and personal social services', in Booth (1979), pp. 173—86.

Schick, A. (1973) 'A death in the bureaucracy: the demise of federal PPB', *Public Administration Review*, 33 (2), 146—56.

Scott, W.G. (1967) *Organisation Theory*, New York, Richard Irwin.

Seebohm Committee (1968) *Report of the Committee on Local Authority and Allied Personal Social Services*, Cmnd 3703, London, HMSO.

Seers, D. (1969) 'The meaning of development', *International Development Review*, 6, December, 2—6.

Select Committee on Estimates (1958) *Treasury Control of Expenditure Sixth Report*, Session 1957—58, HC 254, London, HMSO.

Self, P. (1970) 'Nonsense on stilts: the futility of Roskill', *New Society*, 2 July, 3—11.

Self, P. (1974) 'Is comprehensive planning possible and rational?' *Policy and Politics*, 2 (3), 193—203.

Sharples, A. (1981) 'Alternative economic strategies: labour movement responses to the crisis', in Currie and Smith (1981), pp, 71—92.

Shaw, M. (1972) 'The coming crisis of radical sociology', in R. Blackburn (ed.) *Ideology in Social Science*, London, Fontana, pp. 32—44.

Shearer, A. (1981) 'A framework for independent living', in Walker with Townsend (1981), pp. 73—90.

Showler, B. (1980) 'Political economy and unemployment', in Showler and Sinfield (1980), pp. 27—58.

Showler, B. and Sinfield, A. (eds) (1980) *The Workless State*, Oxford, Martin Robertson.

Simmie, J.M. (1974) *Citizens in Conflict*, London, Hutchinson.

Simon, H.A. (1957) *Administrative Behaviour*, London, Macmillan.

Sinfield, A. (1978) 'Analyses in the social division of welfare', *Journal of Social Policy*, 7 (2), 129—56.

Sinfield, A. (1981) *What Unemployment Means*, Oxford, Martin Robertson.

Skelcher, C. (1982) 'Corporate planning in local government', in S. Leach and J. Stewart (eds), *Approaches in Public Policy*, London, Allen & Unwin, pp. 36—51.

Sleeman, J.F. (1979) *Resources for the Welfare State*, London, Longman.

Smith, A. (1937) *The Wealth of Nations*, New York, Modern Library.

Smith, G. (1980) *Social Need*, London, Routledge & Kegan Paul.

Smith, G. and May, D. (1980) 'The artificial debate between rationalist and incremental models of decision making', *Policy and Politics*, 8 (2), 147–61.

Social Audit (1973) *Social Audit*, 1 (1).

Social Services Committee, House of Commons (1980) *The Government's White Papers on Public Expenditure: The Social Services*, Session 1979–80, vol. 1, HC 702–1, London, HMSO.

Social Services Committee, House of Commons (1981) *Public Expenditure on the Social Services*, Session 1980–81, vol. 1, HC 324–1, London, HMSO.

Social Services Committee, House of Commons (1982) *1982 White Paper: Public Expenditure on the Social Services*, Session 1981–82, vol. 1, HC 306–1, London, HMSO.

SSAC (1982) *First Report of the Social Security Advisory Committee 1981*, London, HMSO.

Stewart, J.D. (1971) *Management in Local Government*, London, Charles Knight.

Stewart, M. (1972) *Keynes and After* (2nd edn), Harmondsworth, Penguin.

Supplementary Benefits Commission (1976) *Annual Report 1975*, London, HMSO.

Sutherland, A.T. (1981) *Disabled We Stand*, London, Souvenir Press.

Sweezy, P. (1977) *American Economic Review, Papers and Proceedings*, 67, 67–8.

Tawney, R.H. (1964) *Equality* (4th edn), London, Unwin Books.

Tawney, R.H. (1966) *The Radical Tradition*, Harmondsworth, Pelican.

Taylor-Gooby, P. and Dale, J. (1981) *Social Theory and Social Welfare*, London, Edward Arnold.

Terrill, R. (1973) *R.H. Tawney and His Times*, London, André Deutsch.

Thomas, P. (1983) 'Social research and government policy' in Loney, et al. (1983) pp. 117–26.

Titmuss, R.M. (1963) *Essays on 'the Welfare State'* (2nd edn), London, Allen & Unwin.

Titmuss, R.M. (1967) *Income Distribution and Social Change*, London, Allen and Unwin.

Titmuss, R.M. (1968) *Commitment to Welfare*, London, Allen & Unwin.

Titmuss, R.M. (1970) *The Gift Relationship*, London, Allen & Unwin.

Titmuss, R.M. (1974) *Social Policy: An Introduction*, London, Allen & Unwin.

Tobin, J. (1972) 'Inflation and unemployment', *American Economic Review*, 62, 1–18.

Townsend, P. (1967) 'The need for a social plan', *New Society*, 14 December, 852–54.

Townsend, P. (1972) 'Social planning and the control of priorities', in Townsend and Bosanquet (1972), pp. 274–301.

Townsend, P. (1974a) 'Inequality and the health service', *Lancet*, 15 June, 1179–90.

Townsend, P. (1974b) 'Poverty as relative deprivation: resources and style of living' in D. Wedderburn (ed.) (1974), *Poverty, Inequality and Class Structure*, London, Cambridge University Press, pp. 15–42.

Townsend, P. (1975) *Sociology and Social Policy*, Harmondsworth, Penguin.

Townsend, P. (1979) *Poverty in the United Kingdom*, London, Allen Lane.

Townsend, P. (1980) 'Social planning and the Treasury' in Bosanquet and Townsend (1980), pp. 3–23.

Townsend, P. (1981a) 'Poverty in the 80s', *New Socialist*, 1 September/October, 25–31.

Townsend, P. (1981b) 'Employment and disability', in Walker with Townsend (1981), pp. 52–72.

Townsend, P. and Bosanquet, N. (1972) (eds) *Labour and Inequality*, London, Fabian Society.

Travers, T. (1981) *Rates, Grants and Accountability*, London, North East London Polytechnic.

Treasury (1969a) *Public Expenditure 1968/69 to 1973/74*, Cmnd 4234, London, HMSO.

Treasury (1969b) *Public Expenditure: A New Presentation*, Cmnd 4017, London, HMSO.

Treasury (1970) *The Reorganisation of Central Government*, Cmnd 4506, London, HMSO.

Treasury (1979) *The Government's Expenditure Plans 1979–80 to 1982–83*, Cmnd 7439, London, HMSO.

Treasury (1980) *The Government's Expenditure Plans 1980–81 to 1983–84*, Cmnd 7831, London, HMSO.

Treasury (1981) *Control of Expenditure: Departmental Responsibilities*, London. HM Treasury.

Treasury (1982) *Macroeconomic Model Technical Manual*, London, HM Treasury.

Treasury (1983) *The Government's Expenditure Plans 1983–84 to 1985–86*, vol. 1, Cmnd 8789–1, London, HMSO.

Treasury and Civil Service Committee (1981) *Monetary Policy*, vol. 1, Session 1980–81, HC 163–1, London, HMSO.

Treasury and Civil Service Committee (1982) *Budgetary Reform*, Sixth Report, Session 1981–82, HC 137, London, HMSO.

TUC (1982) *Programme for Recovery*, London, TUC.

TUC/Labour Party Liaison Committee (1982) *Economic Planning and Industrial Democracy*, London, TUC.

Tudor Hart, J. (1971) 'The inverse care law', *The Lancet*, 27 February, 405–12.

Walker, A. (1976) 'Justice and disability', in K. Jones and S. Baldwin (eds), *The Year Book of Social Policy 1975*, London, Routledge & Kegan Paul, pp. 192–212.

Walker, A. (1980a) 'The social creation of poverty and dependency in old age', *Journal of Social Policy*, 9 (1), 49–75.

Walker, A. (1980b) 'The social origins of impairment, disability and handicap', *Medicine and Society*, 6 (2 and 3), 18–26.

Walker, A. (1981) 'Social policy, social administration and the social construction of welfare', *Sociology*, 15 (2), 225–50.

Walker, A. (1982a) 'Dependency and old age', *Social Policy and Administration*, 16 (2), 115–35.

Walker, A. (ed.) (1982b) *Public Expenditure and Social Policy*, London, Heinemann.

Walker, A. (ed.) (1982c) *The Poverty of Taxation*, Poverty Pamphlet 56, London, CPAG.

Walker, A. (ed.) (1982d) *Community Care*, Oxford, Basil Blackwell and Martin Robertson.

Walker, A. (1982e) 'Why we need a social strategy', *Marxism Today*, September, 26–31.

Walker, A. (1982f) *Unqualified and Underemployed*, London, Macmillan.

Walker, A. (1983) 'Labour's social plans: the limits of welfare statism', *Critical Social Policy*, 8, Autumn, 45–65.

Walker, A., Omerod, P. and Whitty, L. (1979) *Abandoning Social Priorities*, Poverty Pamphlet 44, London, CPAG.

Walker, A. with Townsend, P. (eds) (1981) *Disability in Britain*, Oxford, Martin Robertson.

Walker, A., Winyard, S. and Pond, C. (1983) 'Conservative economic policy: the social consequences', in Bull and Wilding (1983), pp. 13–26.

Walker, C. (1982) 'Social assistance: the reality of open government', *Policy and Politics*, 10 (1), 1–25.

Walker, C. (1983) *Changing Social Policy*, London, Bedford Square Press.

Webb, A.L. and Falk, N. (1974) 'Planning and social services', *Policy and Politics*, 3 (2), 33–54.

Webb, A. and Wistow, G. (1982) 'The personal social services', in A. Walker (1982b), pp. 137–64.

Wedderburn, D. (1965) 'Facts and theories of the welfare state', in R. Miliband and J. Saville (eds), *The Socialist Register 1965*, London, Merlin Press, pp. 127–146.

West, R.J. (1980) 'The essentials of planning in the NHS', *Public Health*, 94 (1), 16–20.

Westergaard, J. (1972) 'Sociology: the myth of classlessness', in R. Blackburn (ed.), *Ideology in Social Science*, London, Fontana, pp. 119–63.

Westergaard, J. and Resler, H. (1975) *Class in a Capitalist Society*, London, Heinemann.

Whitmore, R. and Fuller, R. (1980) 'Priority planning in an area social services team', *British Journal of Social Work*, 10, 277–92.

Wildavsky, A. (1966) 'The political economy of efficiency: cost–benefit analysis, systems analysis and programme budgeting', *Public Administration Review*, 26, 292–310.

Wilding, P. (1982) *Professional Power and Social Welfare*, London, Routledge & Kegan Paul.

Wilensky, H. (1975) *The Welfare State and Equality*, London, University of California Press.

Williams, A. (1972) 'Cost-benefit analysis: bastard science? and/or insidious poison on the body politick?', *Journal of Public Economics*, 1 (2), 199–226.

Winch, D. (1969) *Economics and Policy*, London, Hodder & Stoughton.

Winkler, J. (1976) 'Corporatism', *Archives European Sociologie*, XVII, 100–36.

Wootton, B. (1955) *The Social Foundations of Wage Policy*, London, Allen & Unwin.

Wright, M. (1979) 'Planning and controlling public expenditure', in Booth (1979), pp. 23–50.

Wright, M. (ed.) (1980) *Public Spending Decisions*, London, Allen and Unwin.

Wright, M. (1981) 'Big government in hard times: the restraint of public expenditure', in Hood and Wright (1981), pp. 3–34.

Index